Communications
in Computer and Information Science 396

Weixia Xu   Liquan Xiao   Chengyi Zhang
Jinwen Li   Liyan Yu (Eds.)

Computer Engineering and Technology

17th CCF Conference, NCCET 2013
Xining, China, July 20-22, 2013
Revised Selected Papers

 Springer

Volume Editors

Weixia Xu
Liquan Xiao
Chengyi Zhang
Jinwen Li
Liyan Yu

National University of Defense Technology
School of Computer Science
Changsha, Hunan, P.R. China

E-mail:
weixia_xu@263.net
marshell.xiao@gmail.com
chengyizhang@nudt.edu.cn
lijinwen@sina.com
happyfish1988@126.com

ISSN 1865-0929   e-ISSN 1865-0937
ISBN 978-3-642-41634-7   e-ISBN 978-3-642-41635-4
DOI 10.1007/978-3-642-41635-4
Springer Heidelberg New York Dordrecht London

Library of Congress Control Number: 2013951048

CR Subject Classification (1998): C.1.2, C.1.4, B.7.1, B.4.3, B.3.2, B.2.4, B.8.2

Typesetting: Camera-ready by author, data conversion by Scientific Publishing Services, Chennai, India

Printed on acid-free paper

Springer is part of Springer Science+Business Media (www.springer.com)

Preface

We are pleased to present the proceedings of the 17th Annual Conference on Computer Engineering and Technology (NCCET 2013). Over its short 17-year history, NCCET has established itself as one of the major national conferences dedicated to the important and emerging challenges in the field of computer engineering and technology. Following the previous successful events, NCCET 2013 provided a forum to bring together researchers and practitioners from academia and industry to discuss cutting-edge research on computer engineering and technology.

We are delighted that the conference continues to attract high-quality submissions from a diverse and national group of researchers. This year, we received 234 paper submissions, of which 26 papers were accepted. Each paper received three or four peer reviews from our Technical Program Committee (TPC) comprising 61 TPC members from academia, government, and industry.

The pages of this volume represent only the end result of an enormous endeavor involving hundreds of people. Almost all of this work is voluntary, with some individuals contributing hundreds of hours of their time to the effort. Together, the 61 members of the TPC, the 16 members of the external review committee (ERC), and the 13 other individual reviewers consulted for their expertise wrote nearly 500 reviews.

Every paper received at least two reviews and many had three or more. With the exception of submissions by the TPC, each paper had at least two reviews from the TPC and at least one review from an outside expert. For the second year running, most of the external reviews were done by the ERC, which was selected in advance, and additional external reviews beyond the ERC were requested whenever appropriate or necessary. Reviewing was "first read double-blind," meaning that author identities were withheld from reviewers until they submitted a review. Revealing author names after initial reviews were written allowed reviewers to find related and previous material by the same authors, which helped greatly in many cases in understanding the context of the work, and also ensured that the author feedback and discussions at the PC meeting could be frank and direct. For the first time in many years, we allowed PC members to submit papers to the conference. Submissions co-authored by a TPC member were reviewed exclusively by the ERC and other outside reviewers, and these same reviewers decided whether to accept the PC papers; no PC member reviewed a TPC paper, and no TPC papers were discussed at the TPC meeting.

After the reviewing was complete, the PC met at the National University of Defense Technology, Changsha, during May 25–28 to select the program. Separately, the ERC decided on the PC papers via email and phone discussions. In the end, 26 of the 234 submissions (11%) were accepted for the conference.

First of all, we would like to thank all researchers who submitted manuscripts. Without these submissions, it would be impossible to provide such an interesting technical program. We thank all PC members for helping to organize the conference program. We thank all TPC members for their tremendous time and efforts during the paper review and selection process. The efforts of these individuals were crucial in constructing our successful technical program. Last but not least, we would like to thank the organizations and sponsors that supported NCCET 2013. Finally, we thank all the participants of the conference and hope they had a truly memorable NCCET 2013 in Xining, China.

Weixia Xu
Haixing Zhao
Minxuan Zhang
Liquan Xiao

Organizing Committee

General Co-chairs

Xu Weixia   National University of Defense Technology, Changsha, China

Zhao Haixing   Qinghai Normal University, Xining, China

Zhang Minxuan   National University of Defense Technology, Changsha, China

Program Chair

Xiao Liquan   National University of Defense Technology, Changsha, China

Publicity Co-chairs

Zhang Chengyi   National University of Defense Technology, Changsha, China

Li Jinwen   National University of Defense Technology, Changsha, China

Yu Liyan   National University of Defense Technology, Changsha, China

Local Arrangements Co-chairs

Zhao Haixing   Qinghai Normal University, Xining, China

Li Jinwen   National University of Defense Technology, Changsha, China

Wang Qinghai   Qinghai Normal University, Xining, China

Registration and Finance Co-chairs

Geng Shengling   Qinghai Normal University, Xining, China

Wang Yongwen   National University of Defense Technology, Changsha, China

Li Yuanshan   National University of Defense Technology, Changsha, China

Zhang Junying   National University of Defense Technology, Changsha, China

Program Committee

Han Wei	631 Institute of AVIC, Xi'an, China
Jin Lifeng	Jiangnan Institute of Computing Technology, Wuxi, China
Xiong Tinggang	709 Institute of China Shipbuilding Industry, Wuhan, China
Zhao Xiaofang	Institute of Computing Technology Chinese Academy of Sciences, Beijing, China
Yang Yintang	Xi Dian University, Xi'an, China
Dou Qiang	National University of Defense Technology, Changsha, China
Li Jinwen	National University of Defense Technology, Changsha, China
Zhang Chengyi	National University of Defense Technology, Changsha, China

Technical Program Committee

Chen Shuming	National University of Defense Technology, Changsha, China
Chen Yueyue	Hunan Changsha DIGIT Company, Changsha, China
Dou Qiang	National University of Defense Technology, Changsha, China
Du Huimin	Xi'an University of Posts & Telecommunications, Xi'an, China
Fan Dongrui	Institute of Computing Technology Chinese Academy of Sciences, Beijing, China
Fan Xiaoya	Northwestern Polytechnical University, Xi'an, China
Fang Xing	Jiangnan Institute of Computing Technology, Wuxi, China
Gu Tianlong	Guilin University of Electronic Technology, Guilin, China
Guo Donghui	Xiamen University, Xiamen, China
Guo Wei	Tianjin University, Tianjin, China
Hou Jianru	Institute of Computing Technology Chinese Academy of Sciences, Beijing, China
Huang Jin	Xi Dian University, Xi'an, China
Ji Liqiang	Cesller Company, Shenzhen, China
Jin Jie	Hunan Changsha Fusion Company, Changsha, China
Li Ping	University of Electronic Science and Technology of China, Chengdu, China

Li Qiong	Inspur Information Technology Co. Ltd., Beijing, China
Li Yuanshan	Inspur Information Technology Co. Ltd., Beijing, China
Li Yun	Yangzhou University, Yangzhou, China
Lin Kaizhi	Inspur Information Technology Co. Ltd., Beijing, China
Li Zhenghao	Tongji University, Shanghai, China
Sun Haibo	Inspur Information Technology Co. Ltd., Wuhan, China
Sun Yongjie	Hunan Changsha DIGIT Company, Changsha, China
Tian Ze	631 Institute of AVIC, Xi'an, China
Wang Dong	National University of Defense Technology, Changsha, China
Wang Yaonan	Hunan University, Changsha, China
Wang Yiwen	University of Electronic Science and Technology of China, Chengdu, China
Xing Zuocheng	Hunan Changsha DIGIT Company, Changsha, China
Xue Chengqi	Southeast University, Nanjing, China
Yang Peihe	Jiangnan Institute of Computing Technology, Wuxi, China
Yang Xiaojun	Institute of Computing Technology Chinese Academy of Sciences, Beijing, China
Yin Luosheng	Synopsys Company, Shenzhen, China
Yu Mingyan	Harbin Institute of Technology, Harbin, China
Yu Zongguang	China Electronics Technology Group Corporation No. 58 Research Institute, Wuxi, China
Zeng Tian	709 Institute of China Shipbuilding Industry, Wuhan, China
Zeng Xifang	Hunan Great Wall Information Technology Co. Ltd., Changsha, China
Zeng Yu	Sugon Company, Beijing, China
Zeng Yun	Hunan University, Changsha, China
Zhang Jianyun	PLA Electronic Engineering Institute, Hefei, China
Zhang Lixin	Institute of Computing Technology Chinese Academy of Sciences, Beijing, China
Zhang Shengbing	Northwestern Polytechnical University, Xi'an, China
Zhang Xu	Jiangnan Institute of Computing Technology, Wuxi, China

Table of Contents

Session 1: Application Specific Processors

Session 2: Communication Architecture

Session 3: Computer Application and Software Optimization

Session 4: IC Design and Test

Session 5: Processor Architecture

Session 6: Technology on the Horizon

Design and Implementation
of a Novel Entirely Covered K^2 CORDIC

Jianfeng Zhang[1,*], Wei Ding[2,1], and Hengzhu Liu[1,2]

[1] Institute of Microelectronics and Microprocessor,
School of Computer National University of Defense Technology
Changsha HN, P.R. of China
jianfengzhang@nudt.edu.cn
[2] China Defense Science and Technology Information Center
Beijing, P.R. of China
1988dingwei2827@sina.com

Abstract. The conventional Coordinate Rotation Digital Computer (CORDIC) algorithm has been widely applied in many aspects, whereas it is restricted by the convergence range of the rotation angle, which need use pre-processing and post-processing units to control the quadrant of the angle. This paper proposes a novel CORDIC architecture which covers the entire coordinate space, no further more pre-processing and post-processing modules will be required. Compared with the conventional CORDIC, the Bit Error Position (BEP) of the proposed architecture has been improved, which exceeds the conventional CORDIC 2 bits. In the mean time, both of the mean errors and the hardware overhead are reduced, and the speed accelerates 35%. The proposed k^2 CORDIC architecture has been validated on the Xilinx ML505 FPGA development platform, which has been well applied in Direct Digital Frequency Synthesizer (DDS) and Fast Fourier Transform (FFT).

Keywords: Coordinate Rotation Digital Computer (CORDIC), bit error position (BEP), FPGA, Direct Digital Frequency Synthesizer (DDS), Fast Fourier Transform (FFT).

1   Introduction

The conventional Coordinate Rotation Digital Computer (CORDIC) algorithm is first presented by J. Volder [1], which uses a series of constant and associated with the radix angles to and fro to approach the assigned angle. The corresponding hardware can be implemented in very economic fashion, which is executed merely by shift and adders. Therefore, the algorithm has been applied in many fields, such as replacing the Table Look-up in Direct Digital Frequency Synthesizer (DDS) to implement the trigonometric transformation [2], demanding applications in digital signal processing (DSP) [3], video technology and image processing like Fast Fourier Transform (FFT) [4].

---

[*] Corresponding author.

W. Xu et al. (Eds.): NCCET 2013, CCIS 396, pp. 1–8, 2013.
© Springer-Verlag Berlin Heidelberg 2013

In essence, CORDIC can be operated in two different modes: rotation and vector. The rotation mode, given a vector with the initial coordinate (x_0, y_0) and the target rotation angle (θ_0), aims to compute the final coordinate (x', y') through a series of backward and forward rotation in an iterative manner. While in vector mode, the magnitude and the phase angle of the vector are computed by initial and final coordinates [5]. However, despite these advantages, the conventional CORDIC has some drawbacks, such as excessive rotation times, the scaling compensation and the limited convergence range. The convergence range of the conventional CORDIC is $[-99.8°, 99.8°]$, which just covers the first and fourth quadrants.

Owing to the limited convergence range of the rotation angle, many researchers have done some incremental research work to improve the conventional CORDIC algorithm, such as repeating the first iteration of the conventional CORDIC [6], domain folding technology proposed in the Scaling-Free (SF) CORDIC [7], reduced z-datapath CORDIC [8] and enhanced scaling free CORDIC [9]. However, all of them need pre-processing and post-processing units, and the required iteration times do not be reduced. Therefore, we propose a novel CORDIC architecture which based on the rotation mode, the convergence range of which will be improved to $[-\pi, \pi]$. Compared with the conventional CORDIC, the proposed one eliminates the pre-processing and post-processing units, and the performance, the Bit Error Position (BEP) and the mean error are all improved significantly. The proposed k^2 architecture of CORDIC algorithm has been validated on the FPGA development kit, and applied in Direct Digital Frequency Synthesizer (DDS) and Fast Fourier Transform (FFT).

The following paper is organized as follows. Section II describes the theoretical background of the proposed algorithm, and the architecture of the k^2 CORDIC is illustrated in section III. In section IV, we present the simulation results and give some discussions. Conclusions are discussed in section V.

2   Principle of k^2 CORDIC Algorithm

2.1   Conventional CORDIC

The primary rotation matrix of the Conventional CORDIC can be described as (considering anti-clockwise rotation)

$$\begin{pmatrix} x' \\ y' \end{pmatrix} = \begin{pmatrix} \cos\theta & -\sin\theta \\ \sin\theta & \cos\theta \end{pmatrix} \cdot \begin{pmatrix} x_0 \\ y_0 \end{pmatrix} \tag{1}$$

In equation (1), θ is the target angle of the rotation. In the conventional CORDIC algorithm, θ is the summation of a decreasing series of elementary angles α_i.

$$\theta = \sum_{i=0}^{b-1} \sigma_i \alpha_i \tag{2}$$

$$\alpha_i = \arctan 2^{-i} \tag{3}$$

In expression (2), b is the word length of the machine. σ_i belongs to {-1, 1}, which is the sign of the residual angle of the $(i-1)^{th}$ iteration, and indicates the direction of the ith iteration. When it is positive, the next iteration is anti-clockwise; on the contrary, the next iteration is clockwise.

$$\sigma_i = sign(\theta - \sum_{j=0}^{i-1} \sigma_j \alpha_j) \tag{4}$$

Then substituting (2) into (1) by using (3), we can get

$$\begin{pmatrix} x' \\ y' \end{pmatrix} = k \begin{pmatrix} 1 & -\sigma_i 2^{-i} \\ -\sigma_i 2^{-i} & 1 \end{pmatrix} \cdot \begin{pmatrix} x_0 \\ y_0 \end{pmatrix} \tag{5}$$

$$k = \prod_{i=0}^{b-1} \cos \alpha_i \tag{6}$$

Where k is the scale factor and the range of the rotation angle is $[-99.8°, 99.8°]$. From the hardware implementation, the algorithm only needs shift and addition operations.

2.2 k^2 CORDIC Algorithm

Despite the attractiveness, conventional CORDIC has some drawbacks, especially the limited convergence range. We propose a novel CORDIC architecture in this section. As sine and cosine functions can be expressed as follows

$$\begin{cases} \cos \theta = \cos^2 \dfrac{\theta}{2} - \sin^2 \dfrac{\theta}{2} \\ \sin \theta = 2\cos \dfrac{\theta}{2} \sin \dfrac{\theta}{2} \end{cases} \tag{7}$$

Then substituting expressions (7) into (1)

$$\begin{pmatrix} x' \\ y' \end{pmatrix} = \begin{pmatrix} \cos^2 \dfrac{\theta}{2} - \sin^2 \dfrac{\theta}{2} & -2\cos \dfrac{\theta}{2} \sin \dfrac{\theta}{2} \\ 2\cos \dfrac{\theta}{2} \sin \dfrac{\theta}{2} & \cos^2 \dfrac{\theta}{2} - \sin^2 \dfrac{\theta}{2} \end{pmatrix} \cdot \begin{pmatrix} x_0 \\ y_0 \end{pmatrix} \tag{8}$$

In which we can extract the $\cos^2 \dfrac{\theta}{2}$ factor, the expression will be described as

$$\begin{pmatrix} x' \\ y' \end{pmatrix} = \cos^2 \dfrac{\theta}{2} \begin{pmatrix} 1 - \tan^2 \dfrac{\theta}{2} & -2\tan \dfrac{\theta}{2} \\ 2\tan \dfrac{\theta}{2} & 1 - \tan^2 \dfrac{\theta}{2} \end{pmatrix} \cdot \begin{pmatrix} x_0 \\ y_0 \end{pmatrix} \tag{9}$$

Assigning that θ is the summation of a decreasing series of elementary angle α_i, so that

$$\tan\frac{\theta}{2} = \tan\alpha_i = 2^{-i} \tag{10}$$

When substituting equation (10) into (9)

$$\begin{pmatrix} x' \\ y' \end{pmatrix} = \prod_{i=0}^{b-1}\cos^2\alpha_i \begin{pmatrix} 1-2^{-2i} & -\sigma_i 2^{-i+1} \\ \sigma_i 2^{-i+1} & 1-2^{-2i} \end{pmatrix} \cdot \begin{pmatrix} x_0 \\ y_0 \end{pmatrix} \tag{11}$$

The expression (11) illustrates that the implementation of the expression will only requires shift and adders. As every proposed rotation angle can be described as

$$\theta_i = 2\arctan 2^{-i}(i=0,1,\cdots,b-1) \tag{12}$$

Compared with the conventional CORDIC, the convergence range of the proposed architecture can cover the whole coordinate space, which eliminates the pre-processing and post-processing units. However, the scale factor of the proposed one is changed into $(\prod_{i=0}^{b-1}\cos\alpha_i)^2$, which is the square of the conventional one. Therefore, we name the proposed algorithm k^2 CORDIC algorithm. If using the same bits to represent it, the truncation error would be decreased [10].

3   Architecture of k^2 CORDIC Algorithm

In the architecture of the k^2 CORDIC algorithm, b is the word length of the machine, which is configurable. More specifically, the implementation of a 16 bits CORDIC rotator is described here as an example. All of the discussions presented in this section are suitable for any n bits CORDIC rotator as well.

For the proposed architecture, we assume that the decimal 1 is represented as 16'h4000, the most significant bit is the sign of the data. When right shifting a data more than 14 bits, it would only leave the sign bits and mean no operation, which can be regarded as the machine zero.

In the expression (11), i denotes the ith iteration. If i is larger than decimal 7, the element 2^{-2i} will be regarded as the machine zero, then the element $(1-2^{-2i})$ approaches the decimal 1. The corresponding expression is

$$\begin{pmatrix} x' \\ y' \end{pmatrix} = \prod_{i=8}^{15}\cos^2\alpha_i \begin{pmatrix} 1 & -\sigma_i 2^{-i+1} \\ \sigma_i 2^{-i+1} & 1 \end{pmatrix} \cdot \begin{pmatrix} x_0 \\ y_0 \end{pmatrix} \tag{13}$$

While if i=0, the expression (11) can be described as

$$\begin{pmatrix} x' \\ y' \end{pmatrix} = \cos^2\alpha_0 \begin{pmatrix} 0 & -\sigma_0 2 \\ \sigma_0 2 & 0 \end{pmatrix} \cdot \begin{pmatrix} x_0 \\ y_0 \end{pmatrix} \tag{14}$$

When i=1, the expression (11) will be changed into

$$\begin{pmatrix} x' \\ y' \end{pmatrix} = \cos^2\alpha_1 \begin{pmatrix} 1-2^{-2} & -\sigma_1 \\ \sigma_1 & 1-2^{-2} \end{pmatrix} \cdot \begin{pmatrix} x_0 \\ y_0 \end{pmatrix} \tag{15}$$

Finally, if the value of i fluctuates between decimal 2 and decimal 7, the expression (11) will be

$$\begin{pmatrix} x' \\ y' \end{pmatrix} = \prod_{i=2}^{7} \cos^2 \alpha_i \begin{pmatrix} 1 - 2^{-2i} & -\sigma_i 2^{-i+1} \\ \sigma_i 2^{-i+1} & 1 - 2^{-2i} \end{pmatrix} \cdot \begin{pmatrix} x_0 \\ y_0 \end{pmatrix} \qquad (16)$$

Analyzing these expressions (13)~(16), the architecture of the expression (14) is the simplest, the longest data path of which is one shift, and the expression (13) is one shift and one addition. However, the longest data path of the expression (15) and (16) is one shift and two additions. In the meantime, all of the architecture of the expressions can't work normally without the angle path adder. In order to balance the logic of every stage of the architecture, we put the i=0 and i=1 modules in the same stage. When i is bigger than 8, we synthesize the next two bits in the same stage. The logic of the proposed architecture is shown in Fig.1.

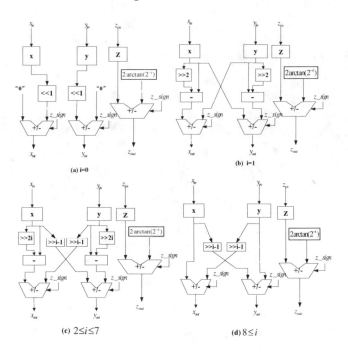

Fig. 1. The architecture of proposed k^2 CORDIC algorithm

Firstly, the initial values of x, y and the rotation angle are sent to the first stage (i=0 and i=1 modules). According to the sign of the input angle to judge the direction of the rotation, when it is positive, the iteration is anti-clockwise; on the contrary, the next iteration is clockwise. Secondly, the signals are handled by the third module (1<i<8) which will execute six times. Finally, the fourth module (i>7) will receive the data streams. Different from the former steps, it will repeat four times.

4   Performance Evaluation and Comparison

In order to evaluate the performance of the proposed k^2 algorithm, we mainly concentrate on three issues: the calculation accuracy of the results, the area consumption and the computation speed.

4.1   Error Analysis

There are two different error sources during the CORDIC algorithm operation [10]:

- Quantization error due to the quantified representation of a rotation angle of the CORDIC by the finite number.
- The truncation or cut-off rounding error due to the word length of arithmetic operations.

The truncation error plays a key role in the error of CORDIC hardware implementation. We analyze the error of the proposed algorithm in terms of the BEP, the expression of which is described as

$$BEP = -\log_2 \left| x_c - x_r \right| \qquad (17)$$

In which, x_c is computed by the machine, and x_r is the real value of the trigonometric function.

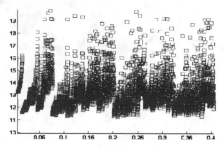

(a) The conventional CORDIC architecture

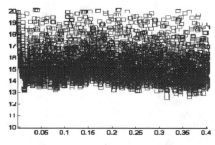

(b) The k^2 CORDIC architecture

Fig. 2. Accuracy errors of Cosine for CORDIC architectures

We generate a pseudorandom sequence of angles lying within the convergence range $[0, \pi/8]$. Using these angles as the input, the corresponding BEP is shown in Fig.2. It is apparent that the maximum error of the conventional CORDIC locates at about the 11th bit position, while the proposed architecture locates at about the 13th, which exceeds conventional CORDIC two bits.

Simultaneously, we analyze the mean error of these architectures, which is shown in Table.1. The mean error of the proposed architecture is the smaller, which means that the value calculated by the proposed one is the more precise.

Table 1. Comparison of Mean Error

Comparison	X mean error	Y mean error	Stages
Conventional	11.261 e-005	5.1572e-005	17
K^2 Architecture	2.1686 e-005	4.4345 e-005	11

Simultaneously, we analyze the mean error of these architectures, which is shown in Table.1. The mean error of the proposed architecture is the smaller, which means that the value calculated by the proposed one is the more precise.

4.2   Area Comparison

We synthesize the proposed architecture and the conventional CORDIC on FPGA XC5VL110T, the hardware overhead is shown in Table2.

Table 2. Comparison of Hardware Overhead

Comparison	Conventional CORDIC	K^2 architecture
Slice Registers	1079	1147
Slice LUTs	1968	894
LUT-FF pairs	840	886

Compared with the conventional CORDIC, the proposed one uses 6% more registers and 5.5% more LUT-FF pairs, but reduces 55% required LUTs. The proposed one is verified on Xilinx FPGA ML505 development platform. Fig.3 shows the chipscope snapshots of the proposed CORDIC. According to the chipscope snapshots, the proposed architecture works normally.

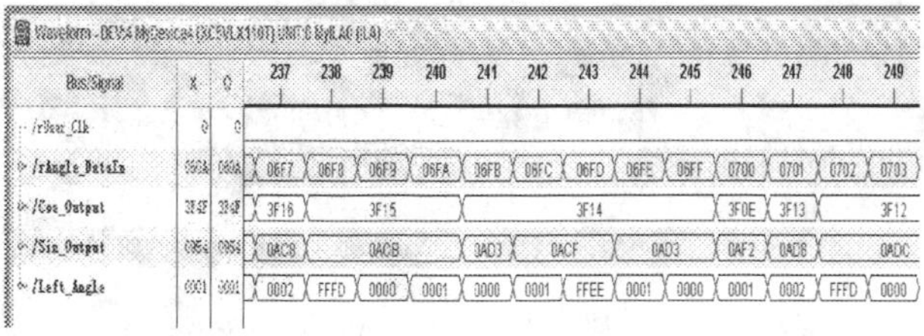

Fig. 3. Chipscope evaluation on Xilinx ML505 development platform

4.3   Speed Comparison

The required stages of varied architectures are also shown in Table.1. The complete pipeline of proposed K^2 architecture contains 11 stages and is 6 cycles less than conventional CORDIC structure, which means that the speed of the proposed one accelerates 35%.

5   Conclusion

In this paper, we present a novel k^2 CORDIC architecture. Compared with conventional CORDIC, the proposed architecture covers the entire coordinate space without pre-processing and post-pressing units. Based on the algorithm, an area-efficient pipeline-balancing architecture is designed. The proposed architecture has been implemented with Verilog HDL, and evaluated by FPGA. The results show the proposed CORDIC exceeds the conventional CORIDC in terms of the computation accuracy, the consumed area and the iteration speed.

Acknowledgments. This work is supported by Research Fund for the Doctoral Program of Higher Education of China (No. 20114307130003).

References

1. Volder, J.E.: The CORDIC trigonometric computing technique. IRE Transactions Electron. Computer EC-8(3), 330–334 (1959)
2. Jridi, M.: Direct Digital Frequency Synthesizer with CORDIC Algorithm and Taylor Series Approximatation for Digital Receivers. European Journal of Scientific Research 30(4), 542–553 (2009)
3. Zhou, L., Liu, H., Zhang, B.: Flexible and High-Efficiency Turbo Product Code Decoder Design. IEICE Electornics Express 9(12), 1044–1050 (2012)
4. Oruklu, E., Xiao, X., Saniie, J.: Reduced Memory and Low Power Architectures for CORDIC-based FFT Processors. Journal of Signal Processing Systems, 1–6 (2011)
5. Walther, J.S.: A unified algorithm for elementary functions. In: AFIPS Spring Joint Computer Conference, pp. 379–385 (1971)
6. Hu, X., Harber, R.G.: Expending the range of convergence of the CORDIC algorithm. IEEE Transactions on Computers 40 (1991)
7. Maharatna, K., Banerjee, S., Grass, E., Krstic, M., Troya, A.: Modified virtually scaling-free adaptive CORDIC rotator algorithm and architecture. IEEE Trans. Circuits Syst. Video Technol. 15(11), 1463–1474 (2005)
8. Maharatna, K., Shabrawy, K.E., Hashimi, B.A.: Reduced z-datapath CORDIC rotator. In: IEEE Int. Symp. for Circuits and System, pp. 3374–3377 (2008)
9. Jaime Francisco, J., Sanchez Miguel, A., Hormigo, J., Villalba, J., Zapata Emilio, L.: Enhanced Scaling-Free CORDIC. IEEE Transactions on Circuits and Systems 57(7), 1654–1662 (2010)
10. Hu, Y.H.: The quantization effects of the CORDIC algorithm. IEEE Transactions Signal Process. 40(4), 834–844 (1992)

The Analysis of Generic SIMT Scheduling Model Extracted from GPU

Yuanxu Xu, Mingyan Yu, Chao Zhang, and Bing Yang

Department of Electronic Information and Technology, Harbin Institute of Technology,
Harbin 150001, China
xuyuanxu_2008@sina.com

Abstract. To improve the performance of processor, more and more companies
during the industrial circle put the single instruction multi-threads (SIMT)
scheduling technology into the processor architecture now, which can develop
the multicore processor multi-thread parallel performance through promote the
ability of processor multi-thread parallel processing. In order to research and
develop the technology of SIMT, this article extracts a generic SIMT scheduling model from Graphic Processing Unit (GPU) which is a kind of processor
that used in the field of high performance computing. Through analyzing the
performance of this scheduling model, this article shows the attributes of this
model and can be an important reference for the use and optimizing of this
model in other processors.

Keywords: Multicore processor, Multi-thread parallel processing, Single instruction multi-threads, Scheduling model, Performance analysis.

1 Introduction

The world is coming into the information era when there are many digital information
need to process, which makes the high performance computing develop quickly. More
and more fields, such as digital signal processing and graphics' visual, have mass of
data and throughput computing applications[1] whose distinguishing feature is that
they have plenty of data level parallelism and the data can be processed independently
and in any order on different processing elements for a similar set of operations such
as filtering, aggregating, ranking,etc. In order to adapt the era developing, the computer processor architecture is turning into the thread level parallelism (TLP) from
instruction level parallelism (ILP). The TLP brings a kind of new energy for the development of processors and promotes the whole of computer field.

During the research of TLP, the efficient scheduling and executing of parallel
threads are the most important parts of TLP. The single instruction multi-thread
(SIMT) technology is a hot selection of achieving the multi-thread parallel
processing, specially the Graphic Processing Unit (GPU) of NVIDIA company which
uses the SIMT scheduling technology perfectly[2]. The SIMT scheduling is the thread
organization and management in the SIMT technology. The SIMT technology in GPU

W. Xu et al. (Eds.): NCCET 2013, CCIS 396, pp. 9–18, 2013.

has its unique thread scheduling architecture which makes its performance exceed many traditional many-core processors[1][3]. So if the SIMT scheduling technology of GPU could be transplanted into other processors, the performance of current processors would be improved greatly.

Before transplanting the SIMT technology of GPU into other architectures, we must understand the SIMT scheduling principle in the GPU and its attribute. In order to research and develop the technology of SIMT in GPU, this article extracts a generic SIMT scheduling model from GPU and shows the attribute of this model which can be an important reference for the use and optimizing of SIMT scheduling technology in other processors through analyzing the performance of this scheduling model.

2   SIMT Scheduling Model of GPU

The SIMT scheduling technology of NVIDIA GPU is based on the CUDA platform[4], which is complex but efficient. The program on the CUDA platform mainly includes the serial part working on the CPU and the parallel part working on the GPU[5]. The parallel part is called kernel core, which will produce many parallel thread groups before issued into the GPU hardware on where the parallel threads execute. The kernel needs to be programed explicitly by the programmer who also needs programing some other preparing programs which include distributing memory space, transmitting data between CPU and GPU, programing the number of threads and dividing the thread blocks. All of the parallel threads formed by the kernel have the same executing code and are scheduled and managed uniformly.

In order to analyze the SIMT scheduling technology of GPU conveniently, this article extracts the SIMT scheduling model from the GPU showing in the figure 1. The SIMT scheduling model has been divided into two parts which are the software scheduling part above the dotted line and the hardware scheduling part below the dotted line.

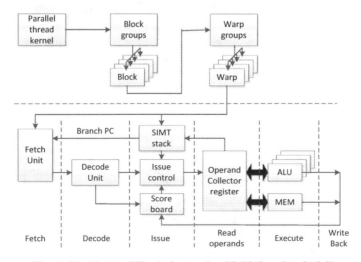

Fig. 1. The Model of Single Instruction Multi-threads scheduling

The software scheduling puts the parallel threads into block groups, each one of which has a number of threads. The threads in every block are divided into many warp groups which are the basic unit of the parallel threads scheduling and executing in the hardware[6]. During the software scheduling, there are three key data structures which are the important parameters of organizing the multi-thread parallelism and will be put into the special memory units of the hardware. The three data structures are the kernel information (figure 2(a)), the thread information (figure 2(b)) and the warp information (figure 2(c)).

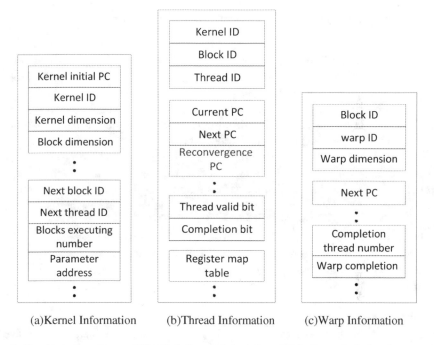

| (a)Kernel Information | (b)Thread Information | (c)Warp Information |

Fig. 2. Key Data Structures of SIMT Software Scheduling (This figure includes the most important parameters during the software scheduling of the SIMT scheduling model. In the thread information figure, the reconvergence PC is a special parameter used for managing the multi-threads branch [7].)

After the software scheduling producing the warp groups, the model puts all the threads in the warp into the hardware scheduling step in warps. There exists six-level-pipeline in the hardware scheduling step of the SIMT scheduling model: 1) *The fetch step*. The fetch unit fetches the instructions from the instruction cache. 2) *The decode step*. The decode unit has some instruction buffers for buffering every warp's instructions. Each warp has its own buffer and each buffer has two instruction entries. 3) *The issue step*. A round robin arbiter chooses a warp to issue from the buffer to rest of the pipeline. Memory instructions are issued to the memory pipeline. The SIMT stack is used for handling control flow of the warp next pc. The score board is in charge of detecting the WAW and RAW hazards. 4) *The read operands step*. After an instruction is decoded, the operand collector register unit is allocated to buffer the source operands of the instruction. 5) *The execute step*. Every thread is executed in each ALU. The SIMT scheduling model has an special memory called shared memory which be shared by threads in the same block. 6) *The write back step*. This is the last step which writes the results into the registers. This step marks that the current thread has completed the execution.

3   Analysis of the SIMT Scheduling Model Attribute

3.1   Influencing Factors of SIMT Scheduling Performance

The major function of SIMT scheduling model is parallel threads executing efficiently. This model has an important attribute, which, using abundant threads number, can hide the delay of the pipeline brought by the memory access and the other problem product by some threads. When threads execution in one of warps stall by some reasons, threads in other warps will fill into the pipeline to make the SIMT model pipeline continue to execute. So it will influence the model performance that the organization and management of the parallel threads change the current executing threads number in the SIMT scheduling model pipeline. During the process of organizing and managing threads, there are three factors that will impact the executing parallel threads in pipeline, which are thread block size, warp size and the number of current thread array (cta). These three factors are relative to each other and together affect the performance of this model.

Thread block size is the number of threads that one block includes, which the programmer designs when programing the workloads. When the model schedules and executes, it issues the threads into the model hardware in each thread-block-unit which affects the number of threads issued on the model hardware. Warp size is the group size of threads divided from each thread block. The model executes the SIMT scheduling and fetching the threads' instructions in each warp-unit, and it has the same executing unit number as the warp size. So the warp size impact the number of threads in the SIMT executing units. What's more, block size and warp size together affect the number of warps, which influences the state of SIMT scheduling and executing. The number of cta is that of thread blocks which the SIMT hardware allows to issue most. The change of cta number will affect the number of parallel threads in the current SIMT hardware and then affect the SIMT scheduling and executing performance. At the same time, the variations of threads number in the hardware are coupled to the register source of hardware, and the latter affects the former behavior to influence the performance of SIMT scheduling model.

In the second section, this article has shown that there exists a shared memory in this model. The shared memory is a special memory shared by all the threads in one block, whose use depends on programmers when they program a workload. It will affect the memory access characteristics of parallel threads in the blocks that whether or not the model uses it.

3.2   Benchmarks

This article uses some general but typical multi-thread programs to test and analyze the SIMT scheduling model. These programs are AES (AES Encryption) [8], LIB (LIBOR Monte Carlo) [9], LPS (3D Laplace Solver) [10], RAY (Ray Tracing) [11] and STO (Store GPU) [12]. The attributes of these programs are shown in table 1, in where the results of three numbers in the kernel dimensions multiplying are the number of thread blocks and those in the thread dimensions multiplying are the number of threads in each thread block. In order to research the influence of SIMT model performance under different memory using strategies, this article uses the typical multi-thread parallel representative program, the matrix multiplication, to test the use of the shared memory. This matrix multiplication program has two factors. The multiplicand is a matrix with 64 lines and 32 columns, and the multiplicator is one with 32 lines and 32 columns. This matrix multiplication workload totally has 2048 threads. This article uses the IPC as the performance index, because the SIMT scheduling is multi-thread technology which means the number of parallel executing instructions in one cycle is an important performance attribute.

Table 1. General Benchmarks

Benchmark	Kernel dimensions	Block dimensions	Thread number	Instruction number	Shared Memory using
AES	(257,1,1)	(256,1,1)	65792	28M	Yes
LIB	(64,1,1)	(64,1,1)	4096	907M	No
LPS	(4,25,1)	(32,4,1)	12800	82M	Yes
RAY	(16,32,1)	(16,8,1)	65536	71M	No
STO	(384,1,1)	(128,1,1)	49152	134M	Yes

3.3   Analysis of Model Attribute Results

With the cta size changing, the result of executing the benchmark on the SIMT scheduling model is shown in the figure 3. When the size of cta expands from small to big, the IPC of all of the workloads firstly rise and then begin to flatten. The reason of this trend can be explained as follows. Increasing the size of cta makes the number of parallel threads in the model hardware grow, which leads a lot of parallel threads to fill into the SIMT pipeline. Following the parallel threads increasing, the stall of some threads' pipelines, which is caused by the memory access delay and exception in some threads, are hidden. The source of hardware has a rising high utilization and the SIMT scheduling model tends to be saturated.

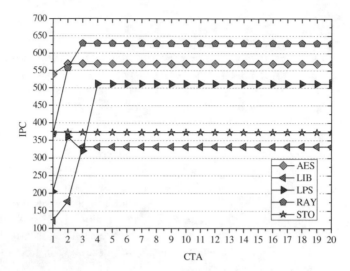

Fig. 3. Changing CTA of General Benchmarks

With the warp size changing, the result of executing the benchmark on the SIMT scheduling model is shown in the figure 4. When the size of warp expands from small to big, the IPC of all of the workloads firstly rise and then begin to drop. The reason of this trend is that the model schedules and executes in each warp-unit and that the warp size has the same number as the executing units in the SIMT hardware.

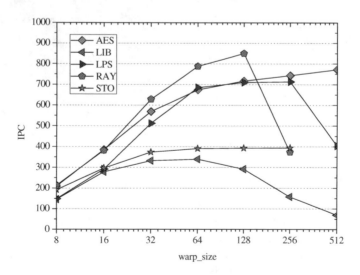

Fig. 4. Changing Warp of General Benchmarks

When the warp size increases, the parallel executing threads grow in quantity, which makes so many threads hide the pipeline stall caused by some threads that the utilization of the hardware source increases leading to reduce the number of appearing the idle state of pipeline executing. However, as more and more threads in a warp, the number of SIMT model executing units is bigger and bigger. When the size of the warp becomes large enough with the total number of threads in the workload so staying the same that making the sum of all the threads issued on the model not increasing, the number of hardware source exceeds that all of the threads needing. So the hardware source is beyond the requirements and is wasted. Its utilization is down to increase the number of appearing the idle state of pipeline executing. The performance of the SIMT scheduling model reduces.

In the SIMT scheduling model the shared memory is another special performance influence factor besides the register in the memory system which can decide this model scheduling and executing efficiency. This article compares the result of using shared memory with that of not using it at the change of thread block size, warp size and cta size. The results are shown at the figure 5 (a), figure 5 (b) and the figure 5 (c).

The figure 5 announces that at the situation of little threads, the performance of using the shared memory is better than that of not using shared memory. That is because the shared memory on chip can keep the threads in blocks from accessing the global memory off the chip too often, which spares the band of memory access and makes full use of the data principle of locality to accelerate the speed of threads accessing the data from the memory and then to improve the performance of the SIMT scheduling model. With the number of threads becoming large, the curvilinear trend, however, changes.

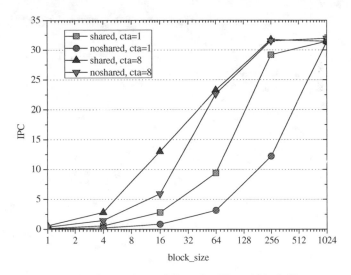

(a)   Comparison of Changing Thread Block Sizes

Fig. 5. Performance Comparison of using shared memory

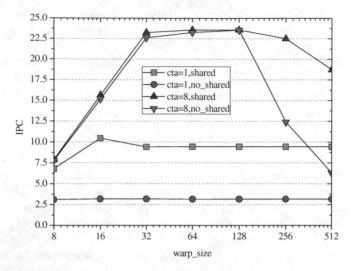

(b) Comparison of Changing Warp Sizes

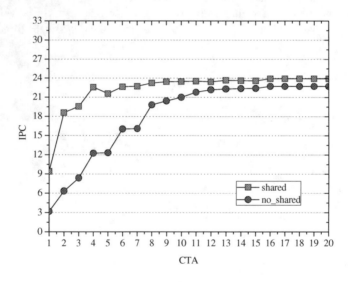

(c) Comparison of Changing CTA Sizes

Fig. 5. (*continued*)

When there are a lot of threads executing, the threads conceal the delay caused by some threads' pipeline stalling, so that the performance rising. After the number of threads is enough to totally hide the delay of threads memory access, the performance of using the shared memory is almost the same as that of not using it. The figure 3-3 has also shown that if the hardware source increased too much that the number of threads is not enough to use hardware sources, the parallel executing threads could not conceal completely the delay caused by the pipeline of some threads stalling, and so the performance falls. Nevertheless, the workloads' performance of using the shared memory decreases more slowly than that of not using it, because that the delay time of former memory access is so less that it has small pipeline stalling time, which makes the demand of the threads hiding the delay time smaller under the use of shared memory.

4   Conclusion

This article extracts a generic SIMT scheduling model from GPU and shows the attribute of this model through analyzing the performance of it, so as to research and develop the technology of SIMT in GPU. Though research the model with benchmarks, this article finds that the workloads having much more threads can take advantage of the SIMT technology better. The sufficient number of threads has the ability to hide the problems existing in threads and makes the source utilization saturation by filling the hardware sources in the SIMT model pipeline. What's more, the programing of workloads must be considered with the executing way of the hardware sources which should be accord with the attribute of the SIMT model to exploit the advantages of it. The architecture of the SIMT model also needs to adapt the program. When someone uses the SIMT architecture, he must consider all of the software and the hardware parts. Only changing one characteristic cannot make a better effect or maybe bring the worse effect with the waste of sources. So a different workload should match its own best fit SIMT hardware structure in order to make full use of its performance. Besides, the special memory technology in SIMT scheduling model leads to a special attribute. When programing the workloads, someone should be as possible as he can to utilize the shared memory source to develop the ability of it for decreasing the pressure of the bandwidth of memory and increasing the speed of data access. In conclusion, the SIMT scheduling model and the results analyzed by this article can be important references for the use and optimizing of SIMT scheduling technology in other processor architectures.

References

[1] Lee, V.W.: Debunking the 100X GPU vs. CPU Myth: An Evaluation of Throughput Computing on CPU and GPU. In: The 37th International Symposium on Computer Architecture, ISCA 2010, Saint-Malo, France, pp. 451–460 (2010)
[2] Luebke, D., Humphreys, G.: How GPUs work. Computer 40(2), 96–100 (2007)
[3] John, N., Dally, W.J.: The GPU Computing Era. Annals Through the Year, pp. 56–69. The IEEE Computer Society (2010)
[4] NVIDIA CUDA: Compute Unified Device Architecture, NVIDIA Corp. (2007)
[5] NVIDIA CUDA C Programming Guide Version 3.2 (M/OL). NVIDIA (2010), http://developer.download.nvidia.com/compute/cuda/3_2/toolkit/docs/CUDA_C_Program-ming_Guide.pdf

[6] Fung, W.W.L., Sham, I., Yuan, G., Aamodt, T.M.: Dynamic Warp Formation and Scheduling for Efficient GPU Control Flow. In: 40th Annual IEEE/ACM International Symposium on Microarchitecture, pp. 407–420. IEEE Press (2007)

[7] Meng, J., Tarjan, D., Skadron, K.: Skadron: Dynamic Warp Subdivision for Integrated Branch and Memory Divergence Tolerance. In: 37th Annual International Symposium on Computer Architecture, ISCA 2010 (June 2010)

[8] Manavski, S.A.: CUDA compatible GPU as an efficient hardware accelerator for AES cryptography. In: ICSPC 2007: Proc. of IEEE Int'l Conf. on Signal Processing and Communication, pp. 65–68 (2007)

[9] Giles, M., Xiaoke, S.: Notes on using the NVIDIA 8800 GTX graphics card, http://people.maths.ox.ac.uk/~gilesm/hpc/

[10] Giles, M.: Jacobi iteration for a Laplace discretisation on a 3D structured grid, http://people.maths.ox.ac.uk/~gilesm/hpc/NVIDIA/laplace3d.pdf

[11] Maxime Ray tracing, http://www.nvidia.com/cuda

[12] Al-Kiswany, S., Gharaibeh, A., Santos-Neto, E., Yuan, G., Ripeanu, M.: StoreGPU: exploiting graphics processing units to accelerate distributed storage systems. In: Proc. 17th Int'l Symp. on High Performance Distributed Computing, pp. 165–174 (2008)

A Unified Cryptographic Processor
for RSA and ECC in RNS

Jizeng Wei*, Wei Guo, Hao Liu, and Ya Tan

School of Computer Science and Technology,
Tianjin Key Laboratory of Cognitive Computing and Application,
Tianjin University, Tianjin, China
{weijizeng,weiguo,liuhao8901,tanya}@tju.edu.cn

Abstract. This paper proposes a unified and programmable crypto-processor with coarse-grained reconfigurable datapath to perform either RSA or elliptic curve cryptosystems (ECC) over prime field GF(p), which uses Residue Number System (RNS) as basic arithmetic to exploit data-level parallelism and Transport Triggered Architecture to improve instruction-level parallelism. The reconfigurable datapath provides three configuration modes to accelerate the RNS Montgomery multiplication(RNSMM). An efficient RNS base, $2^n - c_i$, is chosen to reduce the multiplication complexity of RNSMM. Experimental results show that the proposed processor has better tradeoff among algorithm flexibility, performance and area than other related works.

Keywords: Public-Key Cryptosystems, RSA, ECC, Residue Number System, Transport Triggered Architecture, Reconfigurable Architecture.

1 Introduction

Considering security as well as cost-efficiency, various unified and programmable processors for Public Key Cryptosystems (PKC) such as RSA and Elliptic curve cryptography (ECC) have caused wide concern[2][3][4][5]. For PKC, Montgomery Multiplication (MM) is the foremost cornerstone. Copious literatures have proposed many optimized MM designs, for example, Radix-2 MM[1], systolic array [6] and word-based MM [7]. Nevertheless, above methods do not bridge the gap between the key size of RSA and ECC, producing the low performance/cost ratio in the unified architecture. In this context, residue number system (RNS) has been employed to implement MM called RNSMM. In this way, a large integer can be decomposed into several small and dependent elements with the same width. As a result, RNS owns the attractive ability to execute modular arithmetic in parallel and make the operands of RSA and ECC have the same size. For RSA, A fast parallel RNSMM and the prototype architecture called Cox-Rower

---

* This work is supported by the Natural Science Foundation of Tianjin (No. 11JCZDJC15800), and the National Natural Science Foundation of China (No. 61003306).

W. Xu et al. (Eds.): NCCET 2013, CCIS 396, pp. 19–32, 2013.

is designed[8]. For ECC, [9] and [11] proposed hardware architecture of point multiplier that exploited RNS to speed up elliptic curve point calculations and minimize the area. [10] presented a FPGA implementation of RNS-based ECC, which is resistant against side channel attacks. But there is not yet a RNS-based unified architecture to support both RSA and ECC to the best of our knowledge. Furthermore, above architectures are all based on ASIC, in other words, it must bring the extra area cost for the numbering system conversion between the binary and RNS [9].

In this paper a unified and programmable crypto-processor with coarse-grained reconfigurable datapath is proposed to perform either RSA or ECC over GF(p), which uses RNS as basic arithmetic to exploit data-level parallelism (DLP) and Transport Triggered Architecture to improve instruction-level parallelism (ILP). The reconfigurable datapath provides three configuration modes to accelerate the RNSMM. Moreover, an efficient RNS base, $2^n - c_i$, is chosen to reduce the multiplication complexity of RNSMM.

2 RNS Montgomery Multiplication and Base Selection

2.1 Residue Number System

RNS is defined through a set of co-prime integers $(m_1, m_2, ..., m_k)$, called the base. Any integer X, $0 \leq X < M = \prod_{i=1}^{k} m_i$, has a unique representation, given by the n-tuple $[X]_{RNS} = (x_1, x_2, ..., x_k)$, where $x_i = \langle X \rangle_{m_i} = X \bmod m_i$. In formula (1), residue can also be converted back to binary representation[8][9].

$$x = \sum_{i=1}^{k} x_i M_i \langle M_i^{-1} \rangle_{m_i} \bmod M = \sum_{i=1}^{k} \varepsilon_i M_i - \beta M$$

$$\text{where } M_i = \frac{M}{m_i} \text{ and } \varepsilon_i = (x_i \langle M_i^{-1} \rangle_{m_i}) \bmod m_i \tag{1}$$

Assuming two integers X and Y in RNS representation, i.e. $X = (x_1, x_2, ..., x_k)$ and $Y = (y_1, y_2, ..., y_k)$, then all the operations $\otimes = (+, -, \times)$ can be performed in parallel, as indicated by $X \otimes Y = (\langle x_1 \otimes y_1 \rangle_{m_1}, \langle x_2 \otimes y_2 \rangle_{m_2}, ..., \langle x_k \otimes y_k \rangle_{m_k})$. The parallelism of RNS will greatly accelerate the execution of modular arithmetic in PKC,including modular multiplication.

2.2 RNS Montgomery Multiplication and Data Level Parallelism Analysis

In the form of RNS, almost all operations of RSA and ECC are RNSMM. The only difference is the control flow of invoking RNSMM. So, the data level parallelism of RNSMM will eventually produce a significant impact on the parallel processing capability of proposed crypto-processor. In this paper,a fast parallel

---

Algorithm 1. RNS Montgomery Multiplication

Input: $[X]_{a \cup b}, [Y]_{a \cup b} (X, Y < 2N)$

Output: $[R]_{a \cup b}, (R = XYA^{-1} \bmod N, R < 2N$ and $A = \prod\limits_{i=1}^{k} a_i)$

for $i = 1$ **to** k **do**
   /*k is the number of base elements*/
   step1: $z_i = (x_i \times y_i) \bmod a_i$
   step2: $q_i = (z_i \times \langle -N_i^{-1} \rangle_{a_i}) \bmod a_i$
end for
step3: $[Q]_b = BT([Q]_a, 0)$
/*$[Q]_a = (q_1, q_2, ..., q_i, ..., q_k)$ and $[Q]_b = (q_1, q_2, ..., q_j, ..., q_k)$*/
for $j = 1$ **to** k **do**
   step4: $z_j = (x_j \times y_j) \bmod b_j$
   step5: $w_j = (z_j + q_j \times N_j) \bmod b_j$
   step6: $r_j = (w_i \times \langle A^{-1} \rangle_{b_j}) \bmod b_j$
end for
step7: $[R]_a = BT([R]_b, 0.5)$
/*$[R]_a = (r_1, r_2, ..., r_i, ..., r_k)$ and $[R]_b = (r_1, r_2, ..., r_j, ..., r_k)$*/
return $([R]_{a \cup b})$

Algorithm 2. Base Transformation Algorithm $BT([X]_a, \mu)$

Input: $[X]_a, \mu = 0$ or 0.5
Output: $[X]_b$
$\delta_0 = \mu$
for $i = 1$ **to** k **do**
   /*k is the number of base elements*/
   step1: $\varepsilon_i = x_i \langle A_i^{-1} \rangle_{a_i} \bmod a_i$
   step2: $\delta_i = \delta_{i-1} + trunc(\varepsilon_i)/2^r$
   /*$trunc(\varepsilon_i) = \varepsilon_i \wedge (\underbrace{1...1}_{g}\underbrace{0...0}_{r-g})$ and r is the bit length of base*/

end for
for $j = 1$ **to** k **do**
   $x_{j(0)} = 0$
   for $i = 1$ **to** k **do**
     step3: $x_{ji} = (x_{j(i-1)} + \varepsilon_i \langle A_i \rangle_{b_j}) \bmod b_j$
   end for
   step4: $x_{j(k+1)} = (x_{jk} + (b_j - \delta_k \langle A \rangle_{b_j}) \bmod b_j$
end for
return $x_{j(k+1)}$

RNSMM in Algorithm 1, proposed by [8], is adopted. Two sets of RNS bases, a_i and b_j, are introduced and A is chosen as Montgomery constant. Except for a_i and b_j, the other variables with subscript i and j are the representations on base a_i and b_j. "$<>$" stands for modulus operation. **step 3** and **step 7** in Algorithm 1 are the base transformation (BT) between different base representations, further detailed in Algorithm 2. Another input of Algorithm 2 is correction factor μ for the approximate conversion from RNS to binary. It can be seen that modular multiplication (MM) and modular multiplication-and-accumulation(MMAC) are two main operations in RNSMM. The data dependence graph(DDG) of RNSMM from **step 1** to **step 3** in Algorithm 1 is shown in Fig.1. Fig.1 (a) illustrates the

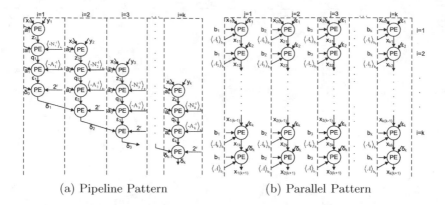

(a) Pipeline Pattern   (b) Parallel Pattern

Fig. 1. The DDG of RNSMM

data dependency of **step 1** and **step 2** in Algorithm 1 and 2, respectively. **step 3** and **step 4** in Algorithm 2 are included in Fig.1 (b). Each circle, denoted by PE, indicates a type of operation in RNSMM such as MM and MMAC.

In Fig.1(a), the ith column completes the ith loop to calculate ε_i and δ_i used by the next loop. Each PE performs one time in the loop. From loop *1* to k, data generated from previous PE is processed by the next PE in pipeline pattern in which four sets of data can be executed concurrently. Therefore, at least four PEs must be designed to meet the requirement in parallel, and each PE is time sharing. The operation time is approximately $E = k + p$, where k is the loop length and p is the pipeline stages. In Fig.1(b), a nested-looping for **step 3** and **step 4** in Algorithm 2 should be performed after ε_i and δ_i are produced. Each column represents one outer loop completing $k + 1$ operations, where k is the loop length of **step 3**, namely inner loop, and "*1*" expresses **step 4**. Each PE processes one time inner loop or **step 4**. In this way, all the PEs are column-sharing and independent each other. This means that the sets of data belonged to the same row can be fully paralleled as long as enough PEs are equipped. The operation time of Fig.1 (b) is about $k \times (k + 1)/N$, where N is the number of PEs. The DDG of **step 4** to **step 7** in Algorithm 1 is almost similar to Fig.1. The only difference is that **step 4** and **step 5** completes one time modular multiplication-and-accumulation instead of modular multiplication of **step 1**. So the RNSMM should consume $2(k + p) + \frac{2k(k+1)}{N} + 1$ operation times.

Stated thus, the RNSMM can be divided into two patterns: ***pipeline*** and ***parallel***, which demands that the connection among PEs can be dynamic changed. A coarse-grained reconfigurable datapath will be introduced in Section 4.

2.3   Base Selection and Efficient Arithmetic Implementation

In RNSMM, MM and MMAC are the most costly operations and MMAC can be further decomposed into MM and modular addition. So, how to implement MM efficiently is a priority. For RNS, the form of base directly determines the computation complexity of MM. In this paper, a highly efficient RNS base is chosen in the form of $2^n - c_i$, where n is the length of RNS base.

Algorithm 3. Modular Multiplication Algorithm $mulmod(a, b, m_i)$

Input: $a, b, m_i, 0 \leq a, b < m$ with $m_i = 2^n - c_i$ and $c_i < 2^t$ and $1 < t < (n-1)/2$
Output: $r = ab \bmod m_i$
step1: $y = a \times b$
step2: $y_1 = y \div 2^n; y_0 = y \bmod 2^n$
step3: $y' = c_i y_1 + y_0$
step4: $y_1' = y' \div 2^n; y_0' = y' \bmod 2^n$
step5: $y'' = c_i y_1' + y_0'$
step6: $y''' = y'' + c_i$
step7:
if $y''' \geq 2^n$ **then**
    $r \leftarrow y''' \bmod 2^n$
else
    $r \leftarrow y''$
end if

Generally, the computation complexity of traditional MM based on Barrett Reduction(BR) algorithm is

$$2n^2 M + S + eA + kS + 4T \ (e = 0 \text{ or } 1, k \geq 0) \tag{2}$$

where M is multiplication of two n bits integer, and S, A and T represent subtraction, addition and shifting operation, respectively. The value of e and k depends on the result of mod operation, which is not fixed. Using RNS base like $2^n - c_i$, the MM is converted into Algorithm 3. BR is given from **step 2** to **step 7**, in which the division and mod operations can be easily implemented by simple shift operation. As c_i is less than 2^t, the complexity of multiplication in **step 3** is ntM. In **step 5**, c_i and y_1' are all less than 2^t, so the complexity of multiplication in this step is ttM. Comparison with formula (2), the whole computation complexity of BR-based MM is decreased to

$$ntM + ttM + 3A + 5T$$

$$= (\delta^2 + \delta)n^2 M + 3A + 5T < 0.75n^2 M + 3A + 5T(\delta = \frac{t}{n} \text{ and } \delta < 0.5). \tag{3}$$

So the considerable reduction of computation complexity of MM, because of specifically selected base, will result in higher performance/cost ratio for the RNSMM hardware implementation.

3   Proposed Cryptographic Processor for RSA and ECC over GF(p)

3.1   Transport Triggered Architecture

Transport Triggered Architecture (TTA) is statically programmed ILP architecture with high resemblance to VLIW at the point of instruction format. It is

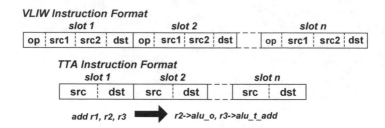

VLIW Instruction Format

slot 1				slot 2					slot n			
op	src1	src2	dst	op	src1	src2	dst	— —	op	src1	src2	dst

TTA Instruction Format

slot 1		slot 2		slot n	
src	dst	src	dst	src	dst

add r1, r2, r3 ➡ r2->alu_o, r3->alu_t_add

Fig. 2. Instruction Format and Programming Method Difference in VLIWs and TTAs. op: operation code. src: source operand register address. dst: destination register address.

organized as a set of functional units (FUs) and register files (RFs) which are connected together with an interconnection network composed of move buses and sockets. Unlike VLIW architectures programmed by specifying the RISC-like operations to trigger data transports, TTAs specify the required data transports of FUs to trigger operations as side effect implicitly. Fig.2 shows the difference of instruction format and programming method between VLIWs and TTAs. In this way, data transports of TTAs are visible at the architecture level, which allows to remove many redundant data hazards, such as write after read (WAR) and write after write (WAW). This characteristic is very important to the pipeline pattern of RNSMM in which strong data hazard exits.

3.2   The Architecture Overview of Proposed Cryptographic Processor

As illustrated in Fig.3, the unified and reconfigurable RSA/ECC processor based on RNS and TTA consists of three key modules: FUs, interconnection network and flow control unit. The data width, depending on the RNS base, is 32-bit. In the view of programmability, there are three levels in the proposed processor.

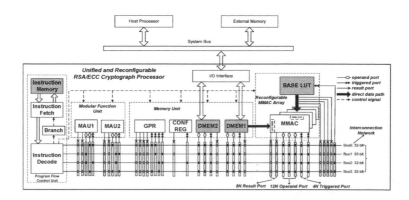

Fig. 3. The Unified and Reconfigurable RSA/ECC Cryptographic Processor

The highest level is RSA modular exponentiation and ECC point multiplication. The middle level is point double and point addition in ECC. And the lowest level is RNSMM associated with the FUs, for example, the modular arithmetic unit (MAU), the coarse-grained reconfigurable MMAC array and the memory units including DMEM1, DMEM2 and BASE LUT.

Coarse-grained MMAC array includes multiple versatile MMAC units, every of which can complete multiplication, MM and MMAC. In MMAC array, four MMAC units compose one group and the MMAC array consists of m groups. Because the pipeline pattern of RNSMM requires at least four PEs to run full-load, every four MMAC units will be configured to cascade connection to process data in pipeline. When getting into parallel patternthe N ($N = 4m$) MMAC units in all groups can be arranged in the parallel connection to achieve N times ($N \leq k$) outer loop simultaneously in the Algorithm 2. The look-up table, BASE LUT, stores all the pre-computed operands related to the selected base. It is divided into multiple banks in order to access multiple 32-bit data in parallel. The details of reconfigurable MMAC array will be discussed in the next section. A configuration register (CONF REG) is adopted to dynamically change the connection of MMAC array. Two on-chip memories, DMEM1 and DMEM2, store the input data of $[X]_{a \cup b}$ and $[Y]_{a \cup b}$ respectively so as to avoid the access conflict. Based on the above FUs.

Instruction Level Parallelism of Proposed Cryptographic Processor. Different from other crypto-processors only concerning the DLP, TTA is adopted as the top architecture to exploit higher ILP. Based on TTA, many redundant data moves, very common in the pipeline pattern of RNSMM, can be avoided by bypass datapath. Fig.4 presents a part of instructions in RNSMM. Instruction 1 and 3 have output dependency on the same destination register which prevents execution in parallel. So these two instructions in the VLIW architecture cannot be issued at a time. It also affects the parallel execution of Instruction 2 and 4, which finally results in a sequential processing. Since the processed results are not required to be written back in TTA-like architecture, the dependency can be ignored and the four instructions can be executed in parallel in two TTA-like instructions. With the help of TTA, the proposed crypto-processor owns higher performance and resource utilization.

4 Coarse-Grained Reconfigurable MMAC Array

4.1 Coarse-Grained Reconfigurable Datapath

As mentioned, the coarse-grained reconfigurable MMAC array is built on the algorithm level instead of operation level, reducing the overhead brought from frequent datapath switching. The MMAC array provides three configuration modes including cascade, parallel and normal. For describing clearly, the MMAC array with only one group is as an example shown in Fig.5. The blue lines stand for the triggered port to keep connecting all the while. The red lines are reconfigurable datapaths that can be switched to transport data in a particular mode.

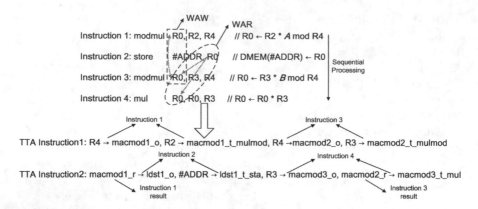

Fig. 4. ILP Exploitation in Proposed Cryptographic Processor

Cascade Configuration Mode:

For the pipeline pattern of RNSMM, four MMAC units are connected one by one, i.e.cascade configuration mode as Fig.5(a). The operands of the first MMAC unit, corresponding to the **step 1** in Algorithm 1, are accessed from BASE LUT and DMEM1. From the 2nd to the 4th MMAC unit that complete the **step 2** in Algorithm 1 and **step 1** and **step 2** in Algorithm 2, the operands are directly provided by the previous one. Furthermore, other operands of MMAC units are fetched from interconnection network. So this configuration mode is suitable to the pipeline pattern of RNSMM in which the atom operations of four steps are executed step by step and each step needs the result of the previous operation.

Parallel Configuration Mode:

As shown in Fig.5(b), operands, such as $\langle A_i \rangle_{b_j}$ and $\langle A \rangle_{b_j}$ in Algorithm 2, are accessed from the multi-bank BASE LUT to accommodate the parallel pattern of RNSMM. Each MMAC unit finishes one outer-loop to produce an accumulated result that is the representation of the input data in another selected base. Modular operands b_j also provided by BASE LUT are not changed. As a result, only one data move instruction is needed at the beginning. The four MMAC units can be seen as fully independent and operands are provided in parallel by BASE LUT default. Like Fig.5(a), other operands, ε_i and δ_i, are transferred from DMEM1 by interconnection network to trigger corresponding operations.

Normal Configuration Mode:

In this mode, all the operands are supplied only by the interconnection network shown in Fig.5(c). So, the MMAC array can be seen as multiple duplicated functional units. This configuration mode is not used in the RNSMM algorithm, but rather in some other sporadic multiplications in RSA or ECC over GF(p), such as the conversion of binary representation and RNS.

For the cascade and parallel mode, the most of operands can be accessed from the direct datapath. In this way, only one start instruction is needed if the data source is not changed. And only specific data is necessary to be moved into the trigger register to make the MMAC array execute as shown in Fig.5. Thereby,

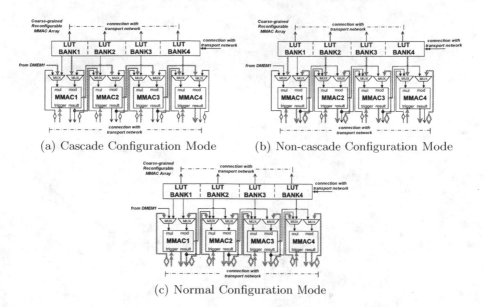

(a) Cascade Configuration Mode   (b) Non-cascade Configuration Mode

(c) Normal Configuration Mode

Fig. 5. The Configuration Modes of Coarse-grained Reconfigurable MMAC Array

only N buses are required to hold $N = 4m$ data simultaneously in one cycle, which is enough to drive N MMAC units running at full capacity.

4.2 Versatile MMAC Unit

Versatile MMAC unit, shown in Fig.6, is the kernel of MMAC array, which can execute three types of operations including multiplication, MM and MMAC. The *macmod_r_ high_reg* saves the high 32-bit of multiplication. The *macmod_r_reg* is for the result of MM, MMAC or the low 32-bit of multiplication. The modulus passing to the next MMAC can be accessed from the *macmod_r_mod_reg* directly.

Three-stage pipeline is applied in the MMAC unit. The first two pipeline stages realize the MM in Algorithm 3, in which there are three multipliers. The multiplier in the first stage is 32-bit because of 32-bit operands in **step 1**. For the multiplication in **step 3**, the c_i is modulus that is less than 14-bit in the selected base and y_1 is the high 32-bit of multiplication result in **step 1**. Therefore, the first multiplier in the second stage is 32-bit × 14-bit. **step 5** contains another multiplication in which c_i is less than 14-bit and y_1' is the high 15-bit of the multiplication result of **step 3**, resulting in another 15-bit × 14-bit multiplier set in the second stage. Comparing with three 32-bit × 32-bit multipliers used in BR, the different width multipliers based on the selected base reduce the design complexity of MMAC unit greatly and derive better performance. The third stage of MMAC unit implements the accumulation operation.

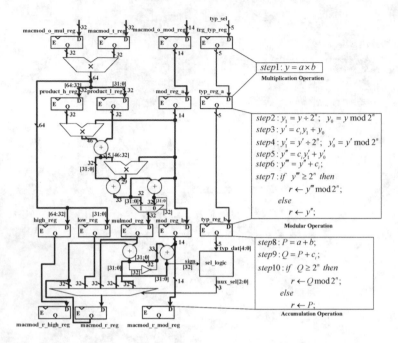

Fig. 6. The Architecture of MMAC Unit

5   Performance Evaluation and Implementation Results

5.1   Performance Evaluation

In this paper, four architecture candidates that are 4MMAC, 8MMAC, 12MMAC and 16MMAC are chosen to be efficiently evaluated. The processing time of RNSMM consists of computation and data preparing time. Upon the DLP analysis, the cycles of RNSMM are approximately equal to $2(k+p) + \frac{2k(k+1)}{N} + 1$. As the delay of DMEM is four cycles and there are $2k$ times loop in the RNSMM, the data preparing time is $4 \times 2k$ cycles. Therefore, the RNSMM consumes $2(k+p) + \frac{2k(k+1)}{N} + 1 + 2 \times 4k$ cycles, where N is the number of MMAC units, k is the number of base elements decided by the key size and p is the number of pipeline stages in the pipeline pattern, which is "4" in this paper.

Upon above formula, Fig.7 plots the impact of different architecture candidates and key sizes on the RNSMM processing time for RSA and ECC. It can be seen that the processing time is reduced with the increase of the number of MMAC units, and when the key size is larger, the downward trend is faster. The decline seems more dramatically for 4096-bit RSA and 384-bit ECC, which can attain 65% and 39% reduction from 4MMAC to 16MMAC. Because, for the parallel pattern, more MMAC units mean that the more parallelism can be offered. Thus, the proposed crypto-processor owns strong scalability. From 512 to 2048-bit key RSA, the reduction of cycles of RNSMM is not significant, when the number of MMAC units is larger than 8. It is also evident for ECC from 160-bit

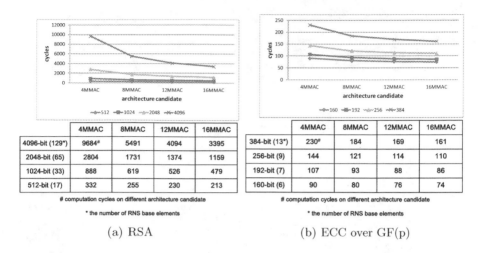

	4MMAC	8MMAC	12MMAC	16MMAC
4096-bit (129*)	9684#	5491	4094	3395
2048-bit (65)	2804	1731	1374	1159
1024-bit (33)	888	619	526	479
512-bit (17)	332	255	230	213

computation cycles on different architecture candidate

* the number of RNS base elements

	4MMAC	8MMAC	12MMAC	16MMAC
384-bit (13*)	230#	184	169	161
256-bit (9)	144	121	114	110
192-bit (7)	107	93	88	86
160-bit (6)	90	80	76	74

computation cycles on different architecture candidate

* the number of RNS base elements

(a) RSA   (b) ECC over GF(p)

Fig. 7. RNSMM Computation Cycles for Different Architecture Candidates and Cipher Key Length

to 256-bit key. The time of ECC with 256-bit key on 12MMAC and 16MMAC are, respectively, only *7* and *11* cycles less than 8MMAC. This is because the number of base elements of 256-bit key is only 9 so that 8MMAC has provided adequate throughput rate. Moreover, as the number of MMAC units increases, more buses are demanded to ensure the MMAC array running at full-load. In TTA, the more buses means the wider instruction word, which results in larger instruction memory. Therefore, the number of MMAC units must be kept within modest bounds. So, 4MMAC and 8MMAC are the better candidates.

5.2   Comparison to Related Works and Implementation Results

Table 1 shows the comparison among different crypto-processers in RNS, in which our design is the only one that adopts the programmable processor solution. So, it breaks the application limits in the ASIC solutions and become the first RNS-based architecture supporting both RSA and ECC over GF(p) of our knowledge to date, which is the biggest advantage of this design. The total area of 4MMAC and 8MMAC are 306kgates and 396kgates, respectively, in which the logic area are 106kgates and 296kgates. Upon 4MMAC architecture, the computation time of 2048-bit RSA and 256-bit ECC can achieve 26.1ms and 3.2ms. When the number of MMAC units increases to 8, the computation time of above to will be reduced to 13.5ms and 2.2ms.

The data in this table may not be compared directly because the implemented platforms are different. [8] has less execution cycles of RSA than ours. The reason is that it equips 11 computation units, while only 8 MMAC units with similar functionality are included in ours. But, because of the programmability, an instruction memory has to be appended, which leads to the area increasing. And more than 8 MMAC units is also a waste to the speed and area of ECC

Table 1. Comparison with Related Cryptographic Processor in RNS

Reference	Year	Technology	Freq. (MHZ)	Area	Func.	Key Length	T_{speed} cycles	ms
[8]	2001	0.25μm	80	221kgates (logic) 57KB ROM 12KB RAM	RSA	1024	336,000	4.2
						2048	2,336,000	29.2
[9]	2009	-	-	66.7kgates	ECC GF(p)	160	-	1.77
				78.9kgates		192	-	2.97
				103kgates		256	-	3.95
[10]	2010	Stratix EP2S30F484C3	165.5	5,896ALM 74DSP	ECC GF(p)	160	52,960	0.32
			160.5	6,203ALM 92DSP		192	70,620	0.44
			157.2	9,177ALM 96DSP		256	106,896	0.68
This Work (4MMAC)	2012	0.13μm	250	306kgates (total) 106kgates (logic) ROM 24KB ROM 2KB RAM	RSA	512	183,708	0.73
						1024	1,003,440	4
						2048	6,519,840	26.1
					ECC GF(p)	160	318,203	1.2
						192	536,343	2.1
						256	791,130	3.2
This Work (8MMAC)				396kgates (total) 196kgates (logic) 24KB ROM 2KB RAM	RSA	512	113,400	0.45
						1024	531,100	2.1
						2048	3,384,000	13.5
					ECC GF(p)	160	294,705	1.1
						192	347,142	1.4
						256	544,322	2.2

[1] the area of data memory used to store parameters of ECC is not included

due to the limitation of the number of base. So it is worth that our design sacrifices some DLP in return for the tradeoff among processing speed and area. The size of ROM and RAM of Kawamura's design is larger than ours. This is because that it supports RNS-based RSA as well as RSA with CRT, which causes it storing many parameters related to base in the CRT mode. [9] and [10] are all the implementation of RNS-based ECC. Because the optimization goal of [9] is area reduction, it only consists of two RNS operation units, which results in slower speed than our design. Moreover, logic area of [9] becomes larger and larger with the increase of key length and is almost close to the area of 4MMAC when the key length is equal to 256-bit. The reason is that there is one RNS-to-binary unit in this solution, increasing the area burden. While, in the this paper, the programmability guarantees the logic area not increasing with the key size increasing and the conversion between RNS and binary can reuse the existing hardware resource as shown in Section 2.3. [10] improves the Cox-Rower architecture, which makes it suitable for ECC over GF(p) and leads to faster speed of scalar multiplication. But it cannot support RSA. In conclusion, the proposed crypto-processor performs a kind of better tradeoff among performance, area and flexibility.

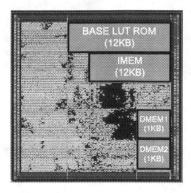

Process Technology	SMIC 0.13Mm CMOS Technology
Die Size	2.5mm x 2.5mm
Power Supply	0.18V
Operation Frequency	250MHZ
Gate counts and Memory	106Kgates and 26KB SRAM Total: about 306Kgates
Decryption Speed	266Kbps for 1024-bit RSA (*1000-bit data packet*)
	490 times scalar multiplication for 192-bit ECC (*184-bit data packet*)

Fig. 8. The Layout and Feature of Proposed Cryptographic Processor with Four MM-MAC Units

With the architecture of 4MMAC, for example, Fig.8 shows the chip layout of the proposed crypto-processor and its features. It is designed with a $0.13\mu m$ SIMC CMOS technology and its area is $2.5 \times 2.5mm^2$ which includes 106K logic gates and 26KB on-chip SRAM. The operating frequency is 250MHZ. Its peak performance can reach to 266Kbps for 1024-bit RSA and 490 times scalar multiplication for 192-bit ECC.

6   Conclusion

An programmable crypto-processor that supports both RSA and ECC over GF(p) using RNS and a coarse-grained reconfigurable datapath was presented. The processor can handle RSA and ECC with arbitrary key size and conversion between binary and RNS by programmability without modifying hardware. RNS and TTA successfully exploited the DLP and ILP of our design. On the selected RNS base, $2^n - c_i$, the reconfigurable datapath composed by MMAC units can complete the RNSMM more efficiently on the level of algorithm. Experimental results show that our design exhibits competitive processing speed, area and flexibility advantages in comparison with related works.

References

1. Hutter, M., Wenger, E.: Fast Multi-precision Multiplication for Public-key Cryptography on Embedded Microprocessors. In: Preneel, B., Takagi, T. (eds.) CHES 2011. LNCS, vol. 6917, pp. 459–474. Springer, Heidelberg (2011)
2. Zeng, X.-Y., et al.: A Reconfigurable Public-key Cryptography Coprocessor. In: IEEE Asia-Pacific Conf. on Advanced System Integrated Circuits (AP-ASIC 2004), pp. 172–175 (2004)
3. Mentens, N., Sakiyama, K., et al.: A Side-channel Attack Resistant Programmable PKC Coprocessor for Embedded Applications. In: Int. Conf. on Embedded Computer Systems: Architectures, Modeling, and Simulation (SAMOS-7), pp. 194–200 (2007)

4. Chen, J.-H., Shieh, M.-D., et al.: A High-performance Unified-field Reconfigurable Cryptographic Processor. IEEE Tran. VLSI. 18(8), 1145–1158 (2010)
5. Smyth, N., et al.: An Adaptable And Scalable Asymmetric Cryptographic Processor. In: IEEE Int. Conf. on Application-Specific Systems, Architectures and Processors (ASAP-17), pp. 341–346 (2006)
6. Wang, Z., Fan, S.-Q.: Efficient Montgomery-Based Semi-Systolic Multiplier for Even-Type GNB of $GF(2^m)$. IEEE Tran. Comp. 61(3), 415–419 (2012)
7. Huang, M.-Q., Gaj, K., et al.: New Hardware Architectures for Montgomery Modular Multiplication Algorithm. IEEE Tran. Comp. 60(7), 923–936 (2011)
8. Kawamura, S.-i., Koike, M., Sano, F., Shimbo, A.: Cox-rower architecture for fast parallel montgomery multiplication. In: Preneel, B. (ed.) EUROCRYPT 2000. LNCS, vol. 1807, pp. 523–538. Springer, Heidelberg (2000)
9. Schinianakis, D.M., et al.: An RNS Implementation of an Fp Elliptic Curve Point Multiplier. IEEE Tran. Circ. Syst. 56(6), 1202–1213 (2009)
10. Guillermin, N.: A high speed coprocessor for elliptic curve scalar multiplications over $\mathbb{F}_p$. In: Mangard, S., Standaert, F.-X. (eds.) CHES 2010. LNCS, vol. 6225, pp. 48–64. Springer, Heidelberg (2010)
11. Schinianakis, et al.: A RNS Montgomery Multiplication Architecture. In: IEEE Int. Symp. on Circuits and Systems (ISCAS), pp.1167–1170 (2011)

Real-Time Implementation of 4x4 MIMO-OFDM System for 3GPP-LTE Based on a Programmable Processor

Ting Chen*, Hengzhu Liu, and Jianghua Wan

Microelectronics and Microprocessor Institute, School of Computer,
National University of Defense Technology,
Changsha 410073, China
{tingchen,hengzhuliu}@nudt.edu.cn

Abstract. MIMO-OFDM is currently being considered as a promising technology for future wideband wireless systems. Meanwhile, the detection of MIMO-OFDM system forms one of the most intensive tasks in baseband signal processing. There have been a great number of algorithms proposed for MIMO-OFDM detection. This paper investigates the real-time implementation of MIMO OFDM systems using programmable multi-SIMD (single instruction multiple data) processor targeting for software defined radio. We analyze the computational characteristic and cost of major algorithms of LPF, symbol synchronization, OFDM modulation, channel estimation and MIMO detection of a 4x4 MIMO-OFDM system based on 3GPP-LTE R-12 standard. The evaluation and implementation results show that our SDR architecture supports 300Mbps LTE system with 20MHz bandwidth. Finally, we discuss the architecture perspective of our SDR processor for future wireless communication standards with higher throughput.

Keywords: MIMO-OFDM, Multi-SIMD, SDR, 3GPP-LTE.

1 Introduction

Multiple Input Multiple Output (MIMO) and Orthogonal Frequency Division Multiplexing (OFDM) have been adopted to increasing the spectrum efficiency by emerging wireless broadband standards, such as the 3rd generation partnership project long term evolution (3GPP-LTE) and WiMax [1]. However, the new techniques bringing the enhancement of data rate in wireless communication always have high computational complexity, a large number of algorithms about OFDM modulation, channel estimation (CE) and MIMO equalization have been proposed [2][3]. Unfortunately, some of them are too complicated to implement in the state-of-the-art digital signal processors (DSP) in real-time though they can provide excellent performance. Consequently, trade-off must be made between performance and complexity for practical and efficient implementation.

---

* Corresponding author.

W. Xu et al. (Eds.): NCCET 2013, CCIS 396, pp. 33–43, 2013.

Many works have been carried out to implement the MIMO-OFDM physical layer by ASIC and VLSI [4][5]. However, they are difficult to be upgraded for the evolving communication standards. Recently, a lot of programmable processor is proposed, e.g., MSC8156 [6], PC205 [7] and TMS320TCI6618 [8]. But they still rely on some accelerators to offload parts of the wireless standard processing to achieve high throughputs. Data movement between accelerators and main memory may push these platforms toward inflexible solutions.

This paper investigates the real-time and hardware-efficient implementation of low pass filter (LPF), symbol synchronization, OFDM modulation, channel estimation and MIMO detection for MIMO-OFDM systems using fully programmable hardware aimed for software defined radio (SDR). A real-time 4x4 MIMO-OFDM system of 3GPP-LTE standard is implemented on a programmable multi-SIMD SDR processor. The remainder of this paper is structured in the following way. In section II, the MIMO-OFDM system is outlined. Then, some algorithms and their complexity for the system are covered in section III. Next in section IV, we describe the architecture of QMBase SDR processor and implementation results. Section V summarizes the challenge and architecture perspective of future wireless communication for SDR processor. In the last section we summarize the major conclusions obtained from this work and future work.

2   Radio System Structure

The system model under consideration is depicted in Fig. 1, which shows the basic function blocks of MIMO-OFDM system with four Tx antennas and four Rx antennas. LTE supports up to 4x4 multi-user MIMO (MU-MIMO) configurations with a maximum bandwidth of 20MHz and 1200 subcarriers per OFDM symbol. The length of every radio frame is 10ms, and one frame consists of 10 subframes. Every subframe contains 14 OFDM symbols with two training sequences (pilot) deployed on the fourth and eleventh OFDM symbols. Transmission and processing are done upon subframe basis within 1ms TTI (Transmission Time Interval)

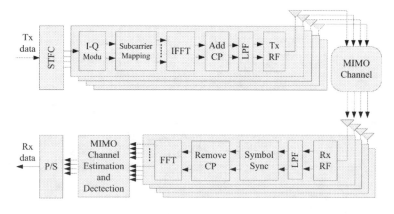

Fig. 1. 4x4 MIMO-OFDM system model

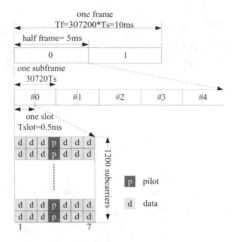

Fig. 2. Radio frame structure

and the throughput is up to 300Mbps. Fig. 2 illustrates the frame structure, the pilot symbols are used for channel estimation and then recovering the data in data symbols.

3   Algorithms Analysis

Since the receiver is much more complex than the transmitter, we focus our discussion on the symbol operations in the receiver. Assuming the frame is perfectly synchronized, so the main operations in receiver include: 1) Low pass filtering (LPF). 2) Symbol synchronization. 3) FFT after removing the cyclic prefixes (CP). 4) MIMO channel estimation. 5) MIMO detection.

3.1   Low Pass Filtering

Finite impulsive response (FIR) low-pass-filter is used for waveform shaping at both transmitter and receiver. An N-point FIR filter with L taps is defined as

$$FIR\_out[n] = \sum_{l=0}^{L-1} data[n+l] * cof[l] \tag{1}$$

Where $data[n]$ and $cof[l]$ are input data and filter coefficient where multiplication and accumulation (MAC) are the primary operations. Every result needs L-1 MACs.

3.2   Symbol Synchronization

CP is the prefixing of OFDM symbol with a repetition of the end. It serves as a guard interval against intersymbol interference from the previous symbol in

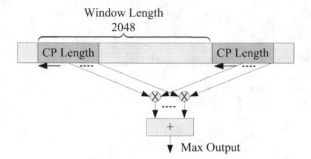

Fig. 3. Symbol synchronization using CP

multi-path channel. The length of CP must be at least equal to the length of the multi-path channel. In the receiver, it makes use of CP to extract the non-interfered symbols and sends them to OFDM demodulation. Fig. 3 shows the primary operations of symbol synchronization are multiplication, accumulation and maximal number searching.

3.3   OFMD (De)modulation

OFDM (de)modulation can be implemented by using discrete Fourier transform (DFT), an N-point DFT is defined as

$$X(k) = \sum_{n=0}^{N-1} e^{-j2\pi nk/N} \tag{2}$$

Where $X(k)$ and $x(n)$ are all complex values. As the literal description, the computational complexity of (2) is $O(N^2)$. The computational complexity can be reduced to $O(Nlog_r^N)$ by using radix-r FFT algorithm [9] which has log_r^N stages with N/r parallelizable radix-r butterfly operations in every stage. Fig. 4 shows the structure of radix-2 butterfly, it implements one complex multiplication and two complex additions.

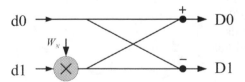

Fig. 4. radix-2 butterfly

3.4 MIMO Channel Estimation

For the OFDM system with transmitter diversity, channel estimation becomes complicated because signals transmitted from different antennas interfere with each other. LTE uplink uses shift-orthogonal training sequence for MIMO channel estimation. The received pilot OFDM symbol first takes advantage of FFT to construct frequency-domain estimator. Then the outputs of the estimator multiply original pilot sequence carrier by carrier and transfer back to time-domain by using inverse FFT (IFFT). A rectangular window is introduced to cut off the time-domain channel taps to obtain the time-domain channel of different users. After being filled with zero in the high delay taps, every channel of users performs FFT to generate frequency-domain channel estimates [10]. Fig. 5 shows the estimation process on one receiving antenna. After estimation of channel matrix on pilot carriers, we use linear interpolation to acquire the channel matrix of data carriers. the primary operations in channel estimation are FFT, IFFT and multiplications.

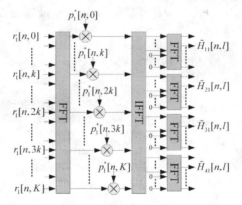

Fig. 5. MIMO channel estimation

3.5 MIMO Detection

The issue of signal detection for MIMO multiplexing systems has been widely discussed with different space-time-frequency-coding (STFC) styles, such as STBC, SFBC and VBLAST encodes [11], of which the VBLAST encode is commonly used for very high data rate communications. A number of detection methods have been proposed based on it, e.g., zero forcing (ZF), minimum mean square estimation (MMSE) and maximum likelihood (ML) methods. Among them, ML method is the optimal detector, but its complexity of full search process grows exponentially with the number of transmit antennas and modulation order. MMSE is one of the most straightforward detection schemes with moderate implementation complexity for channel equalization. It outperforms Zero-Forcing detection by taking noise into consideration [12]. The MMSE detection can be written as

$$X = (H^H H + \sigma^2 I) H^H Y \qquad (3)$$

Where H, σ^2 and Y are channel parameter, variance of additive Gaussian noise and vector signal from the receiver, respectively. Quite a few matrix manipulations such as matrix multiplication and inversion are involved in the MMSE detection which are implemented tone by tone in data symbols.

3.6   Algorithms Summary

According to the analysis above, the main operations at the MIMO-OFDM transceiver are cross- or auto-correlation for waveform shaping and symbol synchronization, FFT/IFFT for OFDM (de)modulation and channel estimation, matrix multiplication and inversion for MIMO detector. All of the data processed is complex number. Besides, these operations have rich inherent task, data parallelism and data access is always linear. Table 1 shows the data parallelism of different algorithms. For example, a 2048-point radix-2 FFT has 1024 parallel butterflies at every stage and MIMO detection is implemented on a tone by tone basis, so the detections of data in 1200 tones can be executed in parallel. The data and task parallelism can always be exchanged in some circumstance. So they are suitable for multi-core system with vector processing.

Table 1. Parallelism analysis of algorithms

algorithms	task parallelism	data parallelism
FIR filter	4×14	L (tap number)
OFDM modulation	4×14	1024(radix-2, 2048-point FFT)
Channel estimation	8	1024(radix-2, 2048-point FFT)
MIMO detector	12	1200

4   Architecture of SDR Processor

The QMBase (Quad Matrix cores for Base station) architecture targets highly parallel application and provides acceleration for wireless communication domain. As shown in Fig. 4. It consists of four vector DSP cores, namely Matrix, with a 1-MB SRAM in each core. There are two inter-core networks on chip. A DMA based QLink [13] which transfers data into packages and sent them to destination cores through a 4x4 crossbar is capable of moving large blocks of data between DSP cores without CPU interference. It can easily extend the system to 8x8 or 16x16 configurations. The fast shared data pool (FSDP) [13] has four groups of memory and control registers, each of which is proprietary to only one core to write but can be read by other cores. Reading will be blocked if the control register corresponded to the read memory is not set. The reading and writing operation is implemented by load and store instructions respectively, so if reading blocked, the entire pipeline of reading core will be stalled to wait until

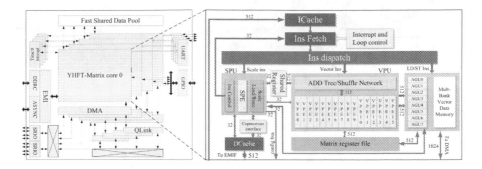

Fig. 6. QMBase architecture

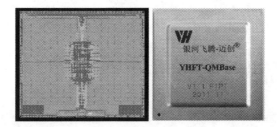

Fig. 7. Micrograph and top photographs

other cores finish what they do and set the control register. Compared to periodic query and interruption methods, FSDP is faster and more power-efficient in data sharing and synchronizations. Besides, some peripherals like external memory interface (EMI) with DDR2 and asynchronous memory control, two 4x3.125Gbps RapidIO interfaces supporting radio remote unit (RRU) are also integrated on the system to provide a complete solution of wireless communication in base station. Fig. 7 shows the micrograph and top photographs of QMBase which was Fabricated in 2011, the processor is clocked at 500MHz with a die size of $168mm^2$ by using 65nm technology.

4.1 Matrix Architecure

Each of Matrix core has a scale processing unit (SPU) and a 16-width SIMD vector processing unit (VPU). It can issue up to ten instructions per cycle, five scale instructions for SPU and five vector instructions for VPU. SPU is responsible for instruction flow control and system configuration. One vector instruction can trigger the 16 vector processing elements (VPE) to do the same operations. Every VPE supports both fixed- and floating-point arithmetic operations. The VPU can deliver sixty four 16-bit fixed-point multiplications or sixteen 32-bit floating MACs simultaneously every cycle. The sixty four fixed-point multiplications can be reconfigured to directly support sixteen complex-value multiplications, which will be of great benefit to FIR, convolution and FFT algorithms. Since matrix operations in MIMO detection are very susceptible to precision limits, causing 16- and even 32-bit fixed-point operations to suffer in performance or simply not work well. The floating-point supporting VPU delivers an efficient MIMO equalizer, with low power consumption, high performance and throughput for the base station.

Every core of QMBase has 1MB SRAM which can be access directly by VPU and SPU. In order to support continuous data flow, the SRAM is divided into two blocks for concurrent data preparation and processing. Every block is further divided into 16 memory banks to support parallel data access and processing in VPU. With dual 512-bit load/store units, every clock 1024 bit Data could be transferred between SRAM and VPU. Data exchange between VPEs can be conducted by SRAM-based 16x16 crossbar shuffle network, with special instructions supporting data reorder operations of FFT calculation. Considering the frequent convolution operation in FIR and symbol synchronization, a reduction tree that sums 16 complex elements from each of VPEs and stores the result into one of them in every clock is accommodated in the VPU.

4.2   System Mapping Scheme

We map the radio system with minimum data movement to reduce data buffer in every processing stage. The map and implementation of MIMO-OFDM system is depicted in Fig. 8. Data is processed in units of TTI with all DSP cores synchronized to start calculation of a new TTI simultaneously. Our hardware system is powerful enough to implement one data stream in one DSP core. Four DSP cores implement LPF, frame synchronization, OFDM demodulation and channel estimation independently at the beginning until MIMO detecting. Before that data and channel state information (CSI) should be relocated in different cores. We cut the 12 data symbols of every antenna into four equal parts in terms of frequency and send three of them to other three cores respectively, same as the channel matrix of pilot carriers. So every core only decodes 300 carriers of 48 data symbol from all the antennas. There are 2x16x300 CSIs deployed in every DSP core in one TTI, if we calculate all the channel matrix of the data symbol first, it needs a large memory to store the CSIs in every core. An alternative way is to calculate them when needed. Since the MIMO detector is performed tone by tone, so we can just exchange part of CSIs and compute the MIMO detecting, the movement of rest of CSIs can be overlapped with prior MIMO detecting. Fig. 8 also shows the execution time of the functional blocks of the system, total processing delay is about 669us, which is much less than the maximum 1ms delay constraints. Because of its massive and irregular data processing that is inefficient for the processor, we don't implement channel coding on the processor. But the remained time is adequate for its implementation on the outside accelerator.

Fig. 9 depicts the uncoded Symbol-Error-Rate (USER) of a 4x4 spatial multiplexing system for different modulation patterns. Frequency-selective fading channels are chosen as channel parameters. In fact, the uncoded SER=10^{-1} performance in different modulations is considered to be acceptable in practice for wireless data communication.

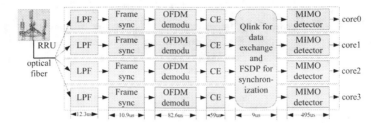

Fig. 8. Mapping scheme on QMBase

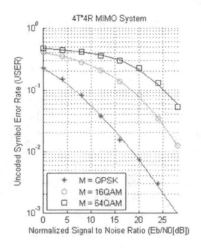

Fig. 9. Uncoded SER of 4x4 MIMO system

5   Opportunities and Challenges

5.1   Fully Programmable Architecure

The QMBase architecture provides a fully programmable SDR platform that implements the complete 3GPP-LTE layer 1 PHY (not including the channel coding) in real time. Multi-core and wide SIMD of the processor takes advantage of the highly task and data parallel nature of the algorithms. And optimized function unit can support direct operation on complex number. In the FIR example, complex multiplication and reduction tree deliver one result every cycle. The auto-correlation operation in symbol synchronization also benefit too. FFT implementation is based on Pease's algorithm for parallel computation. Data alignment is accomplished through dedicate shuffle network. Then each VPE calculate one radix-2 butterfly, eight butterflies are executed in parallel in the VPU. For instance, a 2048-point fixed-point FFT executes in about 2900 cycles in one Matrix core. Similarly in MIMO detecting, implementing one 4x4 MMSE detection depicted in equation 3 takes about 900 cycles per VPE.

Because there is little data movement between VPE within MIMO detecting we can expect gains equal to the width of SIMD. In comparison to the state of-the-art DSP solutions [4][6], our simulation-based performance estimation of different algorithms is 2.5 to 5.3 times higher, for the same clock frequency. Even more, QMBase processor is fully software programmable, thus system operation can be modified post-silicon to adapt to changes and evolutions in the LTE standard, or to support related standards

5.2   Challenges

Many issues remain undissolved regarding the SDR approach for future standards. These challenges are:

Compiler support vectorization-the wide SIMD architecture proposed in this work poses an additional challenge to the programmer. It is impossible to efficiently parallelize all the application automatically from C code. QMBase compiler only supports vectorization of some simple applications like FIR and accumulation. Parallelization of applications with data shuffle is especially difficult, such as FFT algorithm. Besides, the shuffle network is configured explicitly. So the processor is not suitable for the applications with undefined shuffle pattern.

Power efficiency- the entire processor is about 8W when run the FFT application under 1V voltage. Pure-software implementation of all baseband algorithms and large on-chip memory degrade the power efficiency of the processor. This paper is intended as a starting point for us to design an optimized architecture implementing the LTE baseband systems. Wider SIMD, heterogeneous architecture with more specialized function units and streamlined operation may be beneficial not only in performance but also power, which is our next work.

6   Conclusions

The evolving wireless communication standards bring new challenges regarding the huge amount of computation and flexibility required by base station. In this paper, a real-time implementation of 4×4 MIMO-OFDM system with LTE parameters on a programmable processor has been presented. The multi-core and SIMD architecture with optimized function unit deliver a high throughput and flexible solution for future wireless communications. Besides, Potential extensions to exploit the throughput computation capabilities and efficiency are concluded for our next work.

Acknowledgment. The research is supported by the National Science and Technology Major Project of the Ministry of Science and Technology of China under Grant No.2009ZX01034-001-001-006.

References

1. Sampath, H., Talwar, S., Tellado, J., Erceg, V., Paulraj, A.: A Fourth-Generation MIMO-OFDM Broadband Wireless System: Design, Performance, and Field Trial Results. IEEE Communications Magazine 40(9), 143–149 (2002)
2. Li, Y.: Pilot-symbol-aided channel estimation for OFDM in wireless systems. IEEE Trans. Vehicular Technol. 49(4) (2000)
3. Burg, A., Haene, S., Perels, D., Luethi, P., Felber, N., Fichtner, W.: Algorithm and VLSI architecture for linear MMSE detection in MIMO-OFDM systems. In: IEEE International Symposium on Circuits and Systems (ISCAS), pp. 4102–4105 (2006)
4. Perels, D., Haene, S., Luethi, P., Burg, A., Felber, N., Fichtner, W., Bolcskei, H.: ASIC Implementation of a MIMO-OFDM Transceiver for 192 Mbps WLANs. In: Proceedings of the 31st European Solid-State Circuits Conference (ESSCIRC), pp. 215–218 (2005)
5. Yoshizawa, S., Yamauchi, Y., Miyanaga, Y.: A complete pipelined MMSE detection architecture in a 4x4 MIMO-OFDM receiver. In: IEEE International Symposium on Circuits and Systems (ISCAS), pp. 1248–1251 (2008)
6. MSC8156 product brief (Freescale 2011),
   http://cache.freescale.com/files/dsp/doc/prodbrief/MSC8156PB.pdf
7. PC205 product brief, (picoChip 2010),
   http://www.picochip.com/page/76/
8. tms320tci6618, http://www.ti.com/product/tms320tci6618&DCMP=
   tci6618_110214&HQS=Other+PR+tci6618prpf
9. Cooley, J.W., Tukey, J.W.: An algorithm for the machine calculation of complex Fourier series. Math. Computat. 19, 297–301 (1965)
10. Li, Y.: Simplified Channel Estimation for OFDM Systems with Multiple Transmit Antennas. IEEE Transactions on Wireless Communications 1(1), 67–75 (2002)
11. Wolniansky, P., Foschini, G., Golden, G., Valenzuela, R.: V-BLAST: An architecture for realizing very high data rates over the rich scattering wireless channel. In: Proc. ISSSE (1998)
12. Eilert, J., Wu, D., Liu, D.: Implementation of a programmable linear MMSE detector for MIMO-OFDM. In: Proc. IEEE ICASSP, pp. 5396–5399 (2008)
13. Chen, S.M., Wan, J.H., Lu, J.Z., et al.: YHFT-QDSP: High-performance heterogeneous multicore DSP. Journal of Computer Science and Technology 25(2), 214–224 (2010)

A Market Data Feeds Processing Accelerator Based on FPGA

Xiaoyang Shen, Jiang Jiang, Liyuan Zhou, Tianyi Yang, and Li Chen

School of Microelectronics, Shanghai Jiao Tong University, No.800, Dongchuan Road,
200240 Shanghai, China
idwm98@hotmail.com, jiangjiang@ic.sjtu.edu.cn,
zhouliyuan@sjtu.edu.cn, {unremem,woozyqueen}@gmail.com

Abstract. Market data feeds present the current state of the financial market to the customers, with the demand of fast transmission and instant response. The OPRA format with the FAST protocol is one of the most widely-used formats of the market data feeds. This paper provides an accelerator based on FPGA for processing the market data feeds in OPRA format. The accelerator focuses on encoding and decoding the data feeds concerning five of the most important categories, namely categories a, d, k, q and N. Since each OPRA block may have various possibilities of components, which have different lengths, so the latency of our design varies. Under extreme conditions, the encoder portion has the minimum latency of 72 ns and the maximum latency of 424 ns, while the decoder portion has the minimum latency of 48 ns and the maximum latency of 344 ns.

Keywords: FPGA-based, market data feeds handler, low-latency.

1 Introduction

Financial market data feeds refer to the messages of financial market current state that the exchanges provided for customers, which include stock prices, trades, and other related information.

In modern society, the amount, sphere and speed of various financial products are increasing evidently. Meanwhile, the customers would be in superior positions when making critical decisions if they could receive those financial messages in time, and better for earlier. As the consequence, to process the financial data in an efficient way is of great significance. A low-latency market data feeds handler is desired.

Today, the feeds handler are mainly based on software systems. In early 2012, the primary architectures of 55% handlers are based on software, those of 36% are based on hardware and those of 9% are hybrid.[1]

However, the speed of such handler based on software system is highly influenced by the hardware that it runs on. Usually, it takes a relatively longer period of time for software-based market data feeds handler to process these data. So, pure software-based handler will not be a solution for the desire of low-latency.

W. Xu et al. (Eds.): NCCET 2013, CCIS 396, pp. 44–52, 2013.

As for the hardware, there are typically 3 kinds of techniques used for accelerators. One is Field Programmable Gate Array (FPGA), another is Graphics Processing Unit (GPU), and the rest is Application Specific Integrated Circuit (ASIC).

FPGA is a very attractive choice for accelerators. It is easy to reprogram an FPGA and to reconstruct a hardware system. The low power and space requirements are also advantages of the FPGA. To construct a system on FPGA, people should write the program in Hardware Description Language (HDL). The sophistication of such program in HDL is the main disadvantage of FPGA.

GPU pays attention to the calculations of floating-point numbers. It has remarkable performance in the task with abundant such calculations.

ASIC has many similar advantages as FPGA in many aspects, such as high speed, low power consumption and small space requirements. Compared with FPGA, ASIC usually could provide a system with better performance with respect to speed and space requirements. However, the reconfiguration of ASIC-based designs will cost more time and expenses than FPGA-based ones.

As for the market data feeds, the format and protocol are changing in a relatively more frequent trend. The long time cycle and expensive cost of the reconfiguration of an ASIC-based design lead to the inappropriateness to design a market data feeds accelerator based on ASIC. Furthermore, the accelerator has few floating-point numbers calculations. Therefore, FPGA may be the most appropriate solution to the requirement of low-latency market data feeds accelerator.

OPRA is the abbreviation of Option Prices Reporting Authority, it is also the name of the data feed format of this authority. It is one of the most widely-used market data feeds formats. The current participants of OPRA include NASDAQ, AMEX, ARCA and so on.[2] At present, OPRA format uses FAST protocol for information exchange. FAST is the abbreviation of FIX Adapted to Streaming.

This paper proposes a hardware design based on FPGA for low-latency market data feeds accelerator. And the data are in the format of OPRA with FAST protocol. The key points of our design are the followings:

We select some OPRA data which have specific categories to be processed with acceleration. It would be superfluous to process the OPRA data of all categories with acceleration. For example, OPRA data of category f is "equity and index end of day summary"[3], and the exchanges will be closed soon after this message.

We mainly design the encoder portion and decoder portion. Most related work only design for the decoder portion of the whole market data feeds handler system. However, both the acceleration of the encoder portion and the one of the decoder portion are of significance. Our design has 2 core function modules for the 2 portions.

Our design has the combination of both serial and parallel structures. In order to balance the requirements of low-latency, the limitation of the device resources utilization and the maximum speed of data transfer of the given FPGA, we have made the trade-off and design the accelerator with the proper combination of both serial and parallel structures.

There are several related works have been done by others.

An accelerator is designed based on FPGA by Gareth W. Morris, David B. Thomas and Wayne Luk.[4] It eliminates the networking stack of the operating system.

By applying message processing and filtering in FPGA, it could push messages directly into the memory space of software threads. The accelerator uses Xilinx Virtex 5 LX110T FPGA board.

An accelerator is designed based on the novel IBM PowerEN "Edge of Network" processor.[5] The processor integrates network interfaces with functional accelerators and multi-threaded cores. The main decoder function of this design has 3 parts. They are streaming decoder setup, decoding one message and message normalization. Furthermore, it can also run application software on the same platform while processing a message.

Another accelerator based on FPGA is designed by Christian Leber, Benjamin Geib and Heiner Litz.[6] The accelerator uses a Xilinx Virtex-4 FX100 FPGA board. In the paper, 3 systems are realized are compared: the baseline system, the system with Kernel Bypass and the systemwith Kernel Bypass and FASTFix Offloading. Obviously, the last one has reached the best performance.

2   Design and Implements

2.1   Overview

As shown in Fig. 1, our design has 2 main portions, which are the encoder and the decoder.

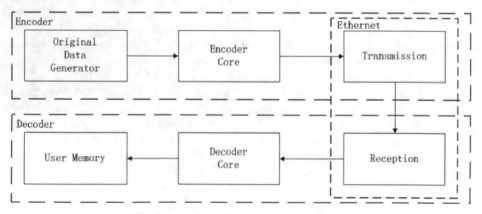

Fig. 1. Overview of the entire system module

The encoder portion is composed of 3 functional modules. The original data generator module generator the original data of OPRA market data feeds and outputs these data in a particular order to the encoder core module through DDR2 memory interaction. The encoder core module receives these data sequently and creates OPRA market data feeds according to FAST protocol. The transmission module sends the mentioned OPRA market data feeds to the Ethernet.

The decoder portion is also composed of 3 functional modules. The reception module receives the OPRA market data feeds from the Ethernet. It also segments the market data feeds in the order of fields. The decoder core module acquires every field value in order according OPRA and FAST protocol. The user memory module writes the field value received into memory through DDR2 memory interaction.

2.2 Original Data Generator

To provide equitable data flow testing the validity of encoding and decoding systems in simulation, abundant original data according to OPRA format is required. We create the original data by designing in a C program due to the fact that available data are scarce in document. The C program is written according to the OPRA field definitions and it writes binary data representing random financial information into file which, read directly into the memory of FPGA in EDK simulation, serves as the data input. Binary data consists of various blocks each containing several messages of different types. Fields is aligned to 64 bits for the convenient of transmitting. The number of fields in one block is limited to 16.

DDR2 memory on Xilinx Virtex-5 XC5VLX50T board is used to store the original data, message sending module functions as reading memory and updating output ports at every clock cycle positive edge. Due to various reasons (Redundant DDR2 control methods in ISE IP core) we practice memory control wrapping the system in EDK project, sending message by PLB connection under software commands. A pack of PLB registers is defined in EDK custom peripheral, when it has downloaded the RTL design onto board, C code in EDK access memory to fetch 32 bits width data then write to register, ready signal is asserted when enough data needed has filled the PLB registers and then activates the system sending message to following module 8 bytes per clock cycle. Process of sending message from memory is predicted to be accelerated and optimized by implementing DMA in EDK, updating registers faster as well as freeing Micro blaze core for other modules.

2.3 Encoder Core Module

The encoder core module is composed of several functional modules as shown in Fig. 2. This section describes the most important modules.

The category control module has the function similar to register. It stores the value of field "Message Category" while processing the very message of an OPRA market data feeds block. Each OPRA market data feeds block has probably two or more messages. According to our design, at each clock cycle, only one field of a particular message is received by the encoder core module. Therefore, should match at first the particular field being processed in each clock cycle. Then, this module stores the value if the current field is "Message Category".

The type control module is extremely similar to the category control module, but it pays attention to the field "Message Type" instead.

The field control module provides the critical control signal to some other modules. The control signal implies which field is being processed. This signal contributes greatly to the following process: to calculate the effective length of current field data, to update the total length of current message, to choose the right input of field register, etc. This signal is decided mainly according to the value of the field "Message Category" and the one of the field "Message Type". Due to the fact that the first three fields of any messages are the same while the second field and the third field are just the field deciding this control signal, there is no additional problem about the sequence.

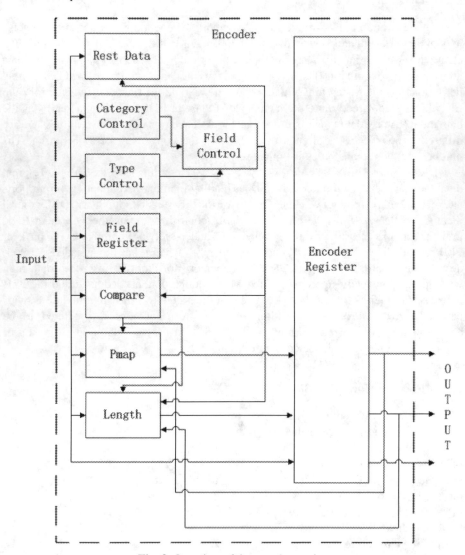

Fig. 2. Overview of the encoder portion

The field register module is critical for FAST protocol encoding. One of the most important parts of FAST protocol is that the value of current field is abridged if the value is exactly the same to the last value of the same field. This module is used for storing the last value of every field. There is no possibility that two sequential fields received are the same field. Therefore, at each positive edge of clock signal, this module outputs the value of every field calculated at last clock cycle. As for the encoder portion, even the input field data of the encoder core module are the same to the value stored in field register, we could just store the input data into the register, in which way we could simplify the logic structure of this module. Because the field control module provides the signal implying which field is the current field, we only need store the input data into the proper field register according to the control signal.

The compare module is also used for FAST protocol. According to the field control signal, this module compares the value in the very field register and the one of the input field data of the encoder core module, and it feedbacks the identity between the two values being compared. This result decides whether the current data should be abridged and how to update the total length of the current message.

The Pmap module is of great importance. The lengths of all the fields are not the same, while some fields in one message could be abridged according to FAST protocol. Sometimes we don't know which field is abridged without Pmap. For example, if there are 3 sequential fields whose lengths are all 4 bytes and the second one of them is abridged by the encoder. Then the decoder doesn't know which field is abridged because it receives 2 data both of 4 bytes, which could also happen when the first or the third field is abridged. Each bit of Pmap implies whether one field is abridged, and it could solve the problem mentioned above. At each clock cycle when the encoder core module process a field data, the Pmap will be updated based on the value at the last clock cycle. The value of the Pmap won't be correct until the last clock cycle of current message.

The length module has the similar function to the Pmap module, but it pays attention to the value of the length of current message. In addition, this module should determine the new length according the field control signal due to the different lengths of various fields.

2.4 Decoder Core Module

As shown in Fig. 3, the decoder core module has several functional modules similar to the ones of the encoder core module. Therefore, this section describes the overall function briefly, and then introduces the modules different with the ones of the encoder core module.

The decoder core module acquires the category data and the type data prior, and then creates several control signals in order to decoder OPRA market data feeds with FAST protocol and to update the data of field register module. For sake of subsequent functions, the decoder core module also provides some signals for the user memory module.

The compare module gets the result directly from the input Pmap data. According to the outputs of the compare module and the data stored in field register, the decoded data module provides the restored data of current field if such data was abridged in the encoder portion, otherwise it provides exactly the data of input.

The category data module assumes that the current field is "Message Category", and then provides the unabridged data or restores the field data if it was abridged. The output of this module is used by the category control module.

The type data module is similar to the category data module, but it pays attention to the field "Message Type" and provides data used by the type control module.

The field register module chooses the input of the current field according to the result of the compare module, instead of always storing the current input data because such data probably was abridged. In such case, it keeps the value of the very register the same.

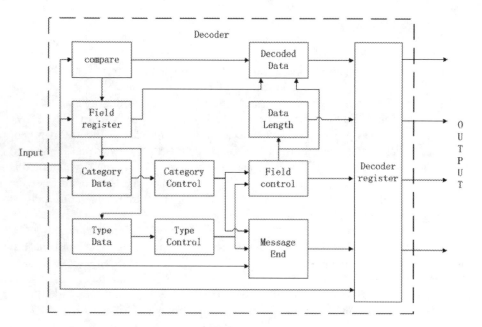

Fig. 3. Overview of the decoder portion

The message end module provides the signal implying whether this clock cycle is the last one of a message. The data length module provides the effective length of current field data. Those signals contribute to subsequent functions in the user memory module.

2.5   Latency Monitor

This module is designed for testing the latency of the encoder portion or the one of the decoder portion. It has a counter with the 125MHz clock signal. The counter begins to work when the very portion begin to encode or to decode data. The counter stops when a signal implying that the process of encoding or decoding has finished. The latency could be calculated by the frequency of the clock signal and the value of the counter.

2.6   Others

The transmission module and reception module use EDK tool to deliver the market data feeds. In addition, the 2 modules are also responsible for reconstructing the data received from the encoder core module or the Ethernet in a correct order by using a series of FIFOs.

3   Experiment Results

To verify the functionality and acceleration performance of our design, we implement the design on FPGA aboard.

3.1   Experiment Environment

A Xilinx Virtex5 XC5VLX50T FPGA board was used for performance test. The clock signal provided by the FPGA board is 125MHz. In addition, we use Xilinx ISE Design Suite 13.2.

3.2   Experiment Results

All modules of our accelerator are designed for such clock period, including the memory control and the Ethernet part. Under several timing constraints, our design meets the requirement of the 8ns clock period.

During active test of the encoder, the latency monitor counts the clock cycles used for encoding the market data feeds. It calculates from the instant when the original data stored in blocks begin to be sorted in the original data generator module to the instant when the encoded data have been reconstructed in a correct order in the transmission module. Because of the different numbers of fields that every OPRA block may contain, the minimum latency of encoder is 72 ns and the maximum is 424 ns. One OPRA block usually contains as many fields as possible if there is enough data waiting to be encoded. Therefore the latency of 424 ns is the more meaningful and representative.

As for the decoder portion, the latency monitor calculates from the instant when the data have been received and wait to be reconstructed to the instant when the decoded data is written into the blocks. The minimum latency of decoder is 48 ns and the maximum one is 344 ns. The more meaningful and representative value is 344 ns.

3.3   Results Comparison

Table 1 shows the comparison of our design and the related works. The reason why we could reach the higher speed is that our design has the reasonable combination of serial and parallel structure. The accelerator takes full advantage of the clock period provided by FPGA board. The latency of the critical path is designed for 8ns, which is appropriate for the FPGA board that we used.

Table 1. Comparison with the related work

Design	Latency	Remarks
Ours	424 ns for the encoder and 344 ns for the decoder	maximum value
[4]	4 μs	constant value
[5]	1.32 μs	decoder portion
[6]	2.6 μs	reception portion included

4   Conclusion

This paper presents an accelerator for processing market data feeds in OPRA format with FAST protocol, which focuses on the encoder and the decoder of the market data feeds of the most resourceful categories, namely categories a, d, k, q and N.

The original data are generated first and stored in the blocks. Then, these data are sorted in a particular order and delivered to the encoder core module. After being encoded, the data of an OPRA block are reconstructed again in order to be in a correct order. Afterwards, the data are delivered out though the Ethernet. The decoder portion receives, sorts and decodes these data. After that, the data are restored and written into memory.

The latency of the encoder portion is 424 ns and the one of decoder portion is 344 ns, irrespective of parts of memory and Ethernet function.

Acknowledgment. This work was supported by a grant of the key project of National High-tech R&D Program of China. The grant number is 2009AA012201.

References

1. Aite Group, http://www.aitegroup.com/Reports/ReportDetail.aspx?recordItemID=901
2. Options Price Reporting Authority, http://www.opradata.com
3. OPRA_Binary_Part_Spec_1.1_091912, http://www.opradata.com/specs/OPRA_Binary_Part_Spec_1.1_091912.pdf
4. Morris, G.W., Thomas, D.B., Luk, W.: FPGA accelerated low-latency market data feed processing. In: 17th IEEE Symposium on High Performance Interconnects, pp. 83–89. IEEE Press, New York (2009)
5. Pasetto, D., Lynch, K., Tucker, R., Maguire, B., Petrini, F., Franke, H.: Ultra low latency market data feed on IBM PowerENTM. J. Computer Science-Research and Development 26(3-4), 307–315 (2011)
6. Leber, C., Geib, B., Litz, H.: High Frequency Trading Acceleration Using FPGAs. In: 2011 International Conference on Field Programmable Logic and Applications, pp. 317–322. IEEE Press, New York (2011)

The Design of Video Accelerator Bus Wrapper

Yan Xu, Longmei Nan, Pengfei Guo, and Jinfu Xu

Zhengzhou Institute of Information Technology
Zhengzhou 450004, China
xy.mail@me.com

Abstract. Novel wrapper implementation technique is used to improve the data communication for video processing accelerator. The wrapper provided the function of flow control, data buffers and protocol analysis. It can reduce video data transfer time up to 50% compared with the conventional CPU based data transfer method. At the same time, the wrapper's area is 9278 μm^2 and the operation clock frequency is 1GHz implemented using 0.13μm CMOS technologies.

Keywords: wrapper, bus, accelerator.

1 Introduction

It is an efficient way to improve the performance for specific applications through adding dedicate accelerators in SoC [1,2]. However, since the accelerators are designed for specific application, they have heavy and non-uniform communication traffic. These properties lead to low communication efficiency between the accelerator and other units.

Usually, the data supplements in SoC are done by CPU or DMA [3,4]. CPU is suitable for small amount of data while DMA for large amount of data [5]. But the non-uniform traffic of custom accelerator is not suitable for the DMA, so designer can only use CPU which leads to low efficiency.

To solve this problem, this paper presents a method to improve the accelerator data supplement. We add a wrapper between bus and the accelerator improved the performance of the accelerator.

2 Background

The accelerator in this paper is designed for the acceleration of video processing. The ports of video accelerator are shown in Table 1.

Following words will describe the working flow of video processing accelerator. Before the accelerator starting to process video data, it needs to be configured. The config_start signal is used to start the configuration of accelerator, the configuration data is feed into accelerator through the config_data port. And the config_end signal is used to info the ending of the configuration data. After the configuration,

W. Xu et al. (Eds.): NCCET 2013, CCIS 396, pp. 53–60, 2013.

accelerator is ready for processing video data and the outside world feed the video data into the data_in0 (or data_in1, or data_in2) port. The port width is 32 bits and length varies from 1 to 16. After the video processing, the accelerator enables the ready signal, and then the result is read from the data_out port. The work flow are shown in Figure 1.

Table 1. Video processing accelerator ports

Port name	Direction	Function
Clk	In	Clock input
Rst_n	In	Accelerator reset
Wen	In	Write enable
Ren	In	Read enable
Config_start	In	Start configuration signal
Config_end	In	Finish configuration signal
Config_data[31:0]	In	Configuration data input signal
Data_in0[31:0]	In	Data input 0
Data_in1[31:0]	In	Data input 1
Data_in2[31:0]	In	Data input 2
Ready	Out	Data processing ready signal
Data_out[31:0]	Out	Data output signal

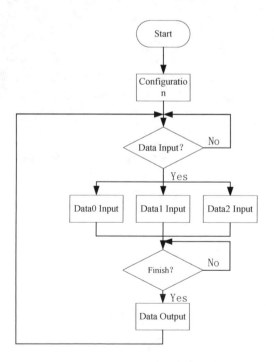

Fig. 1. The connection between the inFIFO and the interface

The length of the accelerator configuration data varies from 1kB to 4kB, and the configuration data is transferred into accelerator only once, so, the configuration data transfer time do not affect the overall SoC performance.

Then we talk about the video data. Suppose the bus is 32 bits and the accelerator only handle 1 to 16 blocks (32 bits each block) video data. If we use DMA to transfer the video data, it only need 2 clock cycles to transfer 1 block data, but the DMA configuration process need about 240 clock cycles, so it is not suitable to use DMA to transfer video data (takes too much time to configure before transfer small mount of data). We can only use CPU to feed the accelerator, and this means 4 to 5 bus cycles per data block which lead to low transfer efficiency.

To solve this problem, we designed a low-cost wrapper between bus and video accelerator, which provide an FIFO to buffer the data from bus.

3   Accelerator Bus Wrapper Structure

Since there is no data buffer in the video accelerator, DMA can not move redundant data to it. If we add a FIFO between bus and the accelerator, it can buffer the extra data. And there is a microcontroller in the wrapper which feed the accelerator with the data stored in the FIFO. It will dramatically improve the performance.

3.1   Wrapper Architecture

As shown in Figure 2, the bus wrapper consists of 8 parts: bus_interface, accelerator_interface, config_unit, FSM, status, controller, inFIFO, outFIFO. Bus_interface module transfers the bus interface signal into inside world. FSM module is used to implement the finite state machine of the wrapper and the status of the wrapper is stored in the status module. Based on the output of the FSM module, controller module generates the accelerator interface signal, inFIFO and outFIFo control signal. And the inFIFO and outFIFO are both asynchronous FIFO.

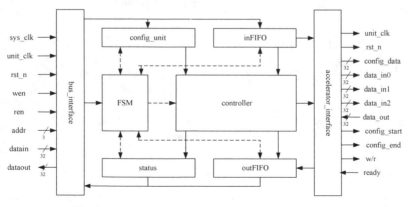

Fig. 2. The architecture of the Accelerator bus wrapper

3.2   The Structure of Data Stored in FIFO

Since the accelerator has 4 different ports (data_in0, data_in1, data_in2, config_data), we buffer the data with the port index into FIFO simultaneously, as shown in Figure 3.

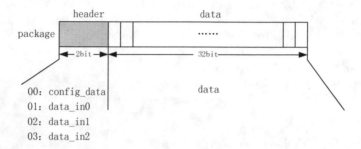

Fig. 3. The structure of the data stored in FIFO

When the wrapper handles the FIFO data, it first needs to analyze the header of the data, determine which port to feed the data. Since the width of SoC data and address bus are both 32 bits, when connected to the bus, the 34 bits input port of the FIFO is connected to the lower 2 bits of the address and all the 32 bits of the data bus, as shown in Figure 4. This method avoids transferring the data and address using two bus cycles.

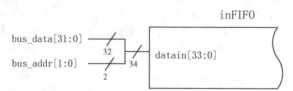

Fig. 4. The connection between the inFIFO and the interface

3.3   FSM Module Design

In our FSM module, there are two finite state machines, one for input control and one for output control.

The input control FSM is shown in Figure 5 (a). When the system starts, the input FSM goes into the idle state. In the idle state, FSM probes whether the FIFO is empty. If not, FSM enter the config_start state, which generates the start signal for the accelerator. Then it enters the configuration state, and the wrapper configure the accelerator using the data stored in the FIFO, if there is not enough data in the FIFO, it will enter the wait_in state. Once there is data in the FIFO, it will go into configuration state again. When the configuration finishes, FSM will go to the config_end state to issue the config_end signal to the accelerator.

When the FSM is in the check_addr state, it will check whether the FIFO is empty, if not, it will pick the data in the FIFO and dispatch the data into different ports depending on the port info stored in the first two bits of the data stored in FIFO.

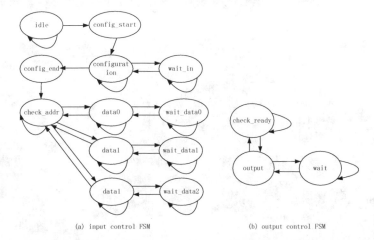

(a) input control FSM   (b) output control FSM

Fig. 5. FSM state diagram

The output control FSM is shown in Figure 5 (b).There are three states in the output control FSM: check_ready, output and wait. When the system starts, the output FSM goes into the check_ready state and check if the computation is completed. If yes, the output FSM will goes into the output state and the wrapper will read the result and transfer it into the outFIFO. When the transfer completed, the FSM will go back to the check_ready state. When the transfer is taking and the outFIFO is full, the FSM will goes to the wait state.

4   Performance Analyzing

4.1   Evaluation Metric and Platform

The wrapper is designed to improve the video data transfer performance. So, the evaluation metric is set to be the video data transfer time. And since the wrapper is used to feed data into accelerator, the total data processing time will affect user experience, so, we compare the data processing time of with and without the wrapper.

Figure 6 shows the platform we used to evaluate our wrapper. There are one CPU and one DMA controller which can transfer data to accelerator. In the platform, there are two uniform video accelerators, one is directly connected to SoC bus and another is connected to SoC bus through the wrapper. The depth of the inFIFO and outFIFO are both 128. The width of inFIFO is 34 bits and the width of outFIFO is 32bits.

An important thing need to explain here is the clock frequency for accelerator A and B is different, since there are FIFOs in wrapper, the input and output of wrapper can be asynchronous, we let accelerator A working at 200MHz, the same frequency as the bus, and accelerator B working at 400MHz.

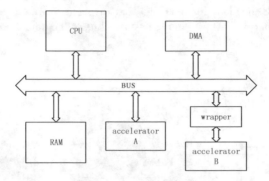

Fig. 6. Wrapper evaluation platform

4.2   Evaluation Result

First comparison is the data transfer time. One transfer time is measured for the time used by CPU transferring data to accelerator A, and the other transfer time is measured for the time used by DMA transferring data to accelerator B.

Figure 7 shows the comparison result. From the result, we can see that: for small amount of data, DMA + wrapper structure shows slight benefit while for large amount of data, DMA + wrapper structure is much better than CPU method. This is because we need to configure DMA before using it to transfer data, and the DMA configuration time is 244 bus cycles per transfer, which is a large number compared with data transfer time. And this is the reason for the low efficiency when DMA directly transfer data to accelerator. The wrapper can provide a buffer that hold large amount of data, and then the DMA can be used to transfer large amount of data.

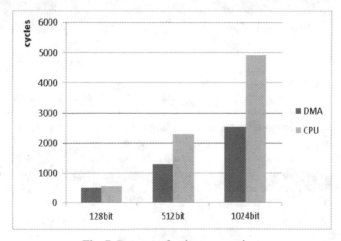

Fig. 7. Data transfer time comparison

Second comparison is the video data processing time. One processing time is measured for the time used by accelerator A to process data plus the data transfer time, and the other processing time is measured for the time used by accelerator B plus the data transfer time.

Figure 8 shows the comparison result. From the result, we can see the DMA + wrapper structure is much faster than the simple CPU structure.

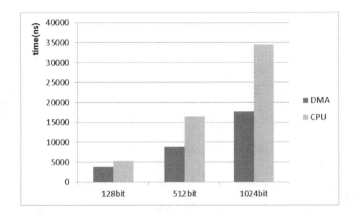

Fig. 8. Data processing time comparison

4.3   Result Analyzing

As shown in Figure 7 and Figure 8, the proposed wrapper improves the performance dramatically. For the original method, we use CPU to transfer data. Since CPU [6, 7] is optimized for general data processing, it uses pipeline technology to enhance performance. The execution of each instruction is divided into several stages, such as IF (instruction fetch), ID (instruction decoder), etc. When CPU moves a data from one location to another, it executes a load instruction, followed by a store instruction. The pipelined execution of load and store instruction lead to low interaction with bus, and will take about 10 ~ 20 clock cycles to transfer 32 bit data from memory to video process accelerator.

DMA [8, 9] is designed for large amount of data transfer. DMA takes about 2 clock cycles to transfer 32 bit data without disturbing CPU. Obviously it saves much more time. But there is a disadvantage that when we transfer a small amount of data, it cannot save much time. This is because we must configure the DMA before we use it. When we transfer a small amount of data, the time consumed to configure DMA cannot be ignored. The warm up time effect is shown in Figure 7 for small amount of data transfer (128 bit), the speed up ratio is smaller than large amount of data transfer (1024 bit).

The asynchronous FIFOs provide the opportunity of using different clock domain on both sides of the wrapper. Then we could let the accelerator working at very high frequency. This improves the performance dramatically, as shown in Figure 8.

4.4   Synthesis Result

To estimate the area cost and the critical path delay of the wrapper, we synthesize it using CMOS 0.13μm technology. Since the size of FIFO varies for different design, we just give the area for the other logics here. Synthesis results show our wrapper can operate at the frequency of 1GHz and occupy the area of 9278 μm^2 without FIFO.

5   Conclusion

This paper presents the design of a wrapper used to improve the data transfer performance for custom video processing accelerator. This design can provide a buffer to hold the data transferred from DMA, which can benefit from the high data transfer rate with small area cost. While the asynchronous FIFO can be used to separate two different clock domain, which provide the opportunity to use high frequency accelerator. Although this wrapper is designed for our video processing SoC, the architecture can be applied to the wrapper for other application.

References

1. van der Wolf, P., Henriksson, T.: Video processing requirements on SoC infrastructures. In: Proceedings of the Conference on Design, Automation and Test in Europe, pp. 1124–1125. ACM, Munich (2008)
2. Ristimaki, T., Nurmi, J.: Reconfigurable IP blocks: A survey [SoC]. In: Proceedings of International Symposium on System-on-Chip (2004)
3. Anjo, K., Okamura, A., Motomura, M.: Wrapper-based bus implementation techniques for performance improvement and cost reduction. IEEE Journal of Solid-State Circuits 39(5), 804–817 (2004)
4. Nikolic, et al.: Wrapper design for a CDMA bus in SOC. In: 2010 IEEE 13th International Symposium on Design and Diagnostics of Electronic Circuits and Systems (DDECS) (2010)
5. Anjo, K., et al.: NECoBus: A high-end SOC bus with a portable and low-latency wrapper-based interface mechanism. In: Proceedings of the IEEE 2002 Custom Integrated Circuits Conference (2002)
6. Ma, H., Wang, D.: The design of five-stage pipeline CPU based on MIPS. In: 2011 International Conference on Electrical and Control Engineering (ICECE) (2011)
7. Hennessy, J.L., Patterson, D.A.: Computer Architecture: A Quantitative Approach, 3rd edn. Morgan Kaufmann Publishers, Inc. (2003)
8. Prokin, M.: DMA transfer method for wide-range speed and frequency measurement. IEEE Transactions on Instrumentation and Measurement 42(4), 842–846
9. Pan, S., Guan, Q., Xu, S.: Optimizing video processing algorithm with multidimensional DMA based on multimedia DSP. In: 2010 International Conference on Computational Problem-Solving, ICCP (2010)

Design and Implementation of Novel Flexible Crypto Coprocessor and Its Application in Security Protocol

Shice Ni, Yong Dou, Kai Chen, and Lin Deng

National Laboratory for Parallel and Distribution Processing,
National University of Defense Technology,
Deya Road, 109#, Changsha, 410073, P.R. China
{nishice,yongdou,chenkai,denglin}@nudt.edu.cn

Abstract. Cryptography is an essential component in modern electronic commerce. Accelerating security protocols is a great challenge in general-purpose processor due to the complexity of crypto algorithms. The ultimate solution to this problem would be an adaptive processor that can provide software-like flexibility with hardware-like performance. After analyzing the characteristics of security protocols, we discover that most crypto algorithms are employed at the function level among different security protocols, and propose a novel flexible crypto coprocessor (FC Coprocessor) architecture that rely on Reconfigurable Cryptographic Blocks (RCBs) to achieve a balance between high performance and flexibility and implement a flexible architecture for security protocols on FPGA. Within the RCBs, the pipelining technique is adopted to realize parallel data and reduce the cost of the host and the coprocessor. We consider several crypto algorithms as examples to illustrate the design of RCB in the FC Coprocessor. Finally, we implement the prototype of the FC coprocessor on Xilinx XC5VLX330 FPGA chip. The experiment results show that the coprocessor, running at 189 MHz, outperforms the software-based Secure Sockets Layer protocol running on an Intel Core i3 530 CPU at 2.93 GHz by a factor of 4.8X for typical crypto algorithm blocks.

Keywords: flexible crypto coprocessor, reconfigurable crypto block, security protocol, accelerator.

1   Introduction

Cryptography is an essential component in modern electronic commerce. With increasing transactions conducted over the Internet, ensuring security of data transfer is critically important. Considerable amounts of money are being exchanged over the network, either through e-commerce sites (e.g., Amazon and Buy.com), auction sites (e.g., eBay), on-line banking (e.g., Citibank and Chase), stock trading (e.g., Schwab), and even governments (e.g., irs.gov). Therefore, many security protocols have been employed to guarantee data privacy and communication channel security, such as virtual private networks [1] and secure IP (IPSec) [2]. Security-related processing can consume the processing capacities of many servers.

W. Xu et al. (Eds.): NCCET 2013, CCIS 396, pp. 61–72, 2013.
© Springer-Verlag Berlin Heidelberg 2013

Accelerating security protocols is a great challenge in the general-purpose processor due to the complexity of crypto algorithms. In general, ciphers use large arithmetic and algebraic modifications, which are not adequate for software implementation. Thus, cipher implementations allocate many system resources in terms of hardware to integrate as components. Additionally, security protocol implementation must also support different algorithms and be upgradeable in the field; otherwise, interoperability among different systems cannot be realized, and any upgrade results in excessive cost. However, most hardware implementations suffer from drawback from the difficulty in the programming model, resulting in upgrading difficulty.

The ultimate solution to this problem would be an adaptive processor that can provide software-like flexibility with hardware-like performance. FPGA chips, which operate at the bit level and serve as custom hardware for different crypto applications, have been considered as a likely option to support efficiently a wide range of cryptographic algorithms and procedures.

After analyzing the characteristics of security protocols, we discovered that most crypto algorithms are employed at the function level among different security protocols. By utilizing the reconfigure feature of FPGA, we propose a novel flexible crypto coprocessor (FC Coprocessor) architecture, which rely on Reconfigurable Cryptographic Blocks (RCBs) to achieve a balance between high performance and flexibility and implement a flexible architecture for security protocols on FPGA. The RCBs are pipeline implementations of crypto algorithms on the reconfigurable chip, with unified interface ports to the host computer and each other. For a specific security protocol, we can adapt the coprocessor architecture and select several correspondent blocks from the module library to realize the entire security protocol on a reconfigurable device.

This paper is organized as follows; Section 2 introduces the related works. Section 3 describes in details the flexible architecture of our proposed coprocessor; Section 4 shows the performance of the crypto blocks and their application to security protocol on FPGA; Section 5 presents the conclusion.

2   Relative Work

Our work encompasses many aspects of cryptographic algorithm accelerations [3–8]. In the following, we summarize some representative works and explain how our paper differs from these.

Many studies focused on the hardware structure to reconfigure unit of ciphers. The Cryptographic Optimized for Block Ciphers Reconfigurable Architecture (COBRA) [9] proposed specialized cryptographic elements (named as reconfigurable cryptographic elements) to construct the COBRA architecture and a methodology to design general-purpose reconfigurable cryptographic elements optimized for block cipher implementation by analyzing the functional requirements of the block ciphers. The Cryptobooster [10] processor adopted modules to implement the IDEA algorithm. The Adaptive Cryptographic Engine (ACE) [11] was proposed to provide the speed and flexibility required by IPSec. ACE consists of an FPGA device, a cryptographic library, and a configuration controller. Using the cryptographic library, the FPGA can be configured at run-time using the configuration controller. Various configuration files are available for selection, similar to COBRA; however, only one crypto algorithm is chosen in the meantime.

Most of the times, security protocol needs more than one crypto algorithm block at once, and integrating all crypto blocks needed by the protocols on a chip can decrease the overhead of communications between the host and the accelerator. Therefore, this paper proposes the novel FC Coprocessor architecture that balances high performance and flexibility.

3   Implementation of the Coprocessor

3.1   Architecture

The crypto coprocessor accelerator comprises one FPGA chip, two SDRAM modules, and an I/O channel interface. The interface channel is responsible for transferring the computed data and results between the accelerator and the host. Figure 1 shows the computation platform consisting of the coprocessor accelerator.

The core of the FC Coprocessor mainly consists of memory controller, register files, a data-path controller, and reconfigurable integrity blocks for the crypto algorithms. The data-path controller controls the dedicated crypto block and performs the interface operations using external devices such as the memory and an I/O bus interface controller. RCB executes various crypto algorithms such as MD5 and SHA-256 (hash algorithms) and other application programs such as the user authentication and IC card interface programs.

The structure of RCB is shown in Figure 2. The input data, e.g., plain text, are transmitted via FIFO, as well as the cipher text. We chose 128 bits as the data width in our implementation because the width of the operands in most crypto algorithms is 128 bits or higher. Through FIFO_I and FIFO_O, different blocks with different operand widths can work synchronously.

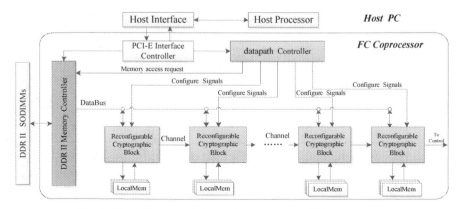

Fig. 1. Block diagram of the hardware design of FC Coprocessor

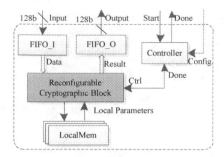

Fig. 2. Block diagram of the hardware design of RCB

A controller module is provided to handle the control signal from the data-path controller. When a start signal is received from the top controller, the module orders the RCB to read the data from FIFO_I sequentially and start the pipeline of RCBs. When the pipeline result is ready, the module produces the control signal to write data back to FIFO_O.

LocalMem is used to store the local parameters of the symmetric algorithms, such as the S-boxes of AES, RC4, and DES. The S-box design is an important work in progress of these algorithms. RCBs are the pipeline implementations of crypto algorithms, described in details in following section.

3.2   Implementations of RCB

RSA

RSA [14] is one of the most popular public-key crypto algorithms. This algorithm is a type of modular exponentiation: $C = M^e \bmod N$. Here, e and N refer to the public-key cryptography, M refers to the plaintext, and C is the calculated cipher text. N, e, and M are large numbers. The width of the operands in the RSA can reach 1,024 bits or higher, indicating that the throughput of the system is too difficult to achieve.

The Montgomery algorithm is used to speed up the modular multiplication and modular exponentiation. The radix-2 Montgomery algorithm without subtraction is presented in [12]. The difficulties of the Montgomery algorithm lie in solving qi and the large-number additions. We propose the following methods to solve these problems:

Solving qi: Before Y is input, we can shift Y to the left of N bits; thus, the calculation of qi would be $q_i = S_i \times n_0' \bmod 2^r$, where $n0'$ is decided by input X. We can truncate the high part of Si because of the mode operation. Then, we can easily and quickly obtain qi.

Large-number additions: Using the CSA contracture, we can split X into Xc and Xs, which indicate the carry of X and the result of X, respectively. Furthermore, the same process with Y can be performed, splitting Y into Yc and Ys. Therefore, the Montgomery algorithm can be modified as shown in Figure 3.

Improved Montgomery Algorithm:
Input: X,Y,N ($0<=$X,Y$<$2N; the length of X,Y,N are all n bits;
    and $n_0 n_0' = -1 \bmod 2^r$)
Output: S = $X \times Y \times 2^{-r(n+1)} \bmod N$

1:     $S_0 = 0$;
2:     for (i =0, i $<$ (n+ r)/ r, i ++)
3:         {
4:                         $q_i = \{S_i + Y \times Equation1^*\} n_0' \bmod 2^r$;
5:                         $S_{i+1} = \{S_i + Y \times Equation1^* + q_i N\}/2^r$;
6:         }
7:     return S_n;

---
*: Equation1$=2^{r-1}x_{ri+r-1}+2^{r-2}x_{ri+r-2}+\cdots+2^1 x_{ri+1}+2^0 x_{ri}$.

Fig. 3. Modified algorithm of the general radix-2^r Montgomery algorithm without subtraction from the radix-2 Montgomery algorithm

Figure 4(a) shows that after X and Y_s are input and width_N cycles carry the save addition in the CSA tree, S_c and S_s are sent to the add module to complete the entire addition. Finally, we can derive the result. The whole Montgomery system requires ($n + r$)/r + n/w cycles (w is the width of the data processing in the Adder module).

The full Adder (FA) module completes the final summation operation of the outputs S_s and S_c in the improved Montgomery algorithm. Figure 4(b) shows its construction. The results of the CSA (S_s and S_c) are sent to Registers A and B, respectively. Subsequently, we derive w bits from A and B to send them to the FA, and the resulting w bits are sent to the lower w bit in the result register. The one-bit carry is sent to C_in to prepare for the next w-bit addition. The result register shifts the w bits to the right following the addition of every w bit.

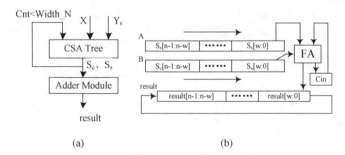

(a)   (b)

Fig. 4. (a) Montgomery multiplier module. (b) Construction of the FA module.

MD5

MD5 is a hash algorithm for message digesting, introduced in 1992 by Rivest; it consists of five steps (for more details, please refer to [13]). The core of MD5 is the algorithm used for processing the message. The algorithm consists of four rounds, each of which comprises 16 steps.

The algorithm is performed as follows: first, the values of A, B, C, and D are stored as temporary variables. Then, every step operation is performed for 64 rounds. For each round, a corresponding nonlinear function exists. Finally, the values of the temporary variables are added to the values obtained from the algorithm, and the results are stored in Registers A, B, C, and D. When all message blocks have been processed, the message digest of M is stored in Registers A, B, C, and D.

Message M is divided into 512-bit blocks, which are processed separately. Data dependence does not exist among the pieces of input data. Hence, we can pipeline the data path in 64 cycles.

A one-round process of MD5 is shown in Figure 5. The Const Unit keeps the data of MD5 constant. The registers store the input message block, and a selection module is available that chooses the response corresponding to the value of Xk in every round. FU is a combinational logic consisting of rotate left, adder, and nonlinear functions.

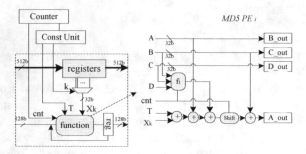

Fig. 5. One round of MD5 algorithm

SHA256

SHA256 15 is another widely used message-digesting algorithm. The SHA-256 algorithm takes a message length of less than 264 bits and outputs a 256-bit long message digest. The digest serves as a concise representation of the message and has the property that any change in the message is very likely to result in a change in the corresponding digest. Initially, we need to initiate several parameters, such as from a to h, as shown in Figure 6, to be used as starting points for the rounds. In the design, parameters a to h are implemented through eight registers whose width are all 32 bits. Subsequently, the message should be scheduled. The next step is an iterative process. Finally, the hash value is updated; the data in registers a to h represent the final result.

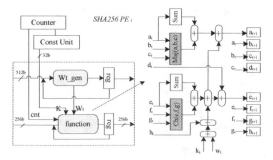

Fig. 6. Iterative progress of SHA256 algorithm

AES

AES [16] was accepted as a FIPS standard in November 2001. The algorithm is composed of four different steps, namely, *byte substitution*, *shift row*, *mix column*, and *key addition*. The number of rounds Nr that the algorithm is repeated is related to the key size that the algorithm used. When a key size of 128 bits is used, the number of rounds is equal to 10. Figure 7 shows the unrolled and fully pipelined implementation of the AES algorithm. The *shift row* step is only for interconnection, and the *key addition* is the XORing of the round data and the round key. The mix column step consists of a chain of XORs to permute the elements of the data in each column. The arithmetic of these three stages can be combined in one pipeline stage for each round.

The *byte substitution* is performed on each byte of the state using a substitution table (S-box). In this phase, the input is considered as an element of $GF(2^8)$. First, the multiplicative inverse of $GF(2^8)$ is calculated. Then, an affine transformation over $GF(2)$ is applied. Here, either all substitute values are calculated in advance and stored in the block RAMs or on-the-fly calculation of the values is logically implemented. We implemented the SubBytes block (S-box) with a block RAM, instead of calculating the multiplicative inverse and affine transform, for simplicity and high performance. We used a 1-kbyte block RAM for the S-box, and S-box was used in the implementation of the AES crypto block.

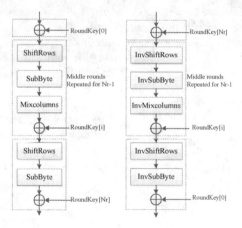

Fig. 7. AES round structure

DES

DES [17] is a block cipher that uses a 64-bit key and operates on 64-bit blocks of data. Because every 8th bit of the 64-bit key is used for parity checking, DES has a 56-bit key. The DES algorithm has 16 rounds of identical operations such as non-linear substitutions and permutations. In each round, 48-bit sub keys are generated, and substitutions using S-box, bitwise shift, and XOR operations are performed.

The 56-bit key length is relatively small by today's standards. For increased security, the DES operation can be performed by three consecutive times, which expands the effective key length to 112 bits. Using DES in this manner is referred to as triple-DES. In this section, we only describe the DES crypto block because the expansion to triple-DES is trivial.

Figure 8 shows one round of the DES algorithm. The left and right halves of each 64-bit input data operand are treated as separate 32-bit data operands L_{i-1} and R_{i-1}. The 32-bit right halves of the data are passed to the next left halves of the data. The left and right halves of each 64-bit input data operand are treated as separate 32-bit data operands L_{i-1} and R_{i-1}. The 32-bit right halves of the data are passed to the next left halves of the data.

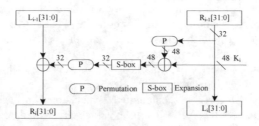

Fig. 8. Structure of one round in DES

RC5

RC5 [18] is a variable key-size stream cipher developed by Ron Rivest for RSA Data Security, Inc. For real-time encrypting, stream cipher is the best choice. Therefore, RC5 is employed in several popular security protocols.

RC5 consists of three components: a key expansion algorithm, an encryption algorithm, and a decryption algorithm. The plain text input to RC5 consists of two words A and B. The algorithm uses an expanded key table $S[0,t-1]$ consisting of $t=2(r+1)$ w-bit words. The key-expansion algorithm initializes S from the user's given secret-key parameter K. (S is not a user, in contrast to that of the DES S-box).

We assume that the input block is given in the two w-bit registers A and B. We assume standard little-endian conventions for packing the bytes into input/output blocks: the first byte goes into the low-order bit position of register A, and so on. We also assume that key expansion has already been performed. The decryption routine is easily derived from the encryption routine.

We implemented RC5 algorithms on FPGA; Figure. 9 shows the structure of RC5, which is composed of three units: Key Setup and Encrypt are the combinational logic, and S-Table is a block RAM that stores in the S-box.

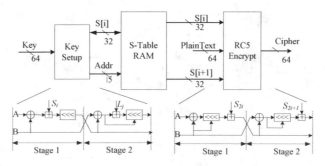

Fig. 9. Structure of RC5

4   Experimental Results

We implemented the crypto coprocessor on a development board and verified the designs on FPGA. The board was composed of one large-scale FPGA chip, Virtex5 XC5VLX330 from Xilinx, two 4 GB DDRII SODIMM modules, and a PCI-E × 8 interface to the host computer.

Our designed target is the FPGA at its fastest speed grade (-2) using ISE 10.1i.03 implementation flow by Xilinx Synthesis Technology. We used the Mentor Graphics ModelSim 6.5a for the behavioral simulation. The software platform included a host PC with Intel Dual-Core i3 530 CPU at 2.93 GHz and 8.0 GB DDR3 1333 memory at level O3 compiler optimization [19].

4.1   Performance of RCB

In this section, we present and analyze the performance of the FC Coprocessor. We compared the representative operation mode of the algorithms in the test. By the term "performance," we mean the throughput of the blocks measured by the minimum time that elapsed between the completions of two independent encrypting operations, which is smaller than the instruction latency because the circuit is pipelined.

➤   *Performance of the RCB*
Table 1 shows the details of the FPGA synthesis results for the basic RCBs. The AES crypto block was implemented with full pipelined-based architecture, and its S-boxes were implemented with FPGA's block RAM. We also chose the pipelining technique for the MD5, SHA256, and DES crypto blocks. Resource cost is usually related to the width of the operand, such as RSA. Because of the mode of operation, the RC4 algorithm block was selected to exploit the sub-pipelining technique.

The achievable maximum frequency of the RCBs is 214.34 MHz. Compared with the same circuit implemented directly on silicon (ASIC), the FPGA implementation, emulated with a very large number of configurable elementary blocks and network of wires, is typically one order of magnitude slower. However, the performance of the FPGAs improved using custom hardware for applications equipped with multiple RCBs working in parallel.

Table 1. Resource and frequency of the algorithms on FPGA

Algorithms	Slice LUT	BRAM	Freq.(MHz)	Perf.(Gbps)
AES 128	14833	32	307.89	39.4
RC5	915	1	353.78	0.91
SHA-256	11,047	55	214.34	10.9
MD5	12,662	20	248.08	53.3
RSA-1024	24,996	1	308.36	2.2×10^{-3}

➤   *Performance comparison with an i3 core*

Table 2 shows that we can obtain better performance compared with the parallel programs running on Intel multi-core processor. We compare the performance of the RCBs with the corresponding parallel program of the multi-core processor. The speedup factor for the RCBs is between 2 and 72. The DES hardware implementation achieves 20.2 Gbps, a factor of 72 times better than the general processor. The AES in the CBC mode results in a performance of 39.4 Gbps and achieves a speedup of 15.8 times. The throughput of the 1,024-bit RSA encryption is 2.2 Mbps.

Table 2. Performance (gigabit per second) comparison with the general processor

Algorithms	Ours (Gbps)	CPU (Gbps)	Speedup
AES-128	39.4	1.16	15.8
RC5	5.6	0.08	66.7
SHA256	10.9	0.12	68.3
MD5	53.3	2.24	29.2
RSA-1024(Sign)	2.2×10^{-3}	1.2×10^{-3}	2.1

➤   *Performance comparison with related works*

In Table 3, we compare the performance of our design with existing designs. From the result, we obtain a better throughput in most algorithms. The performance of AES and SHA256 in our design is approximately the same. For RC5 and MD5 algorithms, the frequency of our design is higher; therefore, the throughput is higher than that of the related works.

Table 3. Performance comparisons with other designs

Algorithms	Implements	chips	Area(slice)	Freq.(Mhz)	Perf.(Gbps)
AES-128	Ours	XC5VLX330	14,833	307.89	39.4
	[20]	XC5vlx30	1,223	289.79	3.71
RC5	Ours	XC5VLX330	915	353.78	5.6
	[21]	XC2V1000	3,618	35	0.05
SHA256	Ours	XC5VLX330	11,047	214.34	10.9
	[22]	Virtex II	3,077	85.9	5.4
MD5	Ours	XC5VLX330	12,662	248.08	53.3
	[23]	EP2SGx90	26,758	66.48	32.0
RSA-1024 (Sign)	Ours	XC5VLX330	24,996	308.36	2.2×10^{-3}
	[24]	XC2V6000	4,956	50	0.3×10^{-3}

4.2   Coprocessor Application in SSL Protocol

To test and verify the method and architecture proposed in this paper, we used the processor to implement SSL ciphered communication in the Virtex5 FPGA. In addition, we evaluated the feasibility of the SSL accelerator based on one-chip architecture using FPGA.

First, we designed RSA by the parallel processing described above. Next, we selected the shared-key cryptography algorithm AES and hash algorithm SHA256 using a shared circuit in sending and receiving and evaluated the efficiency of the area reduction. The circuit area of each algorithm the three algorithms are shown in Table 3.

From these simulation evaluation results, we confirmed the feasibility of SSL accelerator based on the architecture that implements all processes into one chip using FPGA. Finally, we create a prototype of the FC coprocessor on Xilinx Virtex5 XC5VLX330 FPGA chip. The experiment results show that the coprocessor, running at 189 MHz, outperforms the software-based Secure Sockets Layer protocol running on an Intel Core i3 530 CPU at 2.93 GHz by a factor of 4.8X for typical crypto algorithm blocks.

Table 4. Performance comparison of SSL protocol

Modules	Sign/ms	Cipher/ms		Other	Total /ms	Speedup
	RSA1024	AES128	SHA256	Setup		
Avg. time on CPU	0.92	2.3	1.18	0	4.4	4.8
Avg. time on FPGA	0.51	0.15	0.21	0.04	0.91	

5   Conclusion and Future Work

In this paper, we have presented the design and implementation of a novel crypto coprocessor with flexible architecture and reconfigurable crypto blocks. The RCBs of the crypto processor accelerate the private- and public-key crypto algorithms. The crypto processor was evaluated by constructing an acceleration system for SSL protocol. The high performance and flexibility of the crypto processor design enables it for various security applications.

For future work, we plan to develop additional high-performance public-key crypto blocks. To facilitate our crypto processor, we will exploit the high-level synthesis toolchain based on existing architecture for security protocols.

Acknowledgments. This work was supported by the National Science Foundation of China (61125201 and 60921062).

References

1. Freier, A.O., Karlton, P., Kocher, P.C.: Introduction to SSL. IETF draft (1996), https://developer.mozilla.org/zh-CN/docs/Introduction_to_SSL#The_SSL_Protocol
2. Kent, S., Atkinson, R.: Security Architecture for the Internet Protocol. RFC 2401 (November 1998)
3. Taylor, R.R., Goldstein, S.C.: A High-Performance Flexible Architecture for Cryptography. In: Koç, Ç.K., Paar, C. (eds.) CHES 1999. LNCS, vol. 1717, p. 231. Springer, Heidelberg (1999)
4. Antão, S., Chaves, R., Sousa, L.: AES and ECC Cryptography Processor with Runtime Configuration. In: Proceedings of ADCOM (2009)

5. Hodjat, A., Verbauwhede, I.: A 21.54 Gbits/s Fully Pipelined AES Processor on FPGA. In: Proc. FCCM 2004 (2004)
6. Mazzeo, A., Romano, L., Saggese, G.P., et al.: FPGA-based Implementation of a serial RSA processor. In: Proc. DATE 2003 (2003)
7. Michail, H.E., Athanasios, P., et al.: Top-Down Design Methodology for Ultrahigh-Performance Hashing Cores. IEEE Transactions on Dependable and Secure Computing 6(4), 255–268 (2009)
8. Kakarountas, A.P., Michail, H. (eds.): High-Speed FPGA Implementation of Secure Hash Algorithm for IPSec and VPN Applications. The Journal of Supercomputing 37, 179–195 (2006)
9. Elbirt, A.J., Paar, C.: An Instruction-Level Distributed Processor for Symmetric-Key Cryptography. IEEE Transactions on Parallel and Distributed Systems 16(5) (2005)
10. Mosanya, E., Teuscher, C., Restrepo, H.F., Galley, P., Sánchez, E.: CryptoBooster: A Reconfigurable and Modular Cryptographic Coprocessor. In: Koç, Ç.K., Paar, C. (eds.) CHES 1999. LNCS, vol. 1717, pp. 246–256. Springer, Heidelberg (1999)
11. Prasanna, V.K., Dandalis, A.: FPGA-based Cryptography for Internet Security. In: Online Symposium for Electronic Engineers (2000)
12. Li, M., Ji, X., Liu, B.: Analysing and Researching Montgomery Algorithm. Science Technology and Engineering 6, 1628–1631 (2006)
13. Rivest, R.L.: The MD5 Message-Digest Algorithm. RFC 1321, MIT Laboratory for Computer Science and RSA Data Security, Inc. (April 1992)
14. Rivest, R., Shamir, A., Adleman, L.: A Method for Obtaining Digital Signatures and Public-Key Cryptosystems. Communications of the ACM 21, 120–126 (1978)
15. NIST Federal Information Processing Standards Publication, FIPS PUB 180-2 (2002)
16. National Institute of Standards and Technology. Advanced Encryption Standard (AES). Federal Information Processing Standards Publications – FIPS 197 (2001)
17. FIPS PUB 46-3, Data Encryption Standard (DES), Reaffirmed (1977)
18. Rivest, R.L.: The RC5 Encryption Algorithm. In: Preneel, B. (ed.) FSE 1994. LNCS, vol. 1008, pp. 86–96. Springer, Heidelberg (1995)
19. OProfile. OProfile Website (2012), http://oprofile.sourceforge.net/news/
20. Bouhraous, A.: Design feasibility study for a 500Gbits/s advanced encryption standard cipher/decipher engine. IET Computers & Digital Techniques 4(4), 334–348 (2010)
21. de Dormale, G.M., et al.: On Solving RC5 Challenges with FPGAs. In: Proceedings of FCCM (2007)
22. Michail, H.E., et al.: On the Exploitation of a High-Throughput SHA-256 FPGA Design for HMACACM. Transactions on Reconfigurable Technology and Systems 5(1) (2012)
23. Wang, Y., Zhao, Q., Jiang, L., Shao, Y.: Ultra-High Throughput Implementations for MD5 Hash Algorithm on FPGA. In: Zhang, W., Chen, Z., Douglas, C.C., Tong, W. (eds.) HPCA 2009. LNCS, vol. 5938, pp. 433–441. Springer, Heidelberg (2010)
24. Paar, T.B.C.: High-Radix Montgomery Modular Exponentiation on Reconfigurable Hardware. IEEE Transaction on Computer 50(7) (2001)

Wormhole Bubble in Torus Networks

Yongqing Wang and Minxuan Zhang

College of Computer, National University of Defense Technology,
410073 Changsha, China
{yqwang,mxzhang}@nudt.edu.cn

Abstract. Typical bubble schemes are flow control algorithms based on virtual cut-through switching. It can avoid deadlock problems without using virtual channels. In this paper, we extend bubble mechanism to wormhole flow control in torus networks, design a non-blocking moveable bubble scheme combined with a false packet protocol. The minimum buffer space required for each input channel is one maximum-sized packet. We compare the performance of various bubble-based schemes with simulation. The results show that moveable bubble scheme can achieve higher throughput and lower latency than existing bubble schemes, and be comparable with dateline technique with two virtual channels. When buffer size is limited and packet-size is fixed, it even has some advantage over dateline, improving accepted rates at saturation more than 10%.

Keywords: bubble scheme, k-ary n-cube, wormhole flow control, deadlock-free, interconnection network.

1   Introduction

Different flow control techniques have been proposed to control the flow of information in the area of interconnection network. Virtual cut-through (VCT) and wormhole (WH) are the most well-known flow control mechanisms among others. The main difference between VCT and WH routers is the size of their flow control unit. VCT performs flow control at the packet level instead of the smaller data units employed in WH.

Flow control mechanisms can also be classified as being either locally-aware or globally-aware. Locally-aware flow control mechanisms allocate network resources to packets based solely on information local to router nodes. In the contrast, globally-aware flow control mechanisms make resource allocation decisions based on global network conditions that include local status information [1].

Along with routing, network flow control aims to maximize resource utilization. If the routing algorithm and the flow control are not carefully designed, message deadlock can arise. One of the critical issues in the design of large-scale interconnection network is to efficiently handle deadlock anomalies. Deadlocks occur as a result of circular dependencies on network resources by in-flight messages (or packets).

W. Xu et al. (Eds.): NCCET 2013, CCIS 396, pp. 73–80, 2013.
© Springer-Verlag Berlin Heidelberg 2013

2   Related Works

In a full-duplex torus network, the set of unidirectional links along a given direction in a dimension form a unidirectional ring, and intra-dimensional deadlock can occur. A classic solution to this problem is to use a dateline technique where two virtual channels are associated with each physical channel [2]. A drawback of this approach, however, is the requirement of two virtual channels and the corresponding buffer resources.

Carrion [3] first proposed a flow control policy called "bubble" to get rid of the deadlock caused by wraparound links in the virtual cut-through network, reducing the required number of virtual channels under deterministic routing from two down to one.

Puente [4] gave a design of adaptive virtual cut-through router with a combination of adaptive virtual channel and bubble scheme. Bubble flow control (BFC) was adopted in IBM Blue Gene/L [5].

Critical Bubble Scheme (CBS) [1] was proposed as a way to implement globally-aware BFC including special bubble information within the ring, which can reduce the minimum number of channel buffers needed to avoid deadlock to minimal one-packet size as opposed to two of localized version. The principle behind the Critical Bubble Scheme is to mark and track as critical at least one bubble in each directional ring of a network and restrict the use of critical bubble only to packets traveling within dimensions.

MBS[6] was proposed to relieve the potential blocks introduced in CBS. It presented a false packet protocol to make the critical bubble moveable. But like all the other bubble schemes, it works under virtual cut-through switching.

3   Bubble Scheme for Wormhole

In wormhole switching, the unit of flow control is flit. Thus, channel buffer space is multiple of flit size and packet is composed of one or more flits. Also in what follows, a bubble refers to a free flit-sized buffer.

Critical bubble scheme needs to mark and track as "critical" a certain number of free flit-sized buffers (minimally, one per network dimension) and use them correctly to restrict packet injection for preventing deadlock. Thus, free buffers are separated into two classes, normal ones and critical ones. Normal free buffers are those without mark, and critical buffers are those with mark.

Critical bubbles flow within and are confined to certain directional rings.

There are three simple rules when injecting and forwarding of packets across dimensions under wormhole flow control, which are similar to VCT,

1) Forwarding of flit along the same dimension is allowed if the receiving channel buffer has at least one free slot.

2) Injection of a new packet of size S into a dimension is only allowed if the receiving channel buffer has at least S normal free slots and there is at least one additional free buffer located anywhere in the set of queues corresponding to that directional ring.

3) Forwarding of a packet from one dimension to another is treated as a packet injection.

According to rule 1), a flit entering into downstream router generates a bubble at current router. And with rule 2) and 3), the absence of the critical bubble at the immediate destination indicates the existence of a free buffer elsewhere in the ring, ensuring bubble condition.

But just as what was presented in paper [6], using the rules straightforward had a risk of blocking some channel forever, if the critical bubble stayed at some place permanently. This blocking is not a kind of deadlock with resource dependence, but results from the flow control function itself. So we adapt the false packet protocol (FPP) to BUB-WH, and get a moveable bubble scheme for wormhole, named MBS-WH.

The key idea is to assure the transferability of critical bubbles, especially when such kind of buffers doesn't move for a long time. The transfer of critical bubble needs the help from upstream router. If there is any packet from upstream, critical bubble moves automatically. If there is no such flow, a free buffer can also help. A free buffer in upstream can replace the critical bubble in current router.

FPP is used for communications by two neighboring ports connected with a direct link, such as e and w connected in Fig. 1. It includes two phases, request (REQ) and acknowledgement (ACK). During the first phase, a REQ packet is sent and received, and during the second phase, an ACK packet is interchanged. A REQ packet is some kind of control signal and consumes no credit. It can be consumed directly after reception. Whereas the ACK packet acts as a normal data packet of one flit. Credit of one flit buffer is needed to send and receive. At the receiver, it is processed immediately, and there is no further transmitting. Above all, the FPP protocol can generate a temporary data packet to make the critical bubble transfer possible.

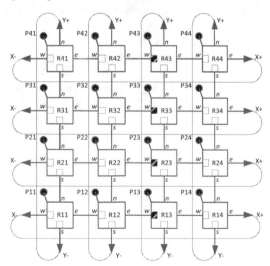

Fig. 1. A 4x4 torus network

In the following, we give the description of the MBS-WH,

1) Initialization: Assume a k-ary n-cube network with bidirectional links. Every dimension is composed of two opposite unidirectional rings. For each unidirectional ring, one or more free flit buffers from any one or more router channels belonging to this direction can be marked as the critical bubbles. The other free buffers operate as normal buffers.

2) Forward rules: In MBS-WH, two rules are defined for the flow control of packets to avoid deadlock. When the flit advances in the same dimension, at least one free slot is needed in the receiving channel, no matter whether it is a normal one or a critical one.

When a packet consisting of S flits is injected to the network or forwarded to a channel belongs to a different dimension, at least S normal slots are needed in the receiving channel. It is prohibited to forward if the size of remaining normal slots is less than S.

3) Migration of Critical Bubble: The primary requirement of the MBS-WH is always to maintain a certain number of free buffers in each unidirectional ring and assure no blocking caused by critical bubbles. For ease of explanation, we take the case in Fig. 1, but assume a general input channel (w in R_{23}) of n free slots and there are m critical bubbles among them, with m <= n. And According to the types of packet forwarding in upstream input channel (w in R_{22}) and the current channel state, there are four cases.

i) When n $-$m $>=S_{max}$ (the number of flits belonging to one maximum-sized packet), there is enough normal free space to accept a maximum-sized packet, and any packet toward this channel is allowed. The critical bubble remains untouched.

ii) When n $-$m $<S_{max}$, and a flit is forwarded from router R_{22} to R_{23} along the same dimension, the critical bubble in router R_{23} transfer backward to router R_{22}.

iii) When n $-$m $<S_{max}$, and the flit in input channel w of R_{22} is not destined for R_{23}, after forwarding, a critical bubble is transfered from R_{23} to R_{22}. Router R_{21} is notified of this change when a credit is returned, and at the same time, the number of critical bubbles in channel e of R_{23} is reduced by one. On the other hand, the normal buffer size is increased by one.

iv) When n $-$m $<S_{max}$, and there is no flit in input channel w of R_{22}, there is a risk of blocking in channel w of R_{23}. So, a timer is set in each output. If n $-$m $>=S_{max}$, the timer is cleared. Otherwise the timer is started. When the timer counts to a threshold, the FPP scheme is triggered. After the ACK packet is processed, the free buffer will be marked as critical and information is sent to R_{21}. Then, the critical bubble count in channel e of R_{22} is reduced by one, avoiding the potential blocking.

4   Evaluation

In this section, we evaluate the proposed wormhole bubble scheme and compare its performance with other techniques. Network throughput and latency are typical metrics used to measure the performance of an interconnection network, so we modify the cycle-accurate simulator, Booksim [2], to model related flow controls and measure the average latency of packets and throughput over a long period, after a sufficient network warm-up. Each point in the plots shows the measured value for a given offered load in flits/node/cycle. The plots present the average packet latency (in clock cycles) and accepted flit rate as a function of offered rate, respectively.

We consider a small network size with bidirectional physical channels, a 16-node (4x4) torus network. Each router node has one injection channel. For our analysis, we consider synthetic traffic patterns, including uniform random and shuffle traffic patterns.

In the following, we assume fixed packet size with 4 flits, while variable packet size from 1 to 4 flits.

For all the figures below, the number of input buffer slots is appended to each scheme, forming a whole name for comparing.

In all cases deterministic (XY) routing is employed.

4.1   Performance with Less Than Two Packet-Sized Buffers

Our simulation exploration starts with a latency and throughput comparison between a locally-aware wormhole bubble (BUB-WH) and the MBS implementation. We first set buffer with least requirements, 4 flits, and then assume that both designs have equal-sized buffers; specifically, 5-flit buffers and 6-flit buffers per input port.

With buffer set to one packet size, MBS passes our test, validating the correctness of MBS-WH.

Fig. 2 depicts how the latency and throughput of MBS change at various buffer sizes. It is evident from the graphs that buffer depth is crucial to performance. As buffer size increasing, the network is able to reach higher throughput. We can also observe from this figure, when packet injection rate is low (< 0.15 flit/cycle), which means the network is empty, their performance is almost the same.

As the flit injection rate increases, network congestion happens, and the packet latency rises dramatically, but the time that congestion happens in MBS is later than BUB-WH. Under uniform traffic pattern, MBS performs a little better than BUB-WH when the packet injection rate is the same. This is because MBS gets more opportunity to forward packets when the network load is heavy.

Under shuffle pattern, curves of MBS-WH-4 and BUB-WH-5 are almost superposed, suggesting that MBS-WH can achieve similar performance with fewer buffers. With equal-sized buffers of 5, MBS-WH-5 substantially outperforms BUB-WH-5.

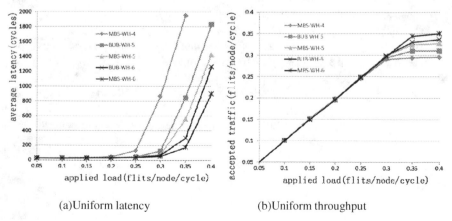

(a)Uniform latency   (b)Uniform throughput

Fig. 2. Performance with Less than eight slots

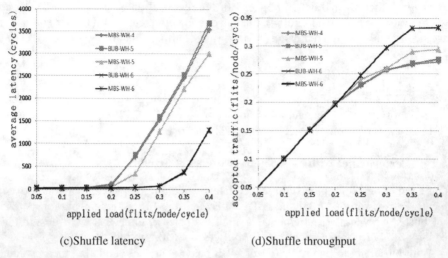

(c)Shuffle latency   (d)Shuffle throughput

Fig. 2. (*continued*)

4.2   Performance with Two Packet-Sized Buffers

Next, we evaluate network performance with the buffer depth set to 8 slots. In the generic dateline design, 8 buffer slots are arranged as 2 VCs, each with a 4-flit depth. Fig. 3 gives the results.

When the applied load rate is low, buffer occupancy is also low in all schemes and the performance is not much different.

In all cases of heavy load, BUB-VCT performs worse than the others, due to its inefficient at moving flits through the router, adopting local bubble scheme with virtual cut-through switching.

Under uniform pattern, MBS-WH and dateline are almost identical with each other. While under shuffle, which are apt to congestion, we can observe MBS-WH provides a competitive latency under load 0.3~0.4 and saturates at higher accepted rates by 15%. The difference comes mainly from the highly efficient buffer utilization of MBS-WH.

This is of profound importance, since dateline is equipped with two virtual channels, while MBS-WH has no virtual channel support. It seems that the use of virtual channels does not make a significant improve under limited buffers.

For bubble schemes with equal-sized configurations, MBS-WH obtains, by far, the best result. It performs clearly better than BUB-WH and BUB-VCT. More importantly, though, MBS-WH saturates at higher injection rates than the generic cases. It shows the benefit of global-awareness.

5   Conclusions

Networks-on-Chip (NoC) have surfaced as a possible solution to escalating wiring delays in future multi-core chips. It is known that router buffers are instrumental in the overall operation of the on-chip network. However, buffers are the largest leakage power and area consumers. It is of great importance to architecting high performance and energy efficient on-chip interconnect with less buffers.

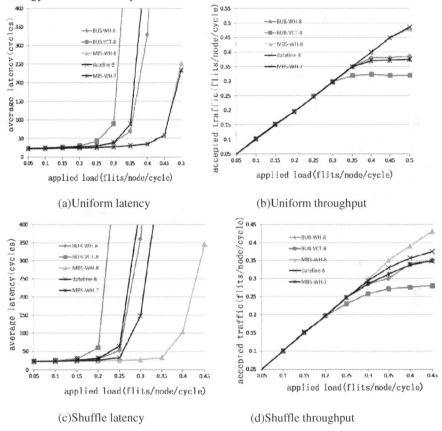

(a)Uniform latency

(b)Uniform throughput

(c)Shuffle latency

(d)Shuffle throughput

Fig. 3. Performance with up to eight slots

It is known that wormhole switching can improve network performance over virtual cut-through. We extend bubble scheme and false packet protocol to wormhole, and present moveable bubble scheme to provide a way to correctly and efficiently implement globally-aware wormhole flow control. The results confirm the benefit of globally-aware wormhole switching. MBS-WH can achieve higher throughput and lower latency than existing bubble schemes, and be comparable with dateline. When buffer size is limited and packet-size is fixed, MBS-WH has some advantage over dateline, improving accepted rates at saturation by 15% for shuffle. Comparing to typical VCT bubble, the accepted rate at saturation can have an increase up to 43%.

Acknowledgements. This work is partly supported by the 863 Project of China under contract 2013AA014301, 2012AA01A301, and National Science Foundation under Contract 61003301.

References

1. Chen, L., Wang, R., Pinkston, T.M.: Critical Bubble Scheme: An Efficient Implementation of Globally Aware Network Flow Control. In: Proceedings of the 2011 IEEE International Parallel & Distributed Processing Symposium, pp. 592–603. IEEE Computer Society, Washington, DC (2011)
2. Dally, W., Towles, B.: Principles and Practices of Interconnection Networks. Morgan Kaufmann, San Francisco (2003)
3. Carrion, C., Beivide, R., Gregorio, J.A.: A Flow Control Mechanism to Avoid Message Deadlock in k-ary n-cube Networks. In: Proceedings of the Fourth International Conference on High-Performance Computing, pp. 322–329. IEEE Computer Society, Washington, DC (1997)
4. Puente, V., Izu, C., Beivide, R.: The Adaptive Bubble Router. J. Parallel Distrib. Comput. 61, 1180–1208 (2001)
5. Adiga, N.R., Blumrich, M.A., Chen, D.: Blue Gene/l Torus Interconnection Network. IBM J. Res. Dev. 49, 265–276 (2005)
6. Wang, Y.Q., Zhang, M.X.: Moveable Bubble Flow Control in k-ary n-cube. Journal of National University of Defense Technology 34(6), 34–38 (2012)

Self-adaptive Scheme to Adjust Redundancy for Network Coding with TCP

Hongyun Zhang*, Wanrong Yu, Chunqing Wu, Xiaofeng Hu,
Liang Zhao, and Xiangdong Cui

School of Computer, The National University of Defense Technology,
410073, Changsha, Hunan, China
{grandcloud88,wangrongyu}@gmail.com

Abstract. Network coding has emerged as an important potential approach to improve the robustness and efficiency of data transmission over lossy wireless network. TPC/NC protocol proposed by Sundararajan et al incorporating network coding into TCP by online coding, TCP/NC has the advantage of naturally adding network coding to current network systems and masking non-congestion packet losses from the congestion control algorithm, However, in TCP/NC the values of redundancy factor R can't be adapted based on the characteristics of the underlying channel.

In this paper we propose a novel self-adaptive scheme to dynamically adjust R based on the collective feedback information of ACKs, which contain the information of sinks decoding matrix. Since the scale of decoding matrix is indicators of the lossy channel condition, the source adjusts R based on the channel conditions, avoiding unnecessary TCP rate reduction and preventing the network from entering in a congestion state. The TCP/NC with our self-adaptive scheme is realized in OM-NET++. Simulation results over realistic network scenarios show that our scheme in conjunction with the standard TCP/NC significantly outperforms the previous redundancy approach in reducing size of decoding matrix , and produces better TCP-throughputs than the standard TCP/NC, TCP-Reno.

Keywords: network coding, TCP, packet loss, redundancy packet.

1 Introduction

It is well known that TCP protocol has an awful performance in the lossy wireless network[2][3][4]. It is because that each loss is interpreted as a congestion signal in TCP. Network Coding allows nodes of a network to send packets that are linear combinations of previously received information, instead of delivering the information to their destination in the standard store-and-forward-manner[1][2].

---

* The work described in this paper is partially supported by the project of National Science Foundation of China under grant No. 61103182; the National High Technology Research and Development Program of China (863 Program) No. 2011AA01A103.

W. Xu et al. (Eds.): NCCET 2013, CCIS 396, pp. 81–91, 2013.

Network coding has emerged as an important potential approach in the operation of communication networks [1].The main benefits of network coding are the potential throughput improvements and a high degree of robustness to packet losses[7]. Despite this potential of network coding, we still seem far from seeing widespread implementation of network coding across networks[5][6].

In [5] Sundararajan et al. propose a new TCP-friendly protocol that successfully implemented the network coding into TCP with minor changes to the protocol stack. The key idea was introducing a new network coding layer between the transport layer and IP layer in TCP/IP stack, which masks non-congestion packet losses from congestion control algorithm. In this layer TCP segments are encoded at the sender and decoded at the receiver. In[6]Sundararajan et al. present a real-world implementation of this protocol that addresses several important practical aspects of incorporating network coding and decoding with TCP's window management mechanism. For every packet that arrives from TCP, $R(>= 1)$linear combinations are sent to the IP layer on average, These packets are used by the receiver to counteract non-congestion losses .

The ideal level of redundancy is to keep R equal to the reciprocal of the probability of successful reception[5]. In TCP/NC, the redundancy factor R is constant. However, when the system is under lossy wireless network where the loss rate is hart to acquire and not constant, the constant R may cause problems, on the one hand, when R is too low to match TCP's sending rate to the rate at which data is received at the receiver, it will lead to the increase of decoding delay and TCP time outs. On the other hand, if R is too large, too many linear combinations are sent to sink, leading to a TCP throughput decrease. Both will impair the performance of the network.

we propose a new scheme which makes use of the implicit collective feedback information of sinks decoding matrix to adjust R adaptively to the real system, aiming to better mask non-congestion packet losses from congestion control algorithm and reducing the size of decoding matrix while increasing throughput.

The remainder of the paper is organized as follows. The TCP/NC protocol is briefly described in Section 2, details about the adaptive algorithm are given in Section 3, simulation results are described in Section 4, and some conclusions and future research directions are drawn in Section 5.

2   TCP/NC Protocol

TCP/NC protocol was presented in 2009[6] which successfully implemented the network coding into TCP with minor changes to the protocol stack. TCP/NC designed with respect to a single source that generates a stream of packets to one sink. It embeds the network coding operations in a separate layer below TCP and above IP in the protocol stack on two end nodes, which masks non-congestion losses from congestion control algorithm. In fact, masking losses from TCP was considered earlier by using link layer retransmission[8]. Yet it has been noted in [9] and [10] that the interaction between link layer retransmission and TCP retransmission is complicated and the performance may suffer due to independent retransmission protocols at different layers. But in TCP/NC, it incorporates the seen scheme which modifies the ACK echo system with congestion control to naturally add network coding to current TCP/IP stack.

Before explain how TCP/NC works, we introduce a definition see packets[11] that will be useful throughout the paper. In TCP/NC, packets are treated as vectors over a finite field $\mathbf{F_q}$ of size q. All the discussion here is with respect to a single source that generates a stream of packets. The K_{th} packet that the source generates is said to have an index k and is denoted as P_k . As a result, a node is said to have seen a packet P_k. if it has enough information to compute a linear combination of the form $(P_k + Q)$, where $Q = \sum_{l>k} \alpha_l P_l$, with $\alpha_l \in \mathbf{F_q}$ for all $l > k$. Thus, Q is a linear combination involving packets with indices larger than k.

In the implementation of TCP/NC, the source side buffers packets generated by TCP in the coding buffer, and for every segment arriving from TCP, R random linear combinations of the most W recently arrived packets in the network coding buffer are sent to IP layer on average, where R is the constant redundancy factor. To convey the combination requires an additional network coding header (contain coding coefficients et al.) that is added to the coded packet.

On the receiver side, upon receiving a linear combination from the sender side, it first retrieves the coding coefficients from the packet header and appends them to the basis matrix of its knowledge space. Then the Gaussian elimination method is adopted to find the newly seen packet and decoded packet. The newly seen packet can be ACKed and the newly decoded packet can be submitted to TCP layer. Fig.1 illustrates an example of encoding and decoding. In addition, any ACK generated by the receiver TCP is suppressed and not sent to the sender. These ACKs may be used for managing the decoding buffer. An important point is that the new NC layer is invisible to the transport layer and IP layer. For more details, the reader is referred to [6].

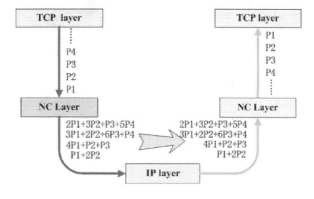

Fig. 1. TCP/NC

3   Self-adaptive TCP/NC Protocol

3.1   Self-adaptive Redundancy Factor

The heart of TCP/NC is that the sink acknowledges every new seen packet even if it does not reveal an original packet immediately. Such heart enables a TCP-compatible sliding-window approach to network coding. It more easy and efficiency add redundant packets by make use of the ability of network coding to mix data across segment. So the redundancy factor R is the key point of masking non-congestion packet losses from congestion control algorithm. If R is too little redundancy, the receiver will not receive enough linear combinations to decode (losses are not masked from TCP), leading to time outs and consequently low throughput. On the other hand, if R is too large, losses are recovered, but at the price of an increased congestion in the network, leading to a TCP throughput decrease. For a loss rate of p_e, with an infinite window W and using TCP Vegas, the theoretically optimal value of R is $1/(1-p_e)$, In TCP/NC redundancy factor R is constantit is impractical to setup R as a constant. Firstly, it is hard to get loss rate of packet in some network scene; secondly, the probability of loss changes over time due to changes on channel conditions.

In this paper we aim to adjust dynamically R to an optimal rate based on the collective feedback information decoding matrix, which indicate the actual network conditions. Our target is to dynamically adjust R in such a way that the losses are effectively masked from the TCP layer, when lost packets are due to the noisy channel, and congestion control algorithm works when a really congestion happened. When the loss rate pe goes up we increase the redundancy to mask the channel losses from TCP. We decrease the redundancy when congestion is present, allowing TCP to sense the congestion and reduce its rate to reduce congestion.

To fulfill our target, we adding a variable to the ACK header, we named it by *Gap*. Before introduce *Gap*, we first expatiate four state of uncoded segment in the receiver side buffer, Fig. 2 shows a typical situation.

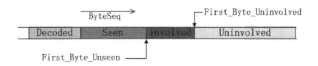

Fig. 2. Four state of segment in receiver buffer

It is easy to understand seen and decoded state, we mainly focus on involved and uninvolved state. When a packet is in involved state means some linear combinations that contain this packet has been receive, but still cant been seen. As for uninvolved state, a packet is in uninvolved state when none linear combinations in receiver side contain this packet.

At the receiver, the difference between $First\_Byte\_Uninvolved$ and $First\_Byte\_Unseen$ is called Gap. When the channel state is stability and R is suited to loss rate, the value of Gap keep stable at the decoding matrix. When channel condition change or R is not suited to loss rate, the value of Gap will also vary. The crux of our scheme is dynamically adjusting R according to the Gap change. Fig. 3 shows a typical situation in the decoding matrix.

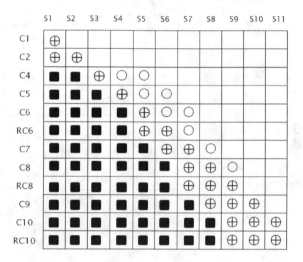

Fig. 3. Typical situation in the decoding matrix

It is safe to assume that the essence of coding packet is a linear combinations of three original segment. The meanings of this mark or symbol on Fig. 3 are are as Table 1:

Table 1. meanings of marks or symbols

Mark/Symbol	Meaning
Si	The ith segment that the source TCP generates
Ci	The ith linear combinations that the source NC layer generates
RCi	A redundant combinations of Ci
⊕	This segment is contained in Ci or RCi and Si has been seen
○	This segment is contained in Ci or RCi and Si still cant been seen
■	This segment has been seen or decoded before receive Ci or RCi

Actually, the number of ○ is the value of Gap when receive Ci of this course. We find when $C3$ is lost, Gap go up to 2, so we should increase the value of R to send more redundant packet for compensation. $C6$ is a effective redundant packet for compensation. When R is too large, just like receiver side find $RC10$ is a redundant packet, at this time receiver side set Gap to -1 to acknowledge send side R is too large.

3.2   Self-adaptation Algorithm for R

In our scheme we perceive the change of loss rate by comparing Gap on NC_ACK (add Gap to the ACK header) with $SGap$ on source side, and thereby dynamically adjust the redundancy factor R. If acked Gap is below $SGap$ which indicates redundancy packet is effective repair packets dropped by the channel impairments, so R should be remain unchanged. On the other hand, if acked Gap is up $SGap$, R should increase (below the upper limit(UL)) to counterbalance channel loss . If acked Gap equals -1, some DUPACKS must have been received, R is decreased until the lower limit(LL). Initially R is set to a value R0 that takes into account the losses in throughput due to the finiteness of the field. The improved algorithm is specified in Algorithm 1 using pseudo-code.

Algorithm 1. Adaptive alg

1: Initialization: $SGap = 0$, R0 $= 1.05$, $R = $ R0 , $UL = 2$, $LL = 1.05$
2: Each time an NC_ACK is received: Pick up Gap in NC_ACK header
3: **if** $Gap == -1$ **then**
4:    **if** $R > LL$ **then**
5:       $R = R - 0.1$
6:    **end if**
7:    $SGap = 0$
8: **else**
9:    **if** $Gap! = SGap$ **then**
10:       **if** $Gap > SGap$ **then**
11:          **if** $R < UL$ **then**
12:             $R = R + (Gap - SGap) * 0.1$
13:          **end if**
14:          $SGap = Gap$
15:       **else**
16:          $R\ remain\ unchanged$
17:          $SGap = Gap$
18:       **end if**
19:    **else**
20:       $R\ remain\ unchanged$
21:       $SGap\ remain\ unchanged$
22:    **end if**
23: **end if**

The reasons for set LL and UL is that R should not below 1, and also R cant be to infinite. What more, if we know much about the network condition or we have some specific requirements on redundancy factor. To implement Algorithm 1 in the network coding layer of source, we make some minor changes to the standard TCP/NC protocol. The changes algorithm is specified below:

Source Side :

NC_ACK arrives from receiver
1) Call *Algorithm*1
2) Remove the $ACKed$ packet from the coding buffer
3) Generate a new ACK by the NC_ACK and send it to the TCP layer

Sink Side :

Packet arrives from source side:
1) Performs Gaussian elimination to update the decoding matrix.
2) Update $First\_Byte\_Uninvolved$ and and $First\_Byte\_Unseen$
3) Generate a new NC_ACK, consisting of the value of Gap which is the difference between $First\_Byte\_Uninvolved$ and $First\_Byte\_Unseen$

4   Simulation Results

The Implementation of TCP with self-adaptive is base on discrete event simulation environment OMNET++ and the open source TCP/IP protocol framework INET. We also use OMNET++ to evaluate and compare the performance of different protocol in network. The topology for the simulations is a tandem network consisting of 7 nodes, three router and 4 host,shown in Fig. 4. The source and sink nodes are at opposite ends of the chain.

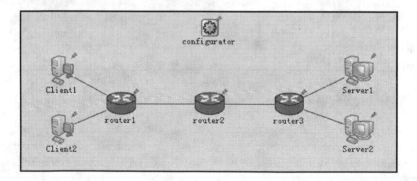

Fig. 4. Topology of network

4.1   Simulation Environment Setup

In this scenario the network carries two flows generated by two FTP applications, the app type of sender side is TCPSessionApp and receiver side is TCPSinkApp. One flow is from Client1 to Server1, and the other is from Client to Server2. They will compete for the intermediate channels. The queue type of wire interface is DropTailQueue which the first item stored is the first item output. The frame capacity of DropTailQueue is 150. All the channels have a bandwidth of 1 Mbps, and the propagation delay between host to router is 10ms, between routers is

50ms. The TCP receive NC layer buffer size is set to 200, and the IP packet size is 556 bytes. TCP-Reno is chosen for the transport layer protocol. The goodput is measured using outputhook(a kind of measure class in INET framework). Each point is averaged over 4 or more iterations of such session, depending on the variability.

4.2   Simulation Results

In order to evaluate the effect of our medication of our simulate protocol on fairness, we first study the fairness of the standard TCP and TCP/NC with our self-adaptive scheme. By fairness, we mean that if two similar flows compete for the same link, they must receive an approximately equal share of the link bandwidth[5]. We figure out the fairness characteristic under three different situation:

*Situation*1: a TCP-Reno flow competes with another flow running TCP/NC with self-adaptive scheme.

*Situation*2: a standard TCP/NC flow competes with another flow running TCP/NC with self-adaptive scheme.

*Situation*3: two TCP/NC flows with self-adaptive scheme compete with each other.

In three cases, the loss rate is set to 0% and the redundancy parameter is set to 1.05 for a fair comparison. The current throughput is calculated at intervals of 1s. TCP/NC with self-adaptive scheme flow start at t=0.1s, the second flow start at t=30s. In situation 1, the second flow is TCP-Reno flow, and it is standard TCP/NC flow in simulation 2, TCP/NC with self-adaptive scheme in simulation 3. Three simulation is all over in 120s. The plot for both three simulation is essentially identical to Fig. 5 (and hence is not shown each simulations respective figure). Both the three simulations show that when the second flow joins in the channel, it quickly shares an equal amount of bandwidth of the channel with the previous TCP/NC with self-adaptive scheme flows, thus proving the fairness of new scheme with TCP/NC.

Next, we try to prove that our new self-adaptive scheme has a better throughput rate and lower decoding delay under lossy channels with variational packet error rate(PER). Packets in the network are subject to these losses in the forward and the reverse direction. The PER can been calculated by a equivalence bit error rate(BER), since the size of packet is stable. We study the variation of receive Seq with time. PER vary over time: 0-50s: 5% PER, PER is set to 40% after 50s. Only flow from client1 to server1 is choose and the size of this flow is 5MB. Fig. 6 shows the evolution of the Seqs sent by the Servers NC layer as a function of time for different values of R, as well as when R is dynamically updated.

We can observe that R plays an important role in TCP/NC. For standard TCP/NC, The peak average throughput achieved is 0.338Mbps(5MB*8/121.02) when R is 1.85, but TCP/NC with our self-adaptive can achieve 0.397Mbps(5MB*8/105.56). We clearly appreciate the improvement obtained in goodput with our scheme.

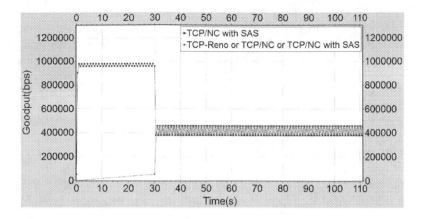

Fig. 5. A TCP/NC compete another TCP flow

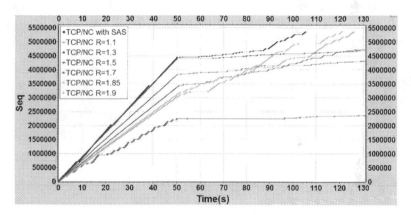

Fig. 6. Revd Seqs vs Time

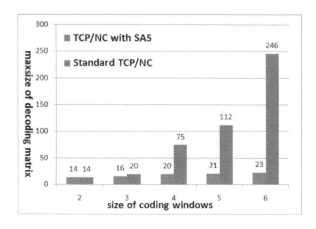

Fig. 7. Decoding Buffer vs Coding Windows

All previous simulations results are get by set coding window as 3. Fig. 7 shows that when PER is 5%, R have been chosen the optimization by trial and error, the maxsize of decoding matrix grows rapidly as coding window increase. In contrast, our scheme also keeps quite a small size and the value does not increase as the coding window increases. Whats more, the decoding delay mainly rests with the size of decoding matrix, a small decoding matrix can achieve a small decoding delay.

5   Conclusions and Future Works

TCP/NC works much better than TCP for loss channels. However, due to the different PER in different period of time in lossy networks, the TCP/NC with constant redundancy factor R cannot effectively solve the non-congestion losses problem.

In this paper, we proposes an approach to dynamically adjust the redundancy factor R in the TCP/NC protocol based on the collective feedback information of sinks decoding matrix, As R is no longer constant, we can update it according to the real current circumstance.

Simulation results show that our scheme significantly outperforms the standard TCP protocol and standard TPC/NC protocol in reducing size of decoding matrix and goodput. In future work, realizations in Linux kernel, scheme of adjust coding window, as well as a study of relation between PER, coding window, R and available computer/memory resource.

References

1. Ahlswede, R., Cai, N., RobertLi, S.Y., Yeung, R.W.: Network information flow. IEEE Transactions on Information Theory 46(4), 1204–1216 (2000)
2. Li, S.R., Yeung, R.W., Cai, N.: Linear Network Coding. IEEE Transactions on Information Theory 49, 371–381 (2003)
3. Polyzos, G.C., Xylomenos, G.: Internet Protocols over Wireless Networks. In: Gibson, J.D. (ed.) Multimedia Communications: Directions and Innovations. Academic Press (2000)
4. Lefevre, F., Vibier, G.: Understanding TCPs behavior over wireless links. In: Proc. IEEE Symposium on Computers and Communications (June 2000)
5. Sundararajan, J.K., Shah, D., Medard, M., Mitzenmacher, M., Barros, J.: Network coding meets TCP. In: Proceedings of IEEE INFOCOM, pp. 280–288 (April 2009)
6. Sundararajan, J.K., Jakubcza, S., Medard, M., Mitzenmacher, M., Barros, J.: Interfacing network coding with TCP: An implementation. In: Proceedings of IEEE INFOCOM, pp. 280–288 (April 2009)
7. Fragouli, C., Le Boudec, J.-Y., Widmer, J.: Network coding: an instant primer. SIGCOMM Comput. Commun. Rev. 36(1), 63–68 (2006), http://doi.acm.org/10.1145/1111322.1111337
8. Paul, S., Ayanoglu, E., Porta, T.F.L., Chen, K.-W.H., Sabnani, K.E., Gitlin, R.D.: An asymmetric protocol for digital cellular communications. In: Proceedings of INFOCOM (1995)

9. DeSimone, A., Chuah, M.C., Yue, O.-C.: Throughput performance of transport-layer protocols over wireless LANs. In: IEEE Global Telecommunications Conference (GLOBECOM 1993), vol. 1, pp. 542–549 (1993)
10. Balakrishnan, H., Seshan, S., Katz, R.H.: Improving reliable transport and handoff performance in cellular wireless networks. ACM Wireless Networks 1(4), 469–481 (1995)
11. Sundararajan, J.K., Shah, D., Medard, M.: ARQ for network coding. In: IEEE ISIT 2008, Toronto, Canada (July 2008)

Research on Shifter Based on iButterfly Network

Zhongxiang Chang[1], Jinshan Hu [2], Chengwei Zheng [1], and Chao Ma[1]

[1] Zhengzhou Information Science and Technology Institute, Zhengzhou 450004
[2] The Air Force Institute of Electronic Technology, Beijing 100195
changzhongxiang0@126.com

Abstract. This paper combines the character of the iButterfly network and the shifter, and study the framework of shifters based on the iButterfly network. Aiming at the circuit of generating route information, the paper put forward a kind of arithmetic to generate the special route information. Through the function simulation and the performance evaluation, we come to a conclusion that the framework of shifters designed in our paper is of important significance and useful value. At last, the paper gives some other research ideas based on interconnection network to construct shifters.

Keywords: iButterfly Network, Route Arithmetic, Shifter.

1 Introduction

Usually, the shifter is integrated into the processor to generate the address and perform arithmetic and logical operations. In addition, it is widely applied in floating point arithmetic, multimedia digital signal processing, encryption and decryption, conversion between serial and parallel data, generation and verification of random data, and so on. Shifter operation is both arithmetic operation and logical operation, and exists in any kind of computers. It can be executed not only independently as a kind of an instruction, but dependently with other instructions as a kind of micro-operation. The shifter instructions and operations are mainly include arithmetic shift left and right, logic shift left and right and circular shift left and right. The forms of the shifter are various, such as barrel shifter, logarithmic shifter, funnel shifter, data flipping shifter based on select switch, data flipping shifter based on mask, shifter based on interconnection network. Among them, logarithmic shifter, funnel shifter and shifter based on interconnection network are typical ones [1–3].

Logarithmic shifter is mainly used for the common cyclic shift left and right operation, and it is not well supported logical shift left logical shift right, short words cyclic shift left, short word cyclic shift right. The funnel shifter needs to extend the initial input data, to ensure the realization of the corresponding function. Although the circuit can achieve various types of shift operation, but the wiring resources are a little bit too large to achieve short word replacement. For shifters based on the interconnection network, the typical one is achieved with the iButterfly network by

Princeton University (Hilewitz Yedidya), but it doesn't make full use of the interconnection function and topology structure of the iButterfly network. Its routing information generation algorithm implemented in hardware is more complex, so the hardware resource consumption is a little too large and the critical path delay is relatively long.

To solve the problems above, this paper combines the features of interconnection functions and topology characteristics of the iButterfly network, then puts forward a special routing information generation algorithm to change the routing information in real time and support multi-step cyclic shift left/right. We add a special post-processing circuit to implement the logical shift left/right operation and the arithmetic shift left/ right operation.

2   The Design of Shifter Architecture

The dynamic interconnection network changes the link status of switches dynamically by setting the active switches and examining the link needs [4–6] As a result, it achieves the connections between different connections and makes the system obtain the ability of self-reconfiguration. Because the interconnection function and the topologies are various, different network has different ability and applies to different occasion, which has become a hot topic.

Dynamic interconnection network is divided into dynamic multi-level blocking network and dynamic multi-level non-blocking network by replacement capacity. The dynamic blocking network can sort the input data partly. With less level and small delay, it's also suitable for the shift operation. What's more, the structure of the dynamic blocking network is simple, and the detachable capacity of it is strong, so it has become the preferred network to achieve a shifter.

2.1   Analysis of the Shifter Based on iButterfly Network

M.C.Pease proposed a multistage interconnection network in 1977, which indirectly used the structure of the cube to achieve the connection between CPUs, making the the number of ports of the processor and have nothing to do with the scale of the system [4–6].

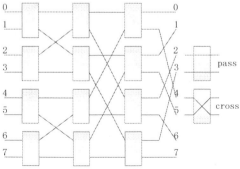

Fig. 1. 8-8 ibutterfly network

As shown in Figure 1, they are successively first grade, second grade and third grade from left to right. The stages are all cube replacements, each of whom is sub-butterfly transformation, and the output ports are the uniform inverse shuffle transform. A N×N network consists of n=log2N two-function switches. The network is a dynamic multi-level blocking network, so it supports many kinds of replacement operations, including cyclic shift, and the routing information of each operation is unique.

The network is detachable and iterative. While removing the outermost layer of a N-N Butterfly network, it can be seen as two (N/2)-(N/2) Butterfly sub-networks. The input and output of the network have a good relationship. For example, when all routing switches are through-state, the state of each level is the same as the initial input. If you want to implement a operation which bit wide is N / 2, you just need to set the outermost layer of the input to be through-state, and configure the other control information properly.

Based on the iButterfly network, the paper studies the shifter architecture. At the same time, we seek a kind of routing information generation algorithm, which support the configuration of the network routing information and the shift function in real-time.

2.2   Shifter Architecture Based on iButterfly Network

The cyclic shift can be supported if the data goes through the iButterfly network one time. Based on it, the paper puts forward the basic architecture of the shifter based on iButterfly network.

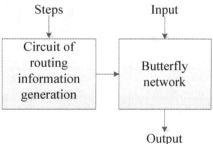

Fig. 2. Basic shifter

As shown in Figure 2, the architecture consists of the circuit of iButterfly network and the circuit of routing information generation. Specifically, the circuit of iButterfly network is responsible for the transmission of data; the circuit of routing information generation determines what mode the data works and whether the cyclic shift operation is supported.

The operation that the data goes through the iButterfly network one time only supports the cyclic shift. In order to support the logical shift operation and the arithmetic shift operation, the paper improves the basic architecture of shifters to propose an enhanced one, which can support both cyclic shift and logical shift.

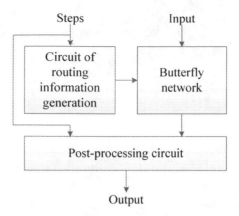

Fig. 3. Enhancement shiter

As shown in Figure 3, we add a post-processing module to the enhanced architecture to post-process the results, so that the logical shift left/right operation and the arithmetic shift left/right operation can be supported.

In shifter architecture, the iButterfly network is achieved by using data selectors. It is too simple, so we needn't give the necessary details. The post-processing circuit has a relatively easy principle, so we just need to analyze it simply. The routing information generating circuit need to generate the routing information according to different types of shift operations in real-time, so it has a higher demand to routing algorithms and hardware circuit. Therefore, we propose a specialized routing algorithm and its implementation in hardware.

3   Design of Key Module

3.1   Extract of Routing Algorithm and Map of Hardware

In order to study effectively, we use figures to indicate the iButterfly network. As shown in figure 4, in a 8-8 iButterfly network, C_{ij} is the switch of every input in each level, u_{ij} is the switch in each level, i is the stage of switch, j is the place of the switch in every stage. when 0 means pass through directly, and 1 means cross through.

In the iButterfly network, the routing information corresponding to different shift results is unique. Based on this, we study the routing algorithm achieved in iButterfly network. Assume that each switch has a control signal, which value is generated from the values of the corresponding switches at the previous stage by a certain Boolean operation.

$$u_{ij} = C_{i(2j)} \bullet C_{i(2j+1)}$$

For example, u_{20} is generated from C_{20} and C_{21} by a certain Boolean operation; u_{21} is generated from C_{22} and C_{23} by a certain Boolean operation;

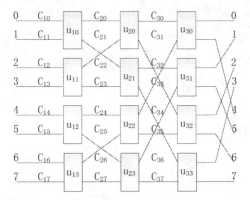

Fig. 4. 8-8 iButterlfy network

There is no previous network before the first network, so the control information of the first network is generated by a dedicated circuit which is called the initial condition. Considering the routing information of shift operation generated by the iButterfly network, the switches at the first stage are straight-through status (namely 0) when the number of the shift steps is even, while the switches at the first stage are cross-through status (namely 1) when the number of the shift steps is odd.

Generally, the interconnection relationship between the switches of different stages is determined, so we just need to consider the relationship between switches at two adjacent stages. We can find the law of Boolean operations in Equation. We seek right and left routing information generation algorithm.

1) right routing information generation algorithm:

$for\ i = 2,..., \log_2 m$
$for\ j = 0,..., m/2$
$if\ (x[i-1] = 0)$

$$\{u_{i0}, u_{i1}, ..., u_{ij}\} = (m/2^i)\ (C_{i(2j)}\, reverseR\ (\wedge^{2^{i-1}}, x[i-2:0])C_{i(2j+1)})$$
$else$

$$\{u_{i0}, u_{i1}, ..., u_{ij}\} = (m/2^i)\ (C_{i(2j)}\, reverseR\ (\sim\wedge^{2^{i-1}}, x[i-2:0])C_{i(2j+1)})$$

2) left routing information generation algorithm.

$for\ i = 2,..., \log_2 m$
$for\ j = 0,..., m/2$
$if\ (x[i-1] = 0)$

$$\{u_{i0}, u_{i1}, ..., u_{ij}\} = (m/2^i)(C_{i(2j)}\, reverseL\ (\wedge^{2^{i-1}}, x[i-2:0])C_{i(2j+1)})$$
$else$

$$\{u_{i0}, u_{i1}, ..., u_{ij}\} = (m/2^i)\ (C_{i(2j)}\, reverseL\ (\sim\wedge^{2^{i-1}}, x[i-2:0])C_{i(2j+1)})$$

If we implement the cyclic shift left operation and the cyclic shift left operation in iButterfly network, we need implement two algorithm in hardware respectively, which will result in a sharp increase in resources. Through the analysis of the two algorithm, we find that reverseR and reverseL are mirror images of each other. Therefore, we integrate the two algorithm above, and put forward a new Boolean operation algorithm supporting cyclic shift left and right.

$for\ i = 2,..., \log_2 m$
$for\ j = 0,..., m/2$
$if\ (x[i-1] = 0)$

$\{u_{i0}, u_{i1}, ..., u_{ij}\} = L\ ?\ (m/2^i)(C_{i(2j)} reverseR\ (\wedge^{2^{i-1}}, x[i-2:0])C_{i(2j+1)})$

$\quad : (m/2^i) \sim (C_{i(2j)} reverseR\ (\wedge^{2^{i-1}}, x[i-2:0])C_{i(2j+1)})$

$else$

$\{u_{i0}, u_{i1}, ..., u_{ij}\} = L\ ?\ (m/2^i)\ (C_{i(2j)} reverseL\ (\wedge^{2^{i-1}}, x[i-2:0])C_{i(2j+1)})$

$\quad : (m/2^i) \sim (C_{i(2j)} reverseL\ (\wedge^{2^{i-1}}, x[i-2:0])C_{i(2j+1)})$

Note: x: expressed as binary in shift; m: the width of the network;

$\wedge^{2^{i-1}}$: 2^{i-1} continuous XOR operations, which respectively correspond to the switches from top to bottom in figure 4;

1: the first stage; $\log_2 m$: the last stage; $\sim$: mirror image;

reverseR : the right of array $\wedge^{2^{i-1}}$ or $\sim\wedge^{2^{i-1}}$ change contrary with x[i-1:0], j=0,1,2,...,m/2 is correspond the reverseR from left to right。

reverseL : the right of array $\wedge^{2^{i-1}}$ or $\sim\wedge^{2^{i-1}}$ change contrary with x[i-1:0], j=0,1,2,...,m/2 is correspond the reverseL from left to right。

According to the Boolean operation law proposed, the routing information generation algorithm is achieved in high-speed hardware circuit. As is shown in Figure 4, the routing information of the shift left operation circuit and the shift right operation circuit is mirror images of each other, so we just need to calculate one operation. For example, the shift left operation is shown as below.

The routing information at the first stage:

$u_{10} = u_{11} = u_{12} = u_{13} = x[0]$

The routing information at the first stage:

$u_{20} = u_{22} = x[1](u_{10} \wedge u_{11})\ |\ !x[1](u_{12} \sim \wedge u_{13})$
$u_{21} = u_{23} = (x[1] \wedge x[0])(u_{10} \sim \wedge u_{11})\ |\ !(x[1] \wedge x[0])(u_{12} \wedge u_{13})$

The routing information at the first stage:

$u_{30} = x[2] (u_{20} \wedge u_{21})\ |\ !x[2](u_{20} \sim \wedge u_{21})$
$u_{31} = (!x[2]\ !x[1]\ |\ x[1]\ (x[2] \sim \wedge x[0]))(u_{20} \wedge u_{21})\ |$
$\quad !(!x[2]\ !x[1]\ |\ x[1]\ (x[2] \sim \wedge x[0]))\ (u_{20} \sim \wedge u_{21})$
$u_{32} = (x[2] \sim \wedge x[1])\ (u_{22} \wedge u_{23})\ |\ !(x[2] \sim \wedge x[1])\ (u_{22} \sim \wedge u_{23})$
$u_{33} = (x[2]\ x[1]\ |\ !x[1]\ (x[2] \sim \wedge x[0]))(u_{22} \wedge u_{23})\ |$
$\quad !(x[2]\ x[1]\ |\ !x[1]\ (x[2] \sim \wedge x[0]))\ (u_{22} \sim \wedge u_{23})$

The minimum delay time of Butterfly network is the delay of the network, which means the time of routing information must short. We calculate the routing information with parallel computing for reducing delay time. Routing information can be achieved by the simplified Boolean function expression. In the expression, the hardware circuits to generate the switches can be multiplexed, reducing the consumption of the hardware circuit effectively.

3.2   Post-processing Circuit and Hardware Implementation

The post-processing circuit uses the data selector to select the results of cyclic shift and the input data outside, achieving the arithmetic shift operation and the logical shift operation.

Table 1. encoder

Steps(x)	Left encoder sel[m-1:0]	Right encoder sel[m-1:0]
0	1^m	1^m
1	$1^{m-1}\|\|0^1$	$0^1\|\|1^{m-1}$
2	$1^{m-2}\|\|0^2$	$0^2\|\|1^{m-2}$
3	$1^{m-3}\|\|0^4$	$0^3\|\|1^{m-3}$
4	$1^{m-4}\|0^4$	$0^4\|\|1^{m-4}$
5	$1^{m-5}\|\|0^5$	$0^5\|\|1^{m-5}$
6	$1^{m-6}\|\|0^6$	$0^6\|\|1^{m-6}$
...	...	...
m	0^m	0^m
right encoder is the mirror as left encoder		
0^m : m continuous 0 ; 1^m : m continuous 0 ; .		

What is shown in Figure 5 is a post-processing circuit. There are encoder circuit and selector circuit. The encoder circuit generates control signal for selector circuit; Selector circuit selects the final result. A has two value, namely 0 or 1, wherein 0 stands for arithmetic shift right operation and 1 stands for arithmetic shift left operation. Mode has two value, namely 0 or 1, wherein 0 stands for shift right and 1 stands for shift left. m-1, ..., 0 stands for the outputs of iButterfly.

4   Performance Evaluation

In order to promise the function and performance of the framework of our design, the paper has achieved the codes and logic synthesis. Now, the cyclic shift operations achieved in references are mostly designed on the basis of 0.18um CMOS process in 64-bit. In order to make the performance comparison more objective, the section completes the functional simulation and the logic synthesis in the bit-width and process.

In Figure 6 and Figure 7, the test_data signal is the standard test data generated in the arithmetic of the software; the odata signal is the output data of the circuit; the shamt signal is the number of the steps in logical shift operation; the L_R signal controls the direction of the logical shift operation, wherein "1"stands for the logical shift left operation and "0" stands for logical shift right operation. The error signal is the XOR result of the test_data signal and the odata signal, so it means the value of circuit's output data (namely odata) is right when error=0. We can see that the value of the error signal is 0, which means the function of the circuit is completely right.

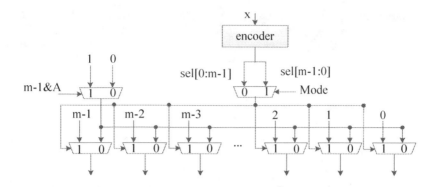

Fig. 5. Post-processing circuit

```
315 error=0,logic=0,L_R=1,shamt=63,odata=0000000000000000000000000000000000001001000101010011010100100100010 test_data=000000
320 error=0,logic=0,L_R=1,shamt= 0,odata=111111111111111111111111111111111111110000001000100101011111010000001 test_data=1111111
325 error=0,logic=0,L_R=1,shamt= 1,odata=111111111111111111111111111111111111100000010001001010111101000001 test_data=1111111
330 error=0,logic=0,L_R=1,shamt= 2,odata=11111111111111111111111111111111111110000001000100101011110100000011 test_data=1111111
335 error=0,logic=0,L_R=1,shamt= 3,odata=11111111111111111111111111111111110000001000100101011110100000011111 test_data=1111111
340 error=0,logic=0,L_R=1,shamt= 4,odata=111111111111111111111111111111111100000010001001010111101000000111 test_data=1111111
345 error=0,logic=0,L_R=1,shamt= 5,odata=11111111111111111111111111111111110000001000100101011110100000011111 test_data=1111111
350 error=0,logic=0,L_R=1,shamt= 6,odata=11111111111111111111111111111110000001000100101011110100000011111111 test_data=1111111
355 error=0,logic=0,L_R=1,shamt= 7,odata=1111111111111111111111111111100000010001001010111101000001111111 test_data=1111111
360 error=0,logic=0,L_R=1,shamt= 8,odata=111111111111111111111111111100000010001001010111101000001111111111 test_data=1111111
365 error=0,logic=0,L_R=1,shamt= 9,odata=11111111111111111111111111110000001000100101011110100000011111111 test_data=1111111
370 error=0,logic=0,L_R=1,shamt=10,odata=111111111111111111111111111000000100010010101111010000001111111111 test_data=111111
375 error=0,logic=0,L_R=1,shamt=11,odata=111111111111111111111111110000001000100101011110100000011111111111 test_data=111111
```

Fig. 6. Rotate left(64-bit)

```
3800 error=0,logic=0,L_R=0,shamt=56,odata=00000000000000000000000000000001111010001101110011010010011110100000000 test_data=000C
3805 error=0,logic=0,L_R=0,shamt=57,odata=0000000000000000000000000000000111101000110111001101001111101000000 test_data=000C
3810 error=0,logic=0,L_R=0,shamt=58,odata=00000000000000000000000000000000111101000110111001101001111101000000 test_data=000C
3815 error=0,logic=0,L_R=0,shamt=59,odata=0000000000000000000000000000000111101000110111001101001111101000 test_data=000C
3820 error=0,logic=0,L_R=0,shamt=60,odata=0000000000000000000000000000000011110100011011100110100111101000 test_data=000C
3825 error=0,logic=0,L_R=0,shamt=61,odata=0000000000000000000000000000000111101000110111001101001111101000 test_data=000C
3830 error=0,logic=0,L_R=0,shamt=62,odata=000000000000000000000000000000011110100011011100110100111101000 test_data=000C
3835 error=0,logic=0,L_R=0,shamt=63,odata=00000000000000000000000000000001111010001101110011010011110100 test_data=000C
3840 error=0,logic=0,L_R=0,shamt= 0,odata=000000000000000000000000000000011101101101010001010111110101101 test_data=0000
3845 error=0,logic=0,L_R=0,shamt= 1,odata=100000000000000000000000000000001110110110101000101011111010110 test_data=1000
```

Fig. 7. Rotate right(64-bit)

Table 2. Performance comparison

Method	Area(NAND gates)	Latency(ns)	Technology(nm)
Barrel shift	1.79K	0.76	180
Funnel shifter	1.75K	0.61	180
References[1]*	3.4K	0.72	180
References [2]	5.8K	0.58	90
References [7]	3.3K	1.3	180
Our(R)	2.32K	0.95	180
Our (R_L)	2.7K	1.01	180
Our(R_L & Logic)	3.2K	1.12	180
Note:* means the width is 128-bit ; R means the design only support rotate right ; R_L means the design supports rotate right/left ; R_L & Logic means the design supports rotate right/left and logical shift right/left ;			

As shown in Table 2, the funnel-shaped shifter has the fastest speed and the smallest area, which is 19.8% faster than the barrel shifter in speed, while 2.2% smaller in area. The funnel shifter uses nearly a double wiring resource to achieve the high-performance requirement. However, it gets the good results without calculating the Interconnect delay and the area. What's more, its flexibility is low because its structure cannot support the short word cyclic shift operation and the parallel insertion and extraction operations.

The reconfigurable shift unit proposed in the reference [1] can support the shift operation of 8~128 bit-wide. In addition, it has a flexible structure and a fast speed. However, it can only shift 31 bits. If the data is more than 64 bits and the number of bits shifted greater than 32, the operation cannot be adapted well.

In the reference [2], the reconfigurable shift unit designed by the PALMS laboratory in Plymouth Princeton University has a similar function with our design. However, it isn't objective to compare their delays with different process. What's more, its control information generation algorithm is more complicated, resulting in difficult hardware implementation and great resource consumption (the scale of the equivalent gates).

The similar route generation algorithm was proposed in the reference [7], but because the complex initial information, which increases the routing information generation time and resources.

5   Summary and Outlook

The paper proposes a architecture of shifter based on iButterfly network, and analyzes the functionality and performance of it. The result shows that, this design has an advantage in shift function which provides a new idea on the interconnection network. So it has reference significances and useful values.

In this paper, routing information generation algorithm use simple adaptation information and complex generation circuit. With the increase of the bits wide in networks, the generation of the network routing information is more complex, and the critical path is much longer. Therefore, we will study the parallel computing routing information of it in next step.

References

[1] Yang, S.: Research of Design Technology of Reconfigurable Shift Unit Based on Multilevel Interconnection. In: 2012 Intelligent System and Applied Material, Advanced Materials Research (March 2012)
[2] Yedidya, H.: Advanced Bit Manipulation Instructions: Architecture, Implementation And Applications. Princeton University, New Jersey (2008)
[3] Ren, X.: The design optimization of Integer arithmetic logic operation components with 64bit at GHz level. National University of Defense Technology, Chang sha (2007)
[4] Pease, M.C.: The Indirect Binary nCube Microprocessor Array. IEEE Trans. on Computers C-26(5) (1977)
[5] Intel Corporation, IA-64 Application Developers' Architecture Guide. Intel Corporation (May 1999)
[6] Lee, R.B.: Precision Architecture. IEEE Computer 22(1), 78–91 (1989)
[7] Lang, T., Stone, H.S.: A Shuffle-Exchange Network with Simplified Control. IEEE Trans. On Computers C-25(1) (January 1976)

A Highly-Efficient Approach to Adaptive Load Balance for Scalable TBGP*

Lei Gao, Mingche Lai, Kefei Wang, and Zhengbin Pang

College of Computer, National University of Defense Technology, Changsha 410073, China
{gaolei,mingchelai}@nudt.edu.cn

Abstract. Multi-threading technique used in BGP protocol empowers the remarkable performance enhancement, but load imbalance on different threads could also become the bottleneck of performance and scalability especially on occurrence of route instability such as route outburst update. To resolve this issue, an effective adaptive route load partition (ARLP) algorithm for TBGP is proposed to provide load balance on different threads and alleviate the influence of route instability. The ARLP algorithm dynamically dispatches sessions on different threads by the statistical number of route update from each neighbor session, and distributes sessions with high load over different threads, to maximize the computing resources and ensure the minimum load difference on threads. Experimental results on dual quad-core Xeon sever show that ARLP algorithm could achieve steady load balance ratio ranging from 0.11 to 0.14 under four thread configurations. We also derive MUTPT as the metric to evaluate the route update performance of TBGP, and the MUTPT samples with ARLP are averagely reduced by 46.2%, 51.8%, 63.2% and 70.3% compared to those with static load-distribution method, yielding good performance improvement and session scalability for TBGP.

Keywords: BGP, multi-threaded, load balance, performance, scalability.

1 Introduction

Border Gateway Protocol (BGP) is widely viewed as the de-facto inter-domain routing criterion, which determines the performance and usability of Internet. In the lifetime of BGP, the routing domain has presented the characteristics of finer-granularity information and denser interconnection, and Internet has grown more than 380,000 routing entries by far[1]. This brings a large number of transient and superfluous update messages produced by BGP to increase the unnecessarily high computing loads imposed on BGP speakers[2]. Furthermore, it also extends the convergence time of routing system and even makes message loss and network congestion, which is unacceptable for the delay-sensitive and real-time applications,

---

* This work was supported by NSFC (No. 61103188 and No. 61070199) and the Specialized Research Fund for the Doctoral Program of Higher Education of China (No. 20114307120011).

W. Xu et al. (Eds.): NCCET 2013, CCIS 396, pp. 101–110, 2013.

e.g. multimedia, E-commerce, network gaming. Apparently, all these issues above have imposed more stringent requirements for higher performance and scalability on the underlying Internet routing system[3].

With the strongly emerging multicore architecture for mainstream as well as high-performance computing, there is an increasing interest for efficient multithreaded BGP architecture that allows maximal exploitation of the available parallelism on multicore platform. We have originally developed on multicore system the TBGP (Threaded BGP) architecture [4] which empowered multiple threads processing in parallel with the decoupled executions among different peer sessions, to efficiently improve BGP performance. Many studies have also presented similar ideas with TBGP to improve BGP computing ability, like [5-7]. However, with the expansion of network scale, BGP route updates on Internet core routers represent obvious instability such as BGP outburst update[8], route oscillations[9], etc., which would lead to great load difference among peer sessions. If sessions are averagely or arbitrarily distributed to threads, it will cause load imbalance on threads and make some threads overload or even crash, decreasing the efficiency of TBGP. Thus, we could find that highly-efficient and scalable TBGP architecture also relies on effective strategies for load balance especially as confronting route instability. Most researches on BGP distributed and parallel processing had adopted static load partition methods[5,6], which were favorable for improving route computation, but still could not adapt to achieving expected performance enhancement when occurring paroxysmal route update or route jitters. Previous researches have provided load-balance alternations for resolving system bottleneck caused by large load difference among nodes. Liu[10] proposed a prediction-based load balancing mechanism to estimate the volume of the inbound traffic that would come to network using outbound traffic and the historical data of inbound traffic, and then assigned links to outbound traffic and the predicted inbound traffic by scheduler. This method still was a static approach which could not provide load balance in a more precision and flexible way. Tong[11] combined static and dynamic balance strategy to reduce the load dispatching time, preventing server skew and improving cluster system performance. Based on the advantage and shortage of load-balance methods with packet-level, connection-level, host-level and AS-level analyzed by [12], Hiroshi [13] proposed a packet-level load balance strategy that dynamically balanced network traffic with MHLB/I protocol which was used to discover multiple BGP paths and set them up while payload traffic was being transmitted through the default BGP path. [14] also proposed a similar approach that used multiple paths to achieve load balance. Load balancing has been shown to significantly improve the guaranteed traffic loads in the networks with regular topologies [15-18]. Kodialam [19] proposed to use two-phase routing in an arbitrary network but it was rather complex since it optimizes the balancing coefficients using linear program with $O(MN^2)$ variables and constraints. To decrease the complexity, [20] also implemented two phase load-balanced routing in OSPF with a LB-SPR protocol that balanced load across the intermediate routers and optimized balancing coefficients to maximize throughput. Although the above researches could reach good load balance effect, they only considered the cases of normal stream on networks but not abnormal cases e.g. unexpected route outburst.

In this paper, an effective adaptive route load partition (ARLP) algorithm for TBGP is proposed to provide load balance of route update packet on different threads, so as to improve performance and scalability even in the case of encountering route instability. The target of the algorithm is designed to ensure the least load difference on threads and make fast load migration among threads. The ARLP algorithm dynamically reconstructs the sessions on different threads by the statistical number of route update from each neighbor session, and distributes sessions with high load over different threads. Experimental results on dual quad-core Xeon sever show that ARLP algorithm could reach steady load balance ratio ranging from 0.11 to 0.14 under four thread configurations. We also derive MUTPT as the metric to evaluate the route update performance of TBGP, and the MUTPT samples with ARLP are averagely reduced 46.2%, 51.8%, 63.2% and 70.3% compared with those of static load-distribution method, yielding good performance improvement and session scalability for TBGP.

2   TBGP Architecture

The router connecting to multiple peer neighbors is always exchanging information through BGP, which represents the decoupled characteristic that the messages from different neighbors can be processed in parallel for their weaker correlations and the ones from the same neighbor have to be processed orderly due to their close correlations. Thus, as the routers shift to multi-core systems, we firstly propose the TBGP protocol to exploit the potential parallelism by dispatching multiple neighbor sessions on different parallelized threads, thereby improving the protocol efficiency. In general, the TBGP is composed of one master thread and multiple slave threads just as shown in Fig.1. The master thread has the responsibility of initializing process, creating slave threads, answering and evenly distributing peer sessions among different slave threads. It monitors and answers the connection requests from neighbor sessions, dispatches a slave thread for the new session, and assigns the socket address to the specified slave thread. The relationship between neighbor sessions and slave threads is recorded in neighbor-thread mapping table. Then, the slave thread is the actual execution entity for a cluster of sessions. For each slave thread, it is responsible for maintaining the Finite State Machine (FSM) operations, keeping session connectivity, processing update messages and managing protocol behaviors by itself. Also, it has its own event queue, so that the multiple sessions triggered by events of different threads may work in parallel. In Fig.1, each thread receives the routes from its corresponding neighbor sessions, and filters them according to the input/output policies from BGP Routing Information Base (RIB). When routes have been processed by local slave thread, they also need to be propagated to other slave threads for announcing to all neighbor sessions, maintaining the behavior consistency with BGP. Then, TBGP deploys a shared routing table to keep the consistent route view for all threads, ensuring to make the correct route decisions and advertise the globally optimal routes. With multi-core systems, the access to the shared routing table supports for the high-bandwidth communication and fast synchronization, thereby addressing the synchronization problem of distributed route storage and providing a better aggregated performance.

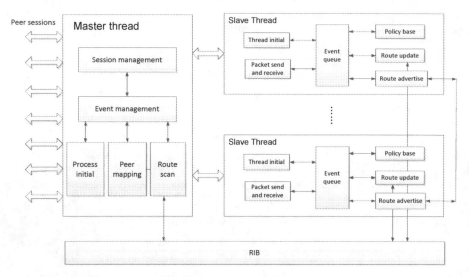

Fig. 1. Architecture of TBGP

Two-level packet pool is adopted in receiving and sending packets among master thread and slave threads, as shown in Fig.2. The first-level packet pool is configured in master thread and maintains a set of packet transfer queues that are used for buffering update packets communicating with neighbor sessions. Each slave thread has a second-level packet pool for receiving or sending update packets with master thread, and different sessions processed on the same slave thread have separate packet transfer queues. As receiving update packets from a neighbor session, master thread puts the packets into the corresponding transfer queues of first-level pool according to neighbor session id. And then it looks up slave thread id in neighbor-thread mapping table by session id and transfers packets to designated slave thread. Packets enter in corresponding transfer queue after reaching the second-level pool in slave thread, waiting to be processed. Similarly with receiving process, slave thread puts local update packets into the sending queues of sessions in second-level pool, where master thread could get into first-level pool the update packets that are to be advertised.

In above multi-threaded structure, each slave thread takes charge a cluster of neighbor sessions, and the update packets will be buffered in two-level packet pool. According to the mapping relationship of neighbor sessions and slave threads, update packets will be dispensed to the transfer queues of designated sessions. As considering the underlying parallelism in BGP, our proposed TBGP architecture implements the parallel computing of update packets on different slave threads, and could also ensure the processing order of packets from the same session, providing route computing acceleration. However, TBGP with traditional session-based load distributing method could not efficiently improve the performance and scalability in actual network environment, especially in case that large load diversity on different sessions incurred by route instability, which could rebate the acceleration effect of multi-threaded parallelism. That's because route outburst update always increases the update packet number sharply in short period on a small fraction of sessions, and leads to the overload of slave thread, which could become the bottleneck of TBGP and prevent the further performance improvement in spite of extending session and slave thread numbers.

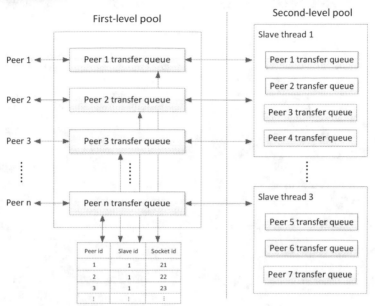

Fig. 2. Structure of two-level packet pool

3   ARLP Algorithm

To resolve load imbalance on slave threads caused by route instability, we propose a highly-efficient load balance algorithm ARLP to dynamically adjust route update number by redistribute neighbor sessions on each slave thread to adaptively regulate load. In general, the ARLP algorithm is triggered in particular intervals by master thread, and in order to ensure the fast load repartition, ARLP algorithm must be completed in a short period.

Therefore, ARLP adopts heuristic-based partition strategy, in which the neighbor sessions are partitioned into multiple session sets according to the route update number of each session, and all session sets reach the least load difference to balance route update number on slave threads.

The ARLP detail is shown in algorithm 1. In step 1-2, the sessions are sorted by the descending order according to the statistical route update number of each session, where f_i denotes route update number by i^{th} session, n is total session number, $F(Q_k)$ denotes the total number of route update by thread Q_k, M is thread number, $r_i[p_i]$ is used to record the location of session in slave thread, and the sort result is demonstrated with $f_{s_1}, \cdots, f_{s_n}$. Then, step 3-4 compute the total number of route update by M threads, then functions **Min_IDX**, **Max_IDX** indicate the lower index of minimum and maximum $F(Q_k)(0 \leq k \leq M-1)$, as represented with Q_α and Q_β.

Algorithm 1: Adaptive Route Load Partition

1   Sort $f_1, f_2, ..., f_n$ by the descending order according to the statistical route update number of each session, and the reorder result is $f_{s_1} \geq \cdots \geq f_{s_n}$;

2    $F(Q_k) \leftarrow 0(k=1,...,M)$, $i \leftarrow 1$; $p_1 = ... = p_M = 0$; $r_1[0] = ... = r_M[0] = 0$; $//r_i[p_i]$ denotes the array of neighbor session set

3    $\alpha \leftarrow$ **Min_IDX** $(F(Q_1),..., F(Q_M))$, $0 < \alpha \leq M$;   //compute the minimal $F(Q_k)$

4    $\beta \leftarrow$ **Max_IDX** $(F(Q_1),..., F(Q_M))$, $0 < \beta \leq M$;   //compute the maximal $F(Q_k)$

5   **if** $(F(Q_\beta) - f_{r_\beta[p_\beta]} > F(Q_\alpha))$ {

    // if Q_β removes its top session $r_\beta[p_\beta]$, and its update number is still bigger than $F(Q_\alpha)$

6    $Q_\beta \leftarrow Q_\beta - \{r_\beta[p_\beta]\} + \{s_i\}$, $Q_\alpha \leftarrow Q_\alpha + \{r_\beta[p_\beta]\}$

    //exchange operation

7    $p_\alpha \leftarrow p_\alpha + 1$, $r_\alpha[p_\alpha] \leftarrow r_\beta[p_\beta]$, $r_\beta[p_\beta] \leftarrow s_i$

8   **if** $(f_{r_\alpha[p_\alpha - 1]} < f_{r_\alpha[p_\alpha]})$

9    $\{tmp \leftarrow r_\alpha[p_\alpha], r_\alpha[p_\alpha] \leftarrow r_\alpha[p_\alpha - 1], r_\alpha[p_\alpha - 1] \leftarrow tmp\}\}$

    // always put the session with minimal update number on top of Q_α

10   **else** $\{Q_\alpha \leftarrow Q_\alpha + \{s_i\}, p_\alpha \leftarrow p_\alpha + 1\}$
    // otherwise, the current session is put into Q_α

The main idea in ARLP algorithm is to put the current session into the set with minimal $F(Q_k)$, thereby limiting the increment of the difference between $F(Q_\beta)$ and $F(Q_\alpha)$ and balancing the update number in each session set. Thus, step 5 first checks the condition $F(Q_\beta) - f_{r_\beta[p_\beta]} > F(Q_\alpha)$ before dispatching each session, and the exchange operation in step 6-7 is performed between sets Q_α and Q_β) if the above condition is satisfied, e.g. $r_\beta[p_\beta]$ and the current session are respectively dispatched to Q_α and Q_β, to further reduce the difference between the maximal and minimal of $F(Q_k)$. Since the route update number of arbitrary session in Q_β is bigger than that of the current session, the algorithm selects the session with minimal update number to exchange with the current session, and performs step 8-9 to put the session on top of Q_β, so that the total update number difference is always the minimum. This conclusion can be confirmed as follows, assuming that the two sets after the exchange are respectively Q_α^* and Q_β^*. Repeat above process until all sessions have been put into session sets, and the algorithm finishes.

Proof: $|F(Q_\beta{}^*) - F(Q_\alpha{}^*)| = |(F(Q_\beta) - f_{r_\beta[p_\beta]} + f_{s_i}) - (F(Q_\alpha) + f_{r_\beta[p_\beta]})|$

$$= |(F(Q_\beta) - f_{r_\beta[p_\beta]}) - F(Q_\alpha) + (f_{s_i} - f_{r_\beta[p_\beta]})|$$

$$< |(F(Q_\beta) - f_{r_\beta[p_\beta]}) - F(Q_\alpha)| + |(f_{s_i} - f_{r_\beta[p_\beta]})|$$

$$= (F(Q_\beta) - f_{r_\beta[p_\beta]}) - F(Q_\alpha) + f_{r_\beta[p_\beta]} - f_{s_i} \quad \square$$

4   Performance Evaluation

We configure the TBGP on Quagga 0.99.9 first and implement the ARLP algorithm as well as load migration. Through adjusting the number of threads, peer sessions and advertised routes, we use the AX4000 series to verify the correctness of proposed load-balance approach by comparing the load balance ratio and route update efficiency with traditional static load distributing method. In this section, with TBGP platform, the performance of ARLP algorithm is measured with prefix database of routing table snapshots extracted from RouteViews[22]. All the experiments are performed on dual quad-core Xeon server with Linux 2.6.18-8AX operation system.

4.1   Load Balance Ratio

The efficiency of our proposed ARLP algorithm is mainly evaluated by the load balance ratio, which represents the load distribution of each slave thread in a period, and could be calculated as equation (1), where $U(t)$ denotes load balance ratio at time interval t, M denotes slave thread number, $PN_i(t)$ records the total route update number of slave thread i at time interval t.

$$U(t) = 1 - \frac{\left(\sum_{i=1}^{M} PN_i(t) \right)^2}{M \sum_{i=1}^{M} \left(PN_i(t) \right)^2} \tag{1}$$

Besides, focusing on the influence of algorithm to TBGP as encountering route outburst update, we also present load difference ratio to evaluate the diversity of route update number among different sessions, and it could be calculated as equation (2):

$$L(t) = \frac{\max_{i=1,\ldots,n} \left(SN_i(t) \right)}{(1/n) \sum_{i=1}^{n} \left(SN_i(t) \right)} \tag{2}$$

Where, $L(t)$ denotes the load difference ratio at time interval t, $SN_i(t)$ denotes the route update number of session i at time interval t, n is neighbor session number, and $\max_{i=1,\ldots,n}(SN(t))$ represents the maximal route update number of all sessions at time interval t.

In this experiment, we use AX4000 series to construct network environment and inject route stream. 100 neighbor sessions are triggered at most and averagely distributed on multiple slave threads at initial, and we select 10% of all sessions as route outburst sources to generate paroxysmal route, the number of which satisfies the load difference ratio could change from 5 to 100. Besides, the trigger interval of ARLP algorithm is set to be 30 minutes. The statistical load balance ratios under four scenarios with configuring 4, 8, 12, 16 slave threads are collected in Fig.3. In all scenarios, it could be observed that the load balance ratios grow slightly with the increase of load difference ratio and slave thread number, and they range from 0.11 to 0.14. That is to say, the ARLP algorithm is not sensitive to load difference and slave thread number, and could yield good load balance effect as well as scalability even occurring strong rout outburst.

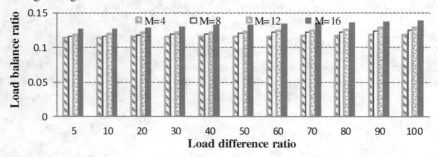

Fig. 3. Results for load balance ratio

4.2   Performance for Route Update

In this section, the performance of route update is experimented and evaluated in terms of Maximal Update Time Per Thread (MUTPT). Following the experiment scenarios in above section, the MUTPT samples are collected with Vtune[TM] toolkit by regulating routes number from one million to ten millions under 4, 8, 12, 16 slave threads, as shown in Fig.4. In four scenarios, it is observed that the MUTPT samples in the case of not using ARLP algorithm increase greatly with the increasing route number, and they are also not obviously reduced with the increase of slave thread number. Although the increase of slave thread number could decrease the load of single slave thread, it still could not effectively resolve the large load difference caused by route outburst on a fraction of sessions. On the other side, those MUTPT samples using ARLP algorithm grows slightly with the increasing route number under four thread configurations, and they have remarkable reductions with the incremental slave thread number, decreased by 46.2%, 51.8%, 63.2% and 70.3% averagely. At the same time, the samples with 16 slave threads are reduced to 78% compared to the ones with 12 slave threads, representing better thread scalability than that not using ARLP algorithm.

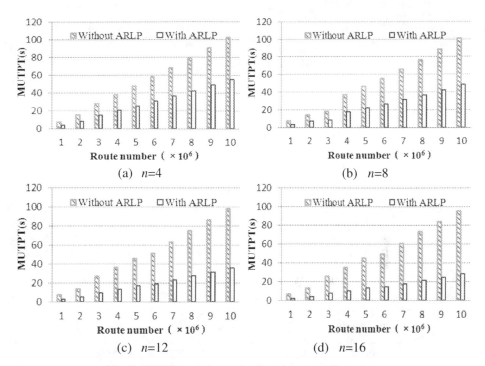

Fig. 4. MUTPT samples under four thread configurations

5   Conclusion

Exploiting thread level parallelism helps in improving the performance of BGP to satisfy the explosive demands on Internet. Our key insight is to resolve load balance issue in TBGP when occurring route instability, such as update outburst, route oscillations, etc., which hinders the performance and scalability improvement of TBGP. In this paper, we originally present a heuristic-based load balance algorithm ARLP to dynamically adjust the load on slave threads according to statistical route update number on each neighbor session. Experimental results on dual quad-core Xeon server show that ARLP algorithm could get good load balance ratio under different thread configurations and MUTPTs with ARLP are averagely reduced by 46.2%, 51.8%, 63.2% and 70.3% compared with that of traditionally static load-distribution method, yielding good performance improvement and session scalability for TBGP.

Acknowledgements. This work was supported by NSFC (No. 61103188 and No. 61070199) and the Specialized Research Fund for the Doctoral Program of Higher Education of China (No. 20114307120011).

References

1. Huston G.: The BGP Report for 2005(EB/OL), http://www.potaroo.net/papers/isoc/2006-06/bgpupds.html, 2006-06-01/2007-05-01
2. Nguyen, K.-K., Jaumard, B.: A scalable and distributed architecture for bgp in next generation routers. In: Proc. of ICC Communications Workshops, pp. 1–5 (2009)
3. Taft, N.: The basics of bgp routing and its performance in today's internet. In: Proc. of RHDM High-speed Networks and Multimedia Workshop, France, pp. 35–42 (2001)
4. Wang, K., Gao, L., et al.: A scalable multithreaded BGP architecture for next generation router. In: EMC 2011, vol. (102), pp. 395–404 (2011)
5. Xu, K., He, H.: BGP parallel computing model based on the iteration tree. Journal of China Universities of Posts and Telcommunications 15(suppl.), 1–8 (2008)
6. Liu, Y., Zhang, S., Wang, B.: MR-PBGP: A multi-root tree model for parallel bgp. In: Proc. of High Performance Computing and Communications, pp. 1211–1218 (2012)
7. Zhang, X., Lu, X., Su, J., et al.: SDBGP: A Scalable, Distributed BGP Routing Protocol Implementation. In: Proc. of the 12th IEEE International Conference on High Performance Switching and Routing, pp. 191–196 (2011)
8. Griffin, T., Shepherd, F.B., Wilfong, G.: The stable paths problem and interdomain routing. IEEE/ACM Transactions on Networking 10(1), 232–234 (2002)
9. Varadhan, K., Govindan, R., Estrin, D.: Persistent route oscillations in inter-domain routing. Computer Networks 32(1), 1–16 (2000)
10. Liu, X., Xiao, L.: Inbound traffic load balancing in BGP multi-homed stub networks. In: Proc. of International Conference on Distributed Computing Systems, pp. 369–376 (2008)
11. Tong, R., Zhu, X.: A Load Balancing Strategy Based on the Combination of Static and Dynamic. In: Proc. of Database Technology and Applications, pp. 1–4 (2011)
12. Guo, F., Chen, J., Li, W., Chiueh, T.: Experiences in Building A Multihoming Load Balancing System. In: Proceedings of IEEE INFOCOM, pp. 1241–1251 (2004)
13. Fujinoki, H.: Improving Reliability for Multi-Home Inbound Traffic: MHLB/I Packet-Level Inter-Domain Load-Balancing. In: Proc. of International Conference on Availability, Reliability and Security, pp. 248–256 (2009)
14. Zhou, S., Chen, J., et al.: Approximate load balance based on id/locator split routing architecture. In: World Congress on Information and Communication Technologies, pp. 981–986 (2012)
15. Smiljanić, A.: Rate and Delay Guarantees Provided by Clos Packet Switches with Load Balancing. IEEE Trans. Netw., 170–181 (February 2008)
16. Antić, M., Smiljanić, A.: Oblivious Routing Scheme Using Load Balancing Over Shortest Paths. In: Proc. ICC 2008 (2008)
17. Antić, M., Smiljanić, A.: Routing with Load Balancing: Increasing the Guaranteed Node Traffics. IEEE Commun. Lett., 450–452 (June 2009)
18. Kostic-Ljubisavljevic, A., Radonjic, V., et al.: Load Balance Routing for Interconnected Next Generation Networks Performances Improvement, pp.42–46 (2011)
19. Kodialam, M., Lakshman, T.V., Sengupta, S.: Traffic-Oblivious Routing for Guaranteed Bandwidth Performance. IEEE Commun. Mag. 45(4), 46–51 (2007)
20. Antić, M., Maksic, N., et al.: Two phase load balanced routing using OSPF. IEEE Journal of Selected Areas in Communications 28(1), 51–59 (2010)
21. Lei, G., Lai, M., Gong, Z.: A practical non-blocking route propagation technology for threaded BGP. In: ICSCC 2010, pp. 206–211 (2010)
22. RouteViews project, http://archive.route-views.org/bgpdata

OpenACC to Intel Offload:
Automatic Translation and Optimization

Cheng Chen, Canqun Yang, Tao Tang, Qiang Wu, and Pengfei Zhang

School of Computer Science
National University of Defense Technology
Changsha, Hunan 410073, China
gaoye23@126.com, {canqun,taotang84}@nudt.edu.cn,
qiangwu.cs.nudt@gmail.com, zhangpengfeii@foxmail.com

Abstract. Heterogeneous architectures with both conventional CPUs and coprocessors become popular in the design of High Performance Computing systems. The programming problems on such architectures are frequently studied. OpenACC standard is proposed to tackle the problem by employing directive-based high-level programming for coprocessors. In this paper, we take advantage of OpenACC to program on the newly Intel MIC coprocessor. We achieve this by automatically translating the OpenACC source code to Intel Offload code. Two optimizations including communication and SIMD optimization are employed. Two kernels i.e. the matrix multiplication and JACOBI, are studied on the MIC-based platform (one knight Corner card) and the GPU-based platform (one NVIDIA Tesla k20c card). Performance evaluation shows that both kernels delivers a speedup of approximately 3 on one knight Corner card than on one Intel Xeon E5-2670 octal-core CPU. Moreover, the two kernels gain better performance on MIC-based platform than on the GPU-based one.

Keywords: OpenACC, Intel Offload, Source to Source, MIC, GPU.

1   Introduction

Nowadays, heterogeneous architecture is a leading candidate under consideration for the design of High Performance Computing (HPC) systems [1]. Such systems typically consist of coprocessors such as GPU, FPGA, and newly Intel MIC coprocessor connecting to hosts. These coprocessors can offer relatively high floating-point rates and memory bandwidth with lower relative power footprints than general-purpose computation platforms [2]. But these coprocessors (e.g. the GPUs) commonly require special programming constructs (e.g. NVIDIA's CUDA [3] language) which poses a significant challenge for developers. There has been growing research and industry interest in lowering the barrier of programming these coprocessors. OpenACC [4], an API consisting of compiler directives to offload loops and regions of C/C++ and Fortran code to coprocessors, is unveiled to support directive-based high-level programming for heterogeneous systems. The simplicity of

W. Xu et al. (Eds.): NCCET 2013, CCIS 396, pp. 111–120, 2013.

the model, the ease of adoption by non-expert users and the support received from the leading companies (PGI, NVDIA and Cray) in this field make us believe that OpenACC is a long-term standard [5]. However, recent OpenACC specification like PGI is mainly designed and optimized for GPUs, which narrows its applying.

In this paper, we take advantage of OpenACC to program on the newly Intel MIC coprocessor. We achieve this by automatically translating the OpenACC source code to Intel Offload code. Our contributions can be concluded as follows:

1)   Mapping task-level and data-level parallelisms of OpenACC to Intel Offload;
2)   Translating OpenACC source code to native Intel Offload source code;
3)   Optimizing the translated code by employing communication optimization and SIMD optimization.

The paper is organized as follows. Section 2 introduces OpenACC and the MIC coprocessor. Section 3 reviews the related work. Section 4 presents our implementation. Section 5 describes our optimization methods. Section 6 gives the experimental results. Conclusion is drawn in Section 7.

2   Overview of OpenACC and the MIC Coprocessor

2.1   OpenACC

The OpenACC standard defines the Application Programming Interface (OpenACC API) for offloading code in C, C++ and Fortran programs from a Host CPU to an attached Device coprocessor. The method provides a model for coprocessor programming that is portable across operating systems and various types of CPUs and coprocessors. In the following we will show more about the execution and memory model.

The execution model targeted by OpenACC API-enabled compilers is Host-directed execution with attached coprocessors [4]. The bulk of a user application executes on the host while the compute intensive regions are offloaded to the coprocessors under control of the host. Most current coprocessors support two or three levels of parallelism. That is coarse-grain parallelism (parallel execution across execution units), fine-grain parallelism (multi threads) and SIMD or vector operations. These multiple levels of parallelism on the coprocessor are exposed to the programmer, who is required to understand the difference and use it effectively.

The memory model of heterogeneous architecture is that the memory on the coprocessor may be completely separate from the host memory. Memory on the coprocessor is not mapped into the host's virtual memory space, so the host may not be able to read or write directly. In OpenACC, the host control data movement between host and coprocessor through runtime library calls which are defined in data transfer directives from the programmer and are managed by the compiler.

2.2   Intel MIC

The Many Integrated Core (MIC) Processor is a new generation of the Intel Architecture (IA), thus supports traditional programming languages such as C, C++, and Fortran. An attractive feature is its support for standard parallel programming models like OpenMP [6] and MPI [7]. By packing up to 60 cores with 512 bits vector unit, a single MIC coprocessor can deliver double precision performance over Tflops. Xeon Phi [8] is the latest generation. When used as a coprocessor, there are two programming models: Co-processor-only Model and Offload Model [9] (Offload for short).

In Co-processor-only Model, the processes reside solely inside the coprocessor. Applications can be launched from the host to the coprocessor with needed libraries. It is usually used for quick development and testing of key kernels [10]. In Offload Model, the MIC acts as GPU, where the code execution begins on the host CPU, and the computing intensive region marked with offload directives are automatically offloaded to MIC. Data transfer via the PCIe bus is also controlled by directives.

3   Related Work

A plenty of researchers have been working on source to source compiler, leading to significant performance boosting on heterogeneous computing. Reyes presents accULL, a novel implementation of the OpenACC standard, based on the combination of a source to source compiler and a runtime library et.al [11]. Dave presents a compiler framework for automatic source-to-source translation of standard OpenMP applications into CUDA-based GPGPU applications et.al [12]. Wei presents a source to source OpenMP compiler framework which translates the program with OpenMP directives to the necessary codes to exploit the parallelism of a sequential program through the different processing elements of the Cell [13]. The Cetus project [14] proposes a source to source compiler framework for automatic translation and optimization. A set of extensions over OpenMP enable it to automatically generate and tune CUDA code. However all these works were done based on GPU and OpenMP, and there is no previous work for MIC. Our work is to achieve the OpenACC source code to native Offload code translation, so that the programmer can use OpenACC API to program on the newly Intel MIC.

4   Automatic Translation of OpenACC to Offload

As OpenACC and Offload are both compiler directives programming API, for effective translation, we should map the OpenACC directives into Offload directives, and then translate OpenACC source code to native Offload source code according to the mapping relationship.

4.1   Mapping OpenACC Directives into Offload Directives

The directives of OpenACC can be divided into three parts: task, data and parallelism management. In this section, we will explain the function of these directives and map them into Offload directives respectively.

(1) Task Management

The Parallel Construct and Kernel Construct define a region of the program that is to be compiled into a sequence of kernels for execution on the accelerator device. These two OpenACC constructs can map into "#pragma offload target( )", which direct to compile the code region offloading to MIC in Offload.

(2) Parallelism Management

In OpenACC standard, when the program encounters an accelerator Parallel Construct or Kernel Construct gangs of workers are created to execute the coprocessor parallel region. Each worker in gangs begins executing the code in the structured block of the construct. Within each worker of the gangs, the vector clause is also allowed. The value of the parameter defines the vector length to use for vector or SIMD operations.

As mentioned in Section 2, the MIC supports OpenMP standard and the Offload modifies OpenMP in parallelism management, so the parallelism management directives from OpenACC can be mapped into OpenMP directives. Table 1 shows congruent relationship of parallelism clause.

Table 1. Congruent relationship of Parallelism clause

OpenACC	collapse()	gang/worker	vector	private	reduction	async
Offload	loop count	num_threads()	vector	private	reduction	nowait

In addition, the Loop directive from OpenACC can describe what type of parallelism to use to execute the loop and declare loop-private variables and arrays and reduction operations. The Loop directives can map into "*#pragma omp parallel for*".

(3) Data Management

The data construct defines scalars, arrays and subarrays to be allocated in the device memory for the duration of the region, whether data should be copied from the host to the device memory upon region entry, and copied from the device to host memory upon region exit.

In Offload Model, we can use "*#pragma offload_transfer target()*" to achieve asynchronous data transfer, or add data transfer clause behind "#pragma offload target()" to achieve synchronous data transfer. The details of congruent relationship of data clause are shown in table 2.

Table 2. Congruent relationship of data clause

OpenACC	Offload	Semantic
if	if	When If condition is true, start transfer
deviceptr	__attribute__ ((target (mic)))	Declare the data point is to coprocessor
copy	inout	Copy data from CPU to coprocessor
copyin	in	Copy data from coprocessor to CPU
copyout	out	Copy both ways
create	nocopy	Data is local to target
present present_or_copy present_or_copyin present_or_copyou t present_or_create		Test whether data is already present in the coprocessor memory before copy data from the host to the coprocessor. If the condition is true, the data will be reused.
	align()	Specify minimum data slignment
[m:n]	length(n-m)	Specify pointer length

4.2   OpenACC to Offload Baseline Translation

The Offload execution model is to offload structured block of the construct to MIC and then parallelize it through OpenMP. To address this, we propose OpenACC source code to native Offload code baseline translation system with two phases: Offload pragma translation and OpenMP pragma translation, shown in Figure 1. At first, it translates the OpenACC program into Intermediate Representation (IR): C + Offload API + parallel label. During this phase the communication optimization is carried out. Then, translates the parallel label into OpenMP directives, and the SIMD optimization is carried out. The communication optimization mainly refers to reduce data transfer via coarse-grain parallelism, and the SIMD optimization refers to the use of 512 bits vector operation based on MIC, which will be discussed in Section 5.

Noted that, data management involves in data transfer between CPU and MIC and data dependence on MIC, we scatter them into the twice translation respectively.

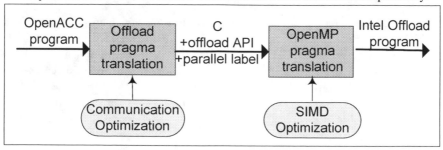

Fig. 1. Two-phase OpenACC-to-Offload translation system

5   Optimization

5.1   Communication Optimization

Data transfer bandwidth between CPU and GPU is about 8GB/s, but the actual measurement of transfer bandwidth between CPU and MIC is about 6GB/s. To fill data transfer bandwidth gap and data ruse on MIC, we carry communication optimization via coarse-grain parallelism, which can reduce data transfer between CPU and MIC.

We use a length of iteration pseudo-code to show the communication optimization. As the synchronous of threads in different block need huge expense, we adopt the strategy of twice iteration correct on GPU while reduction on CPU, the OpenACC source code is shown in Figure 2. If map that kind of code into Offload directly, the twice data transfer will be bottleneck. In our translation, to address the X86 architecture of MIC, we map the iterations into two Parallel Constructs instead of two Kernels, thus cut down data transfer once. The optimized pseudo-code is shown in Figure 3.

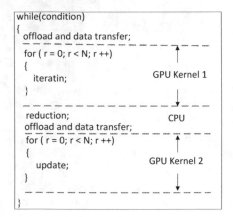

Fig. 2. OpenACC source code

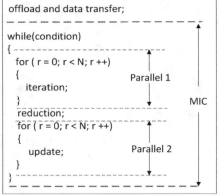

Fig. 3. Translated Offload source code

5.2   SIMD Optimization

The compilers (like PGI) support OpenACC standard translate OpenACC source code into CUDA or OpenCL source code; then generate the target code with native compilers like nvcc. We take CUDA as an example to show our optimization. CUDA uses SIMT (Single Instruction Multi Threads) execution model, and GPU can spread a great mount of light weighted thread. For example, the Tesla k20c, a kind of GPU, owns more than 2400 SM (Stream Multiprocessors). As shown in Figure 4, in the OpenACC source code, nested gangs of workers are created to execute the accelerator parallel region.

A Xeon Phi consists of 60 cores. Each core has 4 hardware threads, and is augmented with a Vector processor (VPU) and Vector register (Zmm register) with 8

64-bit (double precision floating-point) vector lanes. To fully utilize the 8-way SIMD as well as the high thread density of parallel computing technology on Xeon Phi, as shown in Figure 5, we introduce a SIMD optimism: spawning a new team of OpenMP threads to run on all other Xeon Phi cores in outer loop; then inserting the Offload directives "#pragma simd" to automatically vectorize the inner loop by native compilers.

```
#pragma acc kernels loop gang(32), worker(16)
for(j = 0; j < N; j++)
{
    #pragma acc loop gang(32), worker(16)\
      vector(32) independent
    for(i = 0; i < M; i++ )
    {
      ......
    }
}
```

```
#pragma offload target(mic:0)
#pragma omp parallel for num_threads(240)
for(j = 0; j < N; j++)
{
    #pragma simd
    for( i = 0; i < M; i++ )
    {
      ......
    }
}
```

Fig. 4. OpenACC source code   **Fig. 5.** Translated Offload source code

6   Experiments

6.1   Experiments Environment

As the PGI and accULL compilers which support OpenACC Specification cannot compile MIC target code. In order to evaluate our implementation of OpenACC to Offload translation, we have annotated matrix multiplication and JACOBI applications and tested them on CPU+MIC and CPU+GPU platforms. The configurations are listed in Table 3.

Table 3. The configurations of CPU+MIC and CPU+GPU platforms

Setup / Platform	Host			Coprocessor			
	Version	Frequency	Compiler	Version	Frequency	Cores	Peak Performance
CPU+MIC	E5-2670	2.2GHz	icc	Xeon Phi	1.10GHz	60	1.1Tflops
CPU+GPU	E5-2680	2.7GHz	nvcc	k20c	0.71GHz	2496	1.6Tflops

6.2   Experiment Case and Result

In this section we compares the performance of the presented OpenACC source code running on GPU system with the transformed and optimized Offload source code running on MIC system. Figure 6 and Figure 7 show performance of matrix multiplication and JACOBI on GPU and MIC systems.

(1)   Matrix Multiplication

Matrix multiplication (MxM) is a basic kernel frequently used to show the peak performance of GPU computing [15]. Here we use MxM to show the translation efficiency. The OpenACC codes are running on GPU system compiled by PGI; and the translated Offload codes are running on MIC system compiled by native icc. We test the OpenMP version of MxM on CPU to show the peak performance of the two kinds of source code.

Figure 6 shows the performance of different scale of MxM on CPU+MIC and CPU+GPU platform. From Figure 6, we can find that the peak performance of the MxM on MIC is up to 170 Gflops while on GPU is up to 69 Gflops, and the program running on CPU only achieves about 51 Gflops for a 7168×7168 matrix. This simple example demonstrates that with our work the programmer can use OpenACC API to program on the newly Intel MIC. The following experiment will show the efficiency of our optimizations.

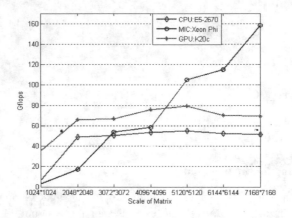

Fig. 6. Performance of MxM in different scales

(2) JACOBI

JACOBI is a widely used kernel containing the main loop of an iterative solver for regular scientific applications [16]. We precede the same test steps like MxM besides that we carry out the communication and SIMD optimization during the translation. Comparing the translated code running on MIC with and without optimization, as shown in Figure 7, the average speedup of the communication optimization is 2.9, and the average speedup of SIMD optimization is 3.9. As the data transfer latency, the MIC base system even get worse performance than CPU without optimization. After both optimizations, the Offload codes achieve better performance than the OpenACC codes on GPU, and get speedup of 3.0 to the octal-core CPU with the same problem.

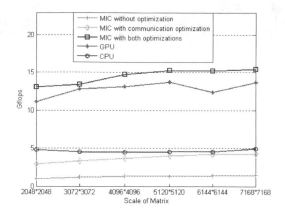

Fig. 7. Performance of JACOBI in different scales

7   Conclusion

In this paper, we take advantage of OpenACC to program on the newly Intel MIC coprocessor by automatically translating the OpenACC source code to Intel Offload code. Two optimizations including communication and SIMD optimization are employed. Performance evaluation shows that, after both optimizations, the Offload codes achieve better performance than the OpenACC codes on GPU, and get speedup of 3.0 to the octal-core CPU running the same problem.

Acknowledgments. This work is supported by the National High Technology Research and Development Program of China (863 Program) No. 2012AA010903, the National Science and Technology Major Project of the Ministry of Science and Technology of China (No.2009ZX01036-001-003), and the National Natural Science Foundation of China (NSFC) NO.61170049.

References

1. Koesterke, L., Boisseau, J., Cazes, J., Milfeld, K., Stanzione, D.: Early Experiences with the Intel Many Integrated Cores Accelerated Computing Technology. In: TeraGrid 2011 (July 2011)
2. Elgar, T.: Intel Many Integrated Core (MIC) Architecture. In: 2nd UK GPU Computing Conference (December 2010)
3. NVIDIA, CUDA programming guide 2.1 (2009), http://developer.download. nvidia.com/compute/cuda/2.1/toolkit/do-cs/NVIDIA_CUDA_ Programming_Guide_2.1.pdf
4. The OpenACC Application Programming Interface, Version 1.0 (November 2011)

5. Wienke, S., Springer, P., Terboven, C., an Mey, D.: OpenACC — first experiences with real-world applications. In: Kaklamanis, C., Papatheodorou, T., Spirakis, P.G. (eds.) Euro-Par 2012. LNCS, vol. 7484, pp. 859–870. Springer, Heidelberg (2012)
6. OpenMP: The OpenMP API Specication for Parallel Programming, http://openmp.org/wp/openmp-specications/
7. MPI-2: Extensions to the Message-Passing Interface, Message Passing Interface Forum (July 1997)
8. I. Corporation. The Intel Xeon phi coprocessor: Parallel processing, unparalleled discover. Intel' Software Network (2007)
9. Knights Corner Software Developers Guide, revision 1.03 (April 27, 2012)
10. Wu, Q., Yang, C., Tang, T., Xiao, L.: MIC Acceleration of Short-Range Molecular Dynamics Simulations. In: CGOW (January 2013)
11. Reyes, R., Lopez, I., Fumero, J.J., de Sande, F.: Sande.accULL: A User-directed Approach to Heterogeneous Programming (2012)
12. Lee, S., Min, S., Eigenmann, R.: OpenMP to GPGPU: A compiler framework for automatic translation and optimization. SIGPLANNot. (February 2009)
13. Wei, H., Yu, J.: Loading OpenMP to Cell: An Effective Compiler Framework for Heterogeneous Multi-core Chip
14. Dave, C., Bae, H., Min, S.-J., Lee, S., Eigenmann, R., Midkiff, S.: Cetus: A source-to-source compiler infrastructure for multicores. Computer 42(12) (2009)
15. Reyes, R., López-Rodríguez, I., Fumero, J.J., de Sande, F.: accULL: An OpenACC Implementation with CUDA and OpenCL Support. In: Kaklamanis, C., Papatheodorou, T., Spirakis, P.G. (eds.) Euro-Par 2012. LNCS, vol. 7484, pp. 871–882. Springer, Heidelberg (2012)
16. Reyes, R., de Sande, F.: Automatic code generation for GPUs in llc. The Journal of Supercomputing 58(3) (March 2011)

Applying Variable Neighborhood Search Algorithm to Multicore Task Scheduling Problem

Chang Wang[1], Jiang Jiang[1], Xianbin Xu[2], Xing Han[1], and Qiang Cao[1]

[1] School of Microelectronics, Shanghai Jiao Tong University
Shanghai, China
{wangchang,jiangjiang,hanxing,caoqiang}@ic.sjtu.edu.cn
[2] School of Computer, Wuhan University
Wuhan, China
xbxu@whu.edu.cn

Abstract. The emergence of multicore processors makes multicore task scheduling a focus of researchers. Since the multicore task scheduling problem is NP-hard, in most cases only approximate algorithms can be adopted to resolve it. This paper provides a detail analysis of the four aspects of applying variable neighborhood search algorithm (VNSA) to the multicore task scheduling problem. We further give a solution: (1) we propose a general solution model named task assignment matrix (TAM) (2) and define relevant element swap operations between the TAM instances; (3) then we present a construction method of the neighborhood and the neighborhood set; (4) finally we introduce a local search strategy for the neighborhood set. We have proved the effectiveness of this scheme through experiments. The results show that the scheduled tasks with different communication to computation ratio have a 1.079-4.258 times performance improvement.

Keywords: VNSA, multicore processor, task scheduling.

1   Introduction

A lot of physical constraints such as the serious heat dissipation problem, the relatively growing transistor interconnect delay and the extremely complex chip design technology results in an insurmountable obstacle for a further performance improvement on uniprocessor. Under this circumstance, multicore processors become very popular. That the multicore processor can better utilize the thread-level parallelism of the applications provides a chance to enhance the performance of the entire computer system.

According to Amdahl's law, the speedup of a program depends on the proportion of the parallel program fraction[1]. The objective of task scheduling on the multicore platform is to make full use of the parallelizable program fraction thus sufficiently utilize processor hardware resources. In order to achieve this goal, applications must be divided into many subtasks and then scheduled to different processor core to execute.

W. Xu et al. (Eds.): NCCET 2013, CCIS 396, pp. 121–130, 2013.
© Springer-Verlag Berlin Heidelberg 2013

Many algorithms have been proposed such as HEFT(Heterogonous Earliest Finished Time) and HCNF(Heterogonous Critical Node First) since this problem has arisen from distributed computing system [2] where lots of tasks are to be dispatched to different processors to execute in an appropriate way. Xiaozhong Geng et al. [3] propose a task scheduling algorithm for CMP based on task duplication which consist of changing task graph from DAG to join structure, generating scheduling set and adjusting scheduling set three steps to minimize communications between different tasks and balance execution costs between different cores. Fengguang Song et al. [4] present a task scheduling approach which put fine-grained computational tasks in a DAG and schedule them dynamically to execute dense linear algebra algorithms on both distributed-memory and shared-memory multicore system. Weimei Chen et al. [5] introduce an energy-efficient algorithm to schedule periodic real-time tasks on multicore system and at the same time this algorithm can preserve system reliability.

As a metaheuristic algorithm, variable neighborhood search algorithm (VNSA) was first proposed by Hansen and Mladenovic in 1997 [6]. By addressing some of the classic combinatorial and global optimization problems, VNSA proves a good performance [2]. We first analyze the four aspects of applying neighborhood search algorithm to the task scheduling problem on the multicore platform. Then we give a solution. Finally we prove its effectiveness through experiments.

The organization of this paper is as follows. Section 2 introduces the basic principle of VNSA. Section 3 is a discussion about the tasks scheduling problem including the tasks graph model and the multicore platform model. Section 4 analyzes applying VNSA to the multicore tasks scheduling problem and presents a solution. Experiment conditions and results are provided in section 5. A conclusion is made in section 6.

2   The Variable Neighborhood Search Algorithm

The combinatorial optimization problem is very common in real world. Multicore task scheduling problem is one of them. Generally, all algorithms developed to solve this problem are either complete or approximate [7]. The complete algorithms can find a global optimal solution by searching the entire solution space. But for the NP-hard problems, the solution space will become large with an exponential rate when the problem size increases. This often leads the problems to unsolvable. On the contrary, the approximate algorithms such as VNSA only searches part of the solution space by using some learning mechanisms thus can find a near-optimal solution in a reasonable amount of time.

The basic idea of VNSA is to change the neighborhood systematically during the search process to expand the search space and find the local optimal solution, and then systematically change the neighborhood based on the obtained local optimal solution to re-expand the search space to find another local optimal solution, and finally find a global optimal solution.

Hansen and Mladenovic have given the rules of basic VNSA [8]. Here we reinterpret some items. x is a solution for the target problem and $N_k(x)$ stands for the k-th neighborhood of x. A neighborhood of solution x is a set of solutions that has the same properties which can be described by a generalized distance function ρ. So the neighborhood structure $N_k(x)$ can be defined as $N_k(x) = \{x' | \rho(x,x') = k\}$ in which k is a natural number. For the basic VNSA, its process is illustrated in Fig. 1.

generate an initial solution x and neighborhood set $\{N_K(x)\}, k = 1, 2, ..., k_{max}$;
set k = 1;
while($k \leq k_{max}$ and termiination condition is not met){
    randomly generate a solution x" in $N_k(x)$;
    explore neighborhood $N_k(x)$ to find a local optimal x' with x" as the initial solution;
    if (x' is better than x){
        set x = x';
        construct a new neighborhood set $\{N_k(x)\}$ with this new x;
        set k = 1;
    }else{set k = k + 1;}
}
return x;

Fig. 1. Process of the Basic VNSA

3 The Multicore Task Scheduling Problem

The essence of multicore task scheduling is to establish a map from a subtask set to a processor core set. The domain is the subtask set and the range is a set of ordered pair which contains a processor core id and the task execution time. If we denote with T the set of subtask, with MC the set of processor· core, then this map function f can be described as $f : T \rightarrow MC \times [0, \infty)$. A complete multicore task scheduling system consists of three parts: the task graph model, the scheduling algorithm and the multicore platform.

3.1 The Task Graph Model

The DAG model is widely used in the researches of multicore task scheduling [3][4][9][10][11]. In order to describe the execution cost of each subtask and the communication overhead between subtasks, weights are added to subtask nodes and edges.

The weighted DAG can be described by a quaternion $G = (V, E, W, M)$, where $V = \{v_0, v_1, v_2, ..., v_{n-1}\}$ stands for the set of subtask nodes and $|V| = n$ is the quantity of the subtask set. $E = \{e_{i,j}\} (0 \leq i \leq n-1, 0 \leq j \leq n-1)$ stands for the set of communication edges between subtasks. $W = \{w_0, w_1, w_2, ..., w_{n-1}\}$ is a set of subtask weight which represents the execution cost of the subtasks. $M = \{m_{i,j}\}$ ($0 \leq i \leq n-1, 0 \leq j \leq n-1$) is a set of communication cost between subtasks in which $m_{i,j}$ stands for the communication cost from subtask v_i to subtask v_j.

There are two types of cost between subtasks. One is the communication cost and the other is the task execution cost. Applications running on computers are either communication-intensive which means there is more communication cost than computation cost or computation-intensive which means the opposite. We use communication to computation ratio (CCR) to indicate this property. Equation (1) illustrates the definition of CCR. The denominator is the execution cost sum of all subtasks and the numerator is the sum of all communication cost.

$$CCR = \frac{\sum_{i=0}^{n-1}\sum_{j=0}^{n-1} m_{i,j}}{\sum_{i=0}^{n-1} w_i} \tag{1}$$

3.2   The Multicore Platform Model

The multicore platform model can be described by a triple $MC = (C, L, R)$ where $C = \{c_0, c_1, c_2, ..., c_{m-1}\}$ stands for the set of processor cores and $|C| = m$ is the quantity of processor core set; $L = \{l_{i,j}\}(0 \le i \le m-1, 0 \le j \le m-1)$ is a set of communication rate in which $l_{i,j}$ stands for the communication speed between processor core c_i and c_j. $R = \{r_0, r_1, r_2, ..., r_{m-1}\}$ is a set of processor core execution speed. In homogeneous system, the speed of every processor core is the same, that is to say $\forall c_i, c_j \in C, r_i = r_j (i \ne j, 0 \le i \le m-1, 0 \le j \le m-1)$. In real world the multicore processor mostly are fully-connected. We can use communication cost between different subtasks to measure the impact caused by the communication limit. So here we just simplify this triple multicore model to a set of processor cores which is $MC' = \{c_0, c_1, c_2, ..., c_{m-1}\}$.

4   Applying VNSA to Multicore Task Scheduling Problem

There are several issues to be tackled when applying VNSA to the multicore task scheduling problem. First, it must be a one-to-one mapping between the formalized solutions and practical solutions, and the formalized solutions should not cause a deadlock. Second, there must be some measures to change a formalized solution to a different one in order to construct a neighborhood and neighborhood set. Finally, when the algorithm searches a neighborhood, a local search strategy is needed and the opportunity to terminate the algorithm is to be determined as well.

4.1   Formalization of the Solution

Assigning a subtask to a processor core is to designate this core to execute this subtask with a priority. We propose a solution model named task assignment matrix (TAM) $A_{m \times n}(a_{i,j}), 0 \le i \le m-1, 0 \le j \le n-1$ illustrated by Fig. 2. In TAM, the row order stands for the core number and the column order stands for the priority of a subtask. Every valid matrix element is a subtask number and the invalid element is represented by σ. By saying $a_{i,j} = t_k$ we mean subtask t_k is assigned to the i-th core with a priority w_j. Here we assume w_0 is the highest priority and w_{n-1} is the lowest priority.

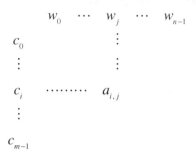

Fig. 2. Task Assignment Matrix

Some notations we used are as follows:

$Pred(t_k)$: a set of predecessor subtask of t_k.

$H(t_k)$: the height of subtask t_k.

$E(h)$: the height interval of h which actually is a set of subtasks with the same height value h.

$W(j)$: the priority of subtask t_j, $W(j) \in \{w_0, w_1, w_2, ..., w_{n-1}\}$.

$C(j)$: the processor core number of subtask t_j, $C(j) \in \{c_0, c_1, c_2, ..., c_{m-1}\}$.

The height of a subtask in TAM is defined by (2)

$$H(t_k) = \begin{cases} 0, if \ Pred(t_k) = \varnothing \\ 1 + max\{H(t_j)\}, else \ if \ t_j \in Pred(t_k) \end{cases} \qquad (2)$$

In (2) we in fact use the partial order relation of the subtask height to represent the communication dependence of subtasks. For example, if $H(t_k) < H(t_j)$, then subtask t_k must have been executed before t_j begin to execute, or it will cause a deadlock. When t_k and t_j are in different processor core, before subtask t_j begin to execute, the communication from t_k to t_j must be accomplished. If $H(t_k) = H(t_j)$, it means there is no communication dependence between them. So these two subtasks can be scheduled to different processor core to execute simultaneously.

Because of the communication dependence, some solutions may cause a deadlock. For eliminating this uncertainty, height interval is introduced in TAM. A height interval is a set of subtasks with the same height value. A subtask in a height interval can't be assigned to a processor core in a different height interval to avoid a deadlock.

4.2   Transformation of the Solution

There are two types of operations in the scheduling process. One is scheduling a subtask from a core to another and the other is changing the priority of a subtask. All other complex operations are composite of these two simple operations. Based on this we define vertical swap operation and horizontal swap operation.

The vertical swap operation is used to schedule a subtask from one processor core to another. In TAM, the vertical swap operation only occurs in the same column. In order to keep the validity of the solution, the operation must be performed between a valid element and an invalid element. Before the swap, if $a_{i_1,j} = t_{k_1}, a_{i_2,j} = \sigma$, and after that $a_{i_1,j} = \sigma, a_{i_2,j} = t_{k_1}$. Fig. 3 shows the process.

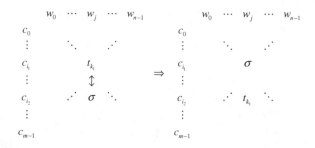

Fig. 3. Process of Vertical Swap Operation

Fig. 4. Process of Horizontal Swap Operation

The horizontal swap operation is used to swap the priorities of two valid elements in the same row and the same height interval. When more than one subtask priority changed, it can be regarded as a composite of some horizontal swap operations. The swap process is illustrated by Fig. 4. Before the swap, $a_{i,j_1} = t_{k_1}, a_{i,j_2} = t_{k_2}$ and after that $a_{i,j_1} = t_{k_2}, a_{i,j_2} = t_{k_1}$.

4.3   Generating the Initial Solution

On the basis of swap operations, we give a method of generating the initial solution. This method takes turns assigning subtask to different processor core. Subtasks with lower height are assigned to the processor core with a higher priority which means the initial solution will not cause a deadlock because the priority relation represented by the weight and the communication dependence represented by the height are consistent. Fig. 5 shows it.

initialize the core number $c = 0$, *subtask weight* $p = 0$, *subtask set* $T = \{t_0, t_1, t_2, ..., t_{n-1}\}$;

while$(T \neq \varnothing)\{$

   select a subtask t with the lowest height, if more than one then randomly select one;

   assign the selected subtask to processor core c with priority w_p;

   $c = (c + 1)\% m$;

   $p = (p + 1)\% n$;

   $T = T - \{t\}$;

$\}$

Fig. 5. Steps of Generating the Initial Solution

4.4   Generating the Neighborhood and the Neighborhood Set

The key to construct a neighborhood is to construct a generalized distance function ρ. Different TAM instance represents different task scheduling solution. In different instances, not all valid element positions are the same. So we can construct a generalized distance function based on the numbers of valid elements in different positions between different instances. Equation (4) is the definition.

$$\rho(x,x') = |\{a_{i',j'}(x') | a_{i,j}(x) = a_{i',j'}(x') \neq \sigma, i \neq i' \text{ or } j \neq j', 0 \leq i\,i' \leq m-1, 0 \leq j\,j' \leq n-1\}| \quad (3)$$

The maximum of the function $\rho(x,x')$ is n because there are at most n valid elements in different positions. If n is too big, the entire neighborhood set will be so huge that the algorithms cannot converge to a solution in a proper time. It's necessary choose some representative neighborhoods to construct the neighborhood set.

One horizontal swap operation will cause one valid element position changed and one vertical operation will cause two. The neighborhood sets showed below are constructed by the representative operation combinations. These neighborhood sets are the whole solution space which the algorithm will search.

- $N_1(x) = \{x' | \rho(x,x') = 1\}$: composed of solutions generated by performing one horizontal swap operation of solution x.
- $N_2(x) = \{x' | \rho(x,x') = 2\}$: composed of solutions generated by performing one vertical swap operation or performing two different horizontal swap operations of solution x.
- $N_3(x) = \{x' | \rho(x,x') = 3\}$: composed of solutions generated by performing one horizontal swap operation and one vertical swap operation of solution x.
- $N_4(x) = \{x' | \rho(x,x') = 4\}$: composed of solutions generated by performing two different vertical swap operations of solution x.

4.5   Local Search Strategy and Termination Conditions

The simplest local search strategy in VNSA is to randomly select a solution in the current neighborhood as the local optimal solution. A more optimized measure is to apply an exhaustive search strategy. Random search strategy is too simple and the exhaustive search strategy is too time-consuming. Moreover, these two algorithms are more likely to converge to a not good enough local optimal solution in most cases.

To prevent the algorithm from trapping into a bad local optimal solution, it's necessary to permit searching a direction which looks not so good. A way is to introduce a probabilistic strategy to determine whether the algorithm should search this new direction when a suboptimal solution yields. We propose a relative probability transition strategy by comparing the difference between the current local optimal solution and the current global optimal solution with the difference between the current local optimal and the previous global optimal solution. If the current local optimal solution is not better than the current global optimal solution, the algorithm will determine whether moving to the new direction based on to what extent the current local optimal solution goes bad. The probability P is calculated by a formula showed in (5). In this formula, x'_{local} is the current local optimal solution, x'_{global} is the current global optimal solution and x''_{global} is the previous global optimal solution.

$$P(x'_{local}, x'_{global}, x''_{global}) = \frac{|x'_{global} - x''_{global}|}{|x'_{global} - x'_{local}|} \tag{4}$$

For approximate algorithms, no direct criteria can be used to judge whether the current global optimal solution is the de facto global optimal solution. A common indirect criterion is the maximum iterations between two consecutive improvements [2] based on the cognition that if an algorithm can't find a better solution in a long enough time, then it's appropriate to regard the current optimal solution as the final global optimal solution. We use the maximum iterations between the two consecutive improvements as the termination condition.

5　　Experiments and Results Analysis

Among the proposed algorithms, HCNF and HEFT show better performance than others[9]. We compare the performance of our algorithm with these two algorithms. We both use random task graphs and real application task graphs. The random task graphs are generated with the method in [12]. The pseudo-code is illustrated in Fig. 6.

1. *initialize the subtasks array Nodes*$[0,...,n-1]$ *and CCR*;

2. *generate the execution cost of each subtask using a uniform distribution*$[2,78]$,
   caculate the average execution time avg_exc;

3. *for*$(i = 0; i <= n-1; i++)$ {
   generate the succssive node number of subtask Nodes$[i]$ *using a uniform distribution*$[0, 0.1*n]$;
   generate the communication cost between subtask Nodes$[i]$ *and*
   each of its successors using uniform distribution$[0, CCR*avg_exc]$;
   }

Fig. 6. Pseudo-code for the process of generating the random task graphs

We choose three types of real application task graphs include the fast Fourier transform (FFT) graph, the gauss elimination graph and the stencil graph [13]. Detail information is in Table 1. We totally test 9450 task graphs with different CCR value in which the random task graphs and the real application task graphs accounted for 55% and 45%, respectively. With bigger CCR, the applications are more communication-intensive. On the contrary the applications are computation-intensive. LCP stands for the length of critical path of task graph and SL is the execution time after the task graph has been scheduled. *NSL* is defined as $NSL = LCP / SL$ which reflects the speedup effects of the algorithm. In order to reduce the negative effect of accidental factors, all results are arithmetic means of a series of experimental data.

Table 1. Detail Information of the Experiment Parameters

Task Graph Type	CCR	Processor Core Number	Subtask Number	Task Graph Number
Random	0.1,0.25,0.5,0.75,1,	2~32	10~100	5200
FFT	2.5,5,7.5,			1100
GE	10,15,20			1650
SA				1500

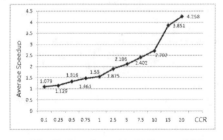

Fig. 7. Speedup with Different CCR   **Fig. 8.** Comparison of algorithms

Fig. 7 illustrates the speedup of task graphs with different CCR. The average speedup of task graphs with bigger CCR is more obvious than task graphs with small CCR. This result shows the algorithm have a good performance improvement for communication-sensitive applications. As CCR value decreases, the performance of the algorithm decreases. Especially when CCR is 0.1, the average speedup of the tasks is less than 10%.

Fig. 8 is the comparison of our algorithm with other two algorithms. We can see, both of HEFT and HCNF have a performance advantage on our algorithm when CCR is small. But when CCR is more than 10, our algorithm has a more obvious performance improvement.

In fact, multicore task scheduling is a balance between tasks communication overhead and tasks execution cost. Putting two tasks with communications on the same processor core can eliminate the communication overhead. But this will lead to an unbalance of tasks execution. The unbalanced tasks execution will directly result the whole tasks execution time become longer. Our algorithm features a good performance for the communication-intensive applications.

6   Conclusion

This paper analyzes the four aspects of applying VNSA to the multicore task scheduling problem and further realizes an algorithm. We (1)use TAM with height interval as the solution model, (2)define relevant element swap operations between different TAM instances, (3)then construct the neighborhood and neighborhood set based on the number of positions of different valid element, (4) and finally prove the effectiveness of our algorithm through experiments. The experiment results show that task graphs with bigger CCR have a performance improvement more than 4 times. When comparing with HEFT and HCNF, our algorithm has a performance advantage when CCR is more than 10.

References

1. Hill, M.D., Marty, M.R.: Amdahl's Law in the Multicore Era. Computer 41, 33–38 (2008)
2. Lusa, A., Potts, C.A.: Variable Neighbourhood Search Algorithm for the Constrained Task Allocation Problem. Journal of the Operational Research Society 59, 812–822 (2007)
3. Geng, X., Xu, G., Wang, D.: A Task Scheduling Algorithm Based on Multicore Processors. In: 2011 International Conference on Mechatronic Science, Electric Engineering and Computer (MEC), pp. 942–945 (2011)
4. Song, F., YarKhan, A., Dongarra, J.: Dynamic Task Scheduling for Linear Algebra Algorithms on Distributed-Memory Multicore Systems. In: Proceedings of the Conference on High Performance Computing Networking, Storage and Analysis (2009)
5. Chen, W., Hung, H.: Energy-efficient Scheduling of Periodic Real-time Tasks for Reliable Multicore Systems. In: Electrical and Control Engineering (ICECE), pp. 5887–5890 (2011)
6. Mladenovic, N., Hansen, P.: Variable Neighborhood Search. Computers & Operations Research 24, 1097–1100 (1997)
7. Blum, C.: Metaheuristics in Combinatorial Optimization: Overview and Conceptual Comparison. ACM Computing Surveys (CSUR) 35, 268–308 (2003)
8. Hansen, P., Mladenović, N.: Variable Neighborhood Search: Principles and Applications. European Journal of Operational Research 130, 449–467 (2001)
9. Cheng, H.: A High Efficient Task Scheduling Algorithm Based on Heterogeneous Multi-Core Processor. In: 2010 2nd Database Technology and Applications (DBTA), pp. 26–29 (2010)
10. Ilavarasan, E., Thambidurai, P.: Low Complexity Performance Effective Task Scheduling Algorithm for Heterogeneous Computing Environments. Journal of Computer Sciences 3, 94–103 (2007)
11. Kwok, Y.-K., Ahmad, I.: Efficient Scheduling of Arbitrary Task Graphs to Multiprocessors Using a Parallel Genetic Algorithm. Journal of Parallel and Distributed Computing 47, 58–77 (1997)
12. Kwok, Y.: Benchmarking the Task Graph Scheduling Algorithms. In: Parallel Processing Symposium, IPPS/SPDP 1998, pp. 531–537 (1998)
13. Olteanu, A., Marin, A.: Generation and Evaluation of Scheduling DAGs: How to Provide Similar Evaluation 1, 57–66 (2011)

Empirical Analysis of Human Behavior Patterns in BBS

Guirong Chen, Wandong Cai, Huijie Xu, and Jianping Wang

School of Computer Science, Northwestern Polytechnical University
710077 Xi,an, People's Republic of China
{guirongchen315,peipei_xiaowu}@163.com,
caiwd@nwpu.edu.cn, xhj004@gmail.com

Abstract. Patterns of human actions have attracted increasing attention, since the quantitative understanding of human behavior has important social and economic significance. This paper focuses on behavior patterns of BBS users by conduct analysis on real data of a famous BBS in China. The results show that the reply number of posts and the post number, reply number of users both follow power-law distribution. We further confirm that the one-day reply number of all the users follows power-law distribution at the population level within a certain range. According to the inflection point of the curve, we find out 100 abnormal reply behaviors. Further analysis to the time and space characteristics of the abnormal reply behaviors, we identify 8 artificial hot posts. We find that they have high time similarity, content similarity, structure similarity and show significant signs of human intervention. We infer that the 8 hot posts are the results of network hypes made by online water army. Our findings are meaningful to network public opinion monitoring and may enable a fast detecting of network hypes and online water army.

Keywords: Human dynamics, User behavior, Power-law distribution, Network hypes, Online water army.

1 Introduction

Understanding human behaviors is helpful to uncover the origins of many socioeconomic phenomena ranging from resource management, transportation control, epidemic prediction, personalized recommendation to public opinion analysis. Thanks to the rapid development of communication and database techniques, most human behaviors with time stamp have been recorded and we can conduct statistical analysis based on real data. Previous studies showed that users' activities follow the heavy-tailed distribution and can be well fitted by a power-law form. Examples of empirical studies include surface mail and email communication [1,2], mobile phone communication [3,4], short message communication [5,6], library loans [7], online activities [8–12], and so on.

With the rapid development of Web2.0, more and more people are interested in online communication. Bulletin Board System (BBS), in which all the registered people can share their opinions freely and anonymously, gets more and more public

W. Xu et al. (Eds.): NCCET 2013, CCIS 396, pp. 131–142, 2013.

attention, and has become one of the most important platforms for public opinions. While people enjoy their online life in BBS, some problems have appeared. Companies which make money by making network hypes are founded, and they employ online water army, who has registered many user names in BBS, to make artificial hot topics (called network hypes) by submitting a huge number of posts or replies in a short period of time. It is more and more different to distinguish true public opinions from false ones. Public opinions are affected seriously.

Because network hypes are newly emerging phenomena and online water army is very clandestine, people know very little about them. To the best of our knowledge, detection of network hypes and online water army has not been addressed in the current literature. While some studies have been done on the detection of sockpuppet [13,14]. Sockpuppet is an online identity used for purposes of deception [15], which means people use different fake identities pretending to be different persons to praise or create the illusion of support for the product. Although online water army and sockpuppet have some similarities, they are different in many aspects. Firstly, online water army usually means huge number of people; secondly, online water army make network hypes by submitting huge number of posts or replies; thirdly, network hypes are formed in a very short period of time(1-2 days). So the detection algorithms of sockpuppets can't be used to detect network hypes and online water army directly. This motivates us to carry out an in-depth analysis to gain insights on user behavior patterns, and find out network hypes hidden in huge number of posts and online water army hidden in normal users.

In this paper, we report an empirical analysis on real data of a famous BBS. The findings will provide a deep understanding on real human behaviors and give clues to the detection of network hypes and online water army.

The paper is organized as follows. In Section 2, we describe the basic statistical characteristics of the dataset used in our empirical analysis. In Section 3, we show our analysis results of the dataset, and present the method to find network hypes and online water army. In Section 4, we summarize our work and close the paper with concluding remarks.

2   Data Set Description

Before the introduction of the dataset used in this paper, we should give some definitions on a few of basic elements of BBS. Usually, content submitted to BBS by a user is called a post. All the posts from the same discussion form a thread. If a post is the first post of a thread, it is called root post, which headline represents the topic of the thread. A thread just has a root post, and all the other posts are replies to the root post. In this paper, we use *post* to represent the root post of a thread, and *reply* to represent the other posts of a thread.

Sina is a famous website in China, and Sina Forum (http://bbs.sina.com.cn/) is very popular. Our data is collected from Sina Entertainment Forum which is a sub forum of Sina Forum. The dataset consists of 9079 posts and 100751 replies submitted by 22537 users over a period of 12 months (between 2010/1/1 and 2010/12/31).

Each record of posts consists of seven elements: post ID, post time, post user ID, headline, content, clicked counts, reply counts, which show the ID of the post, the time when the post is submitted, the user's ID who submits the post, the title of the post, the content of the post, the number that the post has been clicked or browsed, the number that the post has been replied respectively. Each record of replies consists of five elements: reply ID, reply user ID, reply time, content, post ID, which show the reply post's ID, the user's ID who submits the reply, the time when the reply is submitted, the content of the reply, and the root post's ID of the reply respectively. Here, the reply ID of a reply means the ID of the reply post itself and the post ID means the root post to which this reply is submitted to reply. Users who didn't submit a post or a reply during the period of time are excluded from our analyses.

3   Empirical Analysis of Actual Data

3.1   Distribution of the Click Number and Reply Number of Posts

Here, we analyze the click number and reply number of all the posts in the dataset. Fig.1 shows the statistical results. Fig.1 (a) and Fig.1 (b) are both the distributions of click number, and Fig.1 (a) is in semilog coordinate, and Fig.1 (b) is in double logarithmic coordinates. As can be seen in Fig.1 (a) and Fig.1 (b), the distribution doesn't follow Poisson-like or Power law-like distribution. This is consistent with Ref. [16-17], but different with Ref. [18] which shows that the views of posts follow power-law distribution.

The values of the click number focus on 100 and 1000. Further, We find that there are only 5 posts be clicked less than 100 times, 0.05% of the total, and 7650 posts be clicked between 100 and 1000 times, 84.2% of the total, and 1424 posts be clicked more than 1000 times, 15.68% of the total. That is to say more than 99.95% of the posts are browsed more than 100 times, which means that almost all the posts have a certain influence, but the number of posts which are browsed more than 1000 times is not large.

Fig.1 (c) and Fig.1 (d) are both the distribution of reply number in double logarithmic coordinates. For both cases, X-axis represents the distribution we focus on, while $p(X = x)$ in Fig.1 (c) is the distribution function and $p(X \geq x)$ in Fig.1 (d) is the cumulative distribution function. As can be seen in Fig. 1 (c), part of the distribution (1-80) can be fitted by a power-law form $p(\lambda) = \lambda^{-\alpha}$ with exponent 2.06. The exponent is estimated by using the method in Ref. [19]. All the power-law exponents reported in this paper are obtained by such a method. We find that there are 8962 posts be replied less than 80 times, 98.71% of the total, and there are 117 post be replied more than 80 times, 1.29% of the total, which means that most posts have few replies, and only a very few of posts have a very large replies.

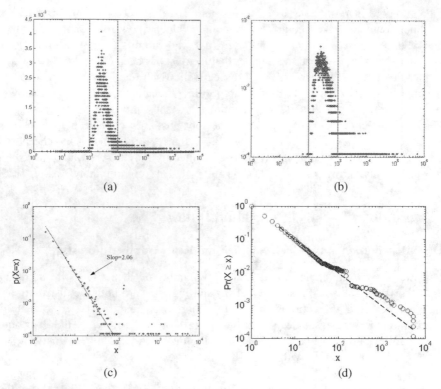

Fig. 1. Distributions of click number and reply number of all the posts. In (a) and (b), X-axis represents click number and Y-axis represents the distribution function. (a) is in semilog coordinate and (b) is in double logarithmic coordinates. (c) is the distribution of reply number, and in (c) X-axis represents reply number, and Y-axis represents the distribution function. (d) is the accumulation distribution function. (c) and (d) are all in double logarithmic coordinates.

3.2   Distribution of the Post Number and Reply Number of Users

In this section, we mainly focus on the distribution of action numbers of users. Since the user's browse behaviors in online forums are not recorded, we can not analyze the browse behavior directly. Here, we analyze the distributions of the post number and reply number submitted by users. Fig. 2 shows the results.

As we can see in Fig.2 (a) and (b), the distribution of post number follow Power-law distribution, and the exponent is 2.48. This means that most users submit few posts and very few users submit a large number of posts. Fig.2 (c) and (d) illustrate the distribution of reply number of all the users. The distribution shows Power-law characteristics, but as Fig. 2(d) shows the curve is not a straight line, when the values are larger than 100, the tail deviates downward, which means that most users rarely reply, and a small part of the users reply more, and users who submitted more than 100 replies are very few. According to Fig. 2(d), users can be divided into two categories, one is less active and one is more active.

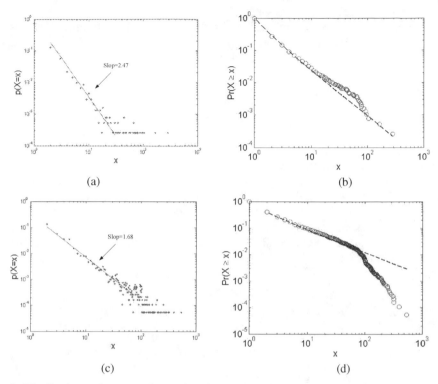

Fig. 2. Distributions of post number and reply number of the users. (a) is the distribution of post number of the users and in (a) X-axis represents the number of posts and Y-axis represents the distribution function. (b) is the accumulation distribution function. (c) is the distribution of reply number of the users and in (c) X-axis represents the number of replies and Y-axis represents the distribution function. (d) is the accumulation distribution function. All of them are all in double logarithmic coordinates.

3.3   Distribution of the One-Day One-User Reply Number on Population Level

We conduct a statistics of one-day reply number of each user, and find that the maximum of one-day reply number is 549, which means that some user has submitted 549 replies in one day, and the minimum of one-day reply number is 0, which means that a user did not submit any reply in that day.

Fig.3 reports the cumulative distribution of one-day one-user reply number on population level. As we see, the distribution shows power law characteristics, which means that most users submit very few replies on most of the days, and a few of users submit a large number of replies on very few days. But as Fig.3 (a) illustrates, the tail of the curve has a downward deviation, which means the phenomenon of one-day reply number exceeds a certain value (the inflection point of the curve) is very rare. That is to say, the behavior submitting a large number of replies (exceeding the inflection point of the curve) is abnormal user behavior which does not comply with the Sina forum user behavioral patterns.

Generally, online water army makes network hypes by submitting a large number of replies in a short period of time. Therefore, we are mainly concerned with the behaviors with large reply numbers. We sort all the records according to the replies submitted on one day, then top *n* records mean the first n records in the sorted record set. Fig.3 (b) and (c) are the distributions of the top 4000 and top 1000 reply behaviors on population level. We can see that they exhibit similar characteristics with Fig.1 (a). To identify the abnormal user behavior, we should determine the inflection point of the curve firstly. We suppose curve deviation occurs when x is equal to *r*. In order to determine the value of *r*, we remove the records greater than *r*, using the maximum likelihood estimation method [19] for power-law curve fitting, estimate the fitting errors. Several experiments found that when *r* is equal to 67, the fitting errors is smallest. Fig.3 (d) is the cumulative distribution of one-day reply number of top 1000 (removing the records larger than 67) on population level. As Fig.3 (d) shows, it follows a power law form strictly in a range. So we set *r* as 67, what means if some one submits more than 67 replies on one day, we think the behavior is abnormal. Further analysis to the whole dataset, we find that there are 100 abnormal behaviors.

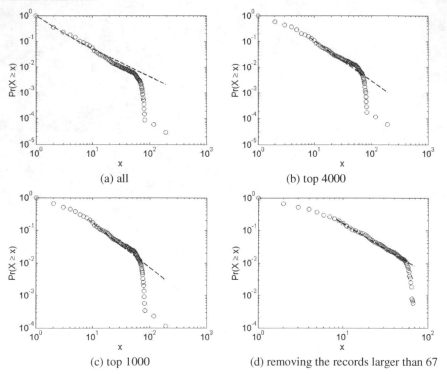

(a) all

(b) top 4000

(c) top 1000

(d) removing the records larger than 67

Fig. 3. Distribution of one-day one-user reply number on population level. (a) All the users. (b) Top 4000. (c) Top 1000. (d) Remove the records larger than 67 from top 1000.

3.4   Distribution of the Abnormal One-Day Reply Behaviors

In this section, we analyze the time and space distributions of the abnormal reply behaviors found in last section. Fig.4 (a) presents the time distribution of the 100 abnormal daily reply behaviors. We find that there are 81 abnormal daily reply behaviors on December 3, 2010, and there are 12 abnormal daily reply behaviors on December 6, 2010, accounting for 93% of the total number. So we suspect that there are network hypes in the Sina Entertainment Forum on that two days.

Further analysis of the dataset, we find that there are 18824 replies on December 3, 2010, and all the replies were submitted to reply 21 different posts. Fig.4 (b) shows the distribution of the replies in different posts. We can see that there are 4 hot posts, which post ID are respectively 774916,775150,775151,775152, and the numbers of replies are respectively 4666, 4686, 4670 and 4687, accounting for a total of 18709, 99.39 % of the total replies of the day. We suspect that the 4 hot posts were network hypes made by online water army.

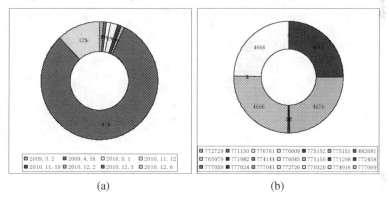

(a)   (b)

Fig. 4. Distributions of the abnormal behaviors. (a) The time distribution of the 100 abnormal behaviors. (b) The space distribution of the replies on December 3, 2010.

In order to confirm whether the 4 posts are network hypes or not, we conduct further analysis to them. Table 1 is the basic information of the 4 hot posts on December 3, 2010. Firstly we analyze the time correlation between these 4 posts, and find that they were all submitted on December 1, 2010, and the difference of the submission time of the last 3 posts were just 2 minutes. Meanwhile, we find that post 775150 and post 775151 were submitted by the same user. So we can suspect that the 3 posts were submitted by the same people, who logged on the BBS with different user names.

We define the life cycle of a post as how many days the post last. Then we analyze the life cycles of the 4 posts, and find that the life cycles of 3 of them are 3 days, that is December 1, 2010, December 2, 2010 and December 3, 2010. They all have no replies on the first day, a lot of replies on the next day, a large number of replies on the third day, and then no replies for ever, which shows burst characteristics such as "short time", "a large number of replies" and so on. The life cycle of post 775150, which is 25 days, does not show burst characteristic. But further analysis of this post shows that the number of replies submitted on the next and third day is 5360, 99.9 % of the total replies. During the next 22 days, there were only 3 replies, which should be submitted by normal users. So we can see that post 775150 shows same burst characteristics with the other 3 posts.

Table 1. The basic information of the 4 hot posts on December 3, 2010

Post ID	User ID	Headline	Submit time	Life Cycle(d)	Reply Number	Click Number	User Number
774916	1883898872	Love art, not money! Kaige Chen was Under the pain behind<The orphan of Zhao>	2010-12-01 14:12:00	3	5335	23964	516
775150	1834813957	<The orphan of Zhao> Kaige Chen's new explain to revenge	2010-12-01 18:52:00	25	5363	26507	521
775151	1834813957	Remodel classic with personality, Kaige Chen give you a new interpretation of the naked human nature	2010-12-01 18:54:00	3	5341	24074	519
775152	1847440812	Does "Black" person get the world in Chinese movie world?	2010-12-01 18:56:00	3	5359	23786	517

Fig.5 (a) reports the time distribution of replies of the 4 abnormal hot posts. We conduct a manual inspection to post 671195 which is a normal hot post and confirm that it does not contain network hype. Fig.5 (b) reports the time distribution of replies of post 671195. As Fig.5 shows, the differences between the time distributions of replies of the 4 hot posts on December 3, 2010 and the real hot posts are big.

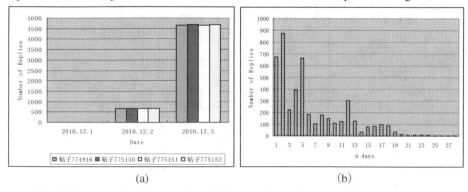

(a)   (b)

Fig. 5. Time distribution of replies. (a) Four abnormal hot posts. (b) A real hot post.

We analyze the content of these 4 hot posts, and find that the 4 posts are all about "Kaige Chen" who is a famous director in China and "The orphan of Zhao" which was Zhao's new film in that time.

In the same way, we analyze the posts and replies submitted on December 6, 2010 deeply. We find that there are 3513 replies on December 6, 2010, and all the replies were submitted to reply 50 different posts. Fig.6 (a) shows the distribution of the replies in the posts. We can see that there are 4 hot posts, which post ID are respectively 777914, 777961, 778102, 778103, the numbers of replies are respectively 1344, 1345, 1204 and 1209, accounting for a total of 3429, 97.61% of the total replies of that day. We suspect that the 4 hot posts were network hypes by online water army.

In order to confirm whether the 4 posts are network hypes or not, we conducted further analysis to them. Table 2 is the basic information of the 4 hot posts on December 6, 2010. As table 2 shows, the 4 posts were all submitted on December 5, 2010, the difference of the submission time of post 777914 and post 777961 is 20 minutes. Post 778102 and Post 778103 were submitted by the same user in two minutes. So we can suspect that the 3 posts were submitted by the same people, who logged on the BBS with different user names. Fig. 6 (b) shows the distribution of the daily replies of the 4 hot posts on December 6, 2010. As we see, the replies of the 4 posts focus on 2 days, accounting for 99.9%, 100%, 100% and 100% of the total, which shows burst characteristics.

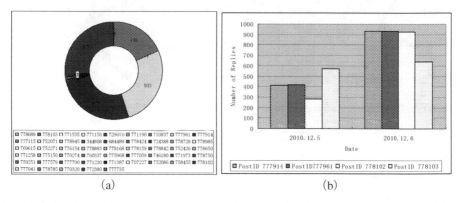

(a)   (b)

Fig. 6. Distribution of the 4 hot posts on December 6, 2010. (a) The space distribution of the replies on December 6, 2010. (b) Reply number of the 4 posts.

Similarly, we analyze the content of the 4 posts, and find that the 4 posts are all about "Kaige Chen" and "The orphan of Zhao". Therefore, we infer that the 4 hot posts on December 3, 2010 and the 4 hot posts on December 6, 2010 are all network hypes conducted by online water army. The content of the two network hypes is Kaige Chen's new film < The orphan of Zhao >. The first network hype was conducted on December 3, 2010, which aim is to make 4 hot posts, each of which having more than 5000 replies, and the second network hype was conducted on December 6, 2010, which aim is to make 4 hot posts, each of which having more than 1200 replies.

In short, the 100 abnormal reply behaviors distributed on 8 days, 93% of which focused on 2 days, when we suspect that there were network hypes. Further analysis on the posts and replies on the 2 days, we find that the replies focus on 8 posts, which have high time, content and structure similarity. Obviously, the 8 posts are network hypes made by online water army. And the users who replied abnormal on the 2 days must be online water army.

Table 2. The basic information of the 4 hot posts on December 6, 2010

Post ID	User ID	Headline	Submit time	Life Cycle(d)	Reply Number	Click Number	User Number
777914	1882937535	On the first day of release <The orphan of Zhao > gets a lot of praise	2010-12-05 12:15:00	19	1344	16229	380
777961	1832901995	<The orphan of Zhao > celebrates the new year as the overlord style	2010-12-05 12:35:00	2	1345	15823	378
778102	1705258735	Cheng Ying who has walked down from the altar	2010-12-05 17:55:00	2	1204	14474	342
778103	1705258735	<The orphan of Zhao >: no enemy but you and me	2010-12-05 17:57:00	2	1209	16434	210

In order to confirm the difference between network hypes and real network hot posts, we compared the 8 artificial hot posts with a real hot post we got by manual analysis from reply count, clicked count, life cycle, user count, average reply number per day, average reply number per user and the ratio of clicked count and reply count.

Fig.7 shows the results, in which post 671195 is a real hot post and other posts are network hypes. We can see that network hypes and real hot posts both have a large number of replies, but the replies of the same network hypes are very close which depends on the tasks of the online water army. The clicked counts of the network hypes are lower than what of the real hot posts having the same number of replies. Network hypes have burst characteristics, so their life cycles are very short, generally only 2-3 days, while real hot posts replied spontaneously by users last longer. The number of different users involved in network hypes is smaller than that of a real hot post having the same number of replies, because in network hypes online water army submit a lot of replies using the same user name. The one-day average replies and one-user average replies of network hypes are much larger that of real hot posts. The ratio of clicked count and reply count reflect the average number of users who have browsed the post will reply the post, and this indicator is very important to identify the network hype. As Fig.7 shows the ratio of network hypes is much smaller than that of real hot posts, which shows that there are many replies are not submitted by users who have browsed the post and wanted to give his or her ideas about it, but submitted by online water army to make a artificial hot post or network hypes, having obvious traces of human intervention.

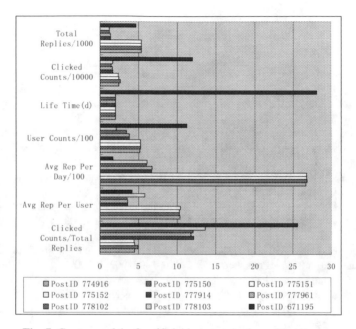

Fig. 7. Compare of the 8 artificial hot posts and a real hot post

4   Discussion and Conclusions

The main contribution of this paper is reflected in two aspects. Firstly, we confirm that the reply number of posts, the post number, reply number, one-day reply number of users all follow power-law distributions. This is meaningful to the modeling the online user behavior, whether what the model is, the post behaviors and reply behaviors should follow power-law distributions. Secondly, we propose a method of detecting network hypes and online water army. The method includes 3 steps, firstly analyze the one-day one-user reply behavior on population level to find abnormal user behaviors, then find out the network hypes by locating the time and the posts the abnormal behaviors focus on, finally identify the online water army by find out the users who have abnormal behaviors during the time when the network hypes occur. The results of empirical analysis to the dataset prove that our method is effective and efficient.

Our method can identify network hype phenomenon which was formed by online water army using extreme measures such as submitting a large number of replies in a short period of time. But sometimes online water army makes network hypes by submitting a large number of replies using a large number of user names in a short time, which means they just reply several times using one user name. On this situation, they masquerade as normal users and we can not find the abnormal behaviors using our method. Because the cost of this speculation mode is too high, needing to spend too much time and effort, so generally online water army does not use it. Even so, we also need to study the network user behavior characteristics more deeply, and constantly improve the accuracy and efficient of the detection of network hypes and online water army.

References

1. Barabási, A.L.: The origin of bursts and heavy tails in human dynamics. Nature 435, 207–211 (2005)
2. Oliveira, J.G., Barabási, A.L.: Human dynamics: Darwin and Einstein correspondence patterns. Nature 437, 1251–1251 (2005)
3. Candia, J., González, M.C., Wang, P.: Uncovering individual and collective human dynamics from mobile phone records. J. Phys. A: Math. Theor. 41, 224015-1–224015-11 (2008)
4. Jiang, Z.Q., Xie, W.J., Li, M.X.: Calling patterns in human communication dynamics. J. PLNA 110, 1600–1605 (2013)
5. Zhao, Z.D., Xia, H., Shang, M.S., Zhou, T.: Empirical analysis on the human dynamics of a large-scale short message communication system. Chin. Phys. Lett. 28, 068901-1–068901-3 (2011)
6. Hong, W., Han, X.P., Zhou, T., Wang, B.H.: Heavy-tailed statistics in short-message communication. Chin. Phys. Lett. 26, 028902-1–028902-3 (2009)
7. Fan, C., Guo, J.L., Zha, Y.L.: Fractal analysis on human dynamics of library loans. Physica A: Statistical Mechanics and its Applications 391, 6617–6625 (2012)
8. Zhou, T., Kiet, H.A.T., Kim, B.J.: Role of activity in human dynamics. EPL. 82, 28002-p1–28002-p5 (2008)
9. Dezsö, Z., Almaas, E., Lukács, A.: Dynamics of information access on the web. Phys. Rev. E. 73, 066132-1–066132-6 (2006)
10. Zhao, Z.D., Zhou, T.: Empirical analysis of online human dynamics. Physica A: Statistical Mechanics and its Applications 391, 3308–3315 (2012)
11. Zhao, Z.D., Cai, S.M., Huang, J.: Scaling behavior of online human activity. EPL. 100, 48004-p1–48004-p6 (2012)
12. Xiong, F., Liu, Y.: Empirical Analysis and Modeling of Users' Topic Interests in Online Forums. PloS One. 7, e50912-1– e50912-7 (2012)
13. Bu, Z., Xia, Z., Wang, J.: A sock puppet detection algorithm on virtual spaces. Knowledge-Based Systems. 37, 366–377 (2013)
14. Zheng, X., Lai, Y.M., Chow, K.P.: Sockpuppet detection in online discussion forums. In: 2011 Seventh International Conference on Intelligent Information Hiding and Multimedia Signal Processing (IIH-MSP), pp. 374–377. IEEE (2011)
15. http://en.wikipedia.org/wiki/Sockpuppet_(Internet)
16. Si, X.M., Liu, Y.: Empirical analysis of interpersonal interacting behavior in virtual community. Acta Phys. Sin. 60, 859–866 (2011)
17. Ding, F., Liu, Y., Cheng, H.: Read and reply behaviors in a BBS social network. Advanced Computer Control (ICACC) 4, 571–576 (2010)
18. Yu, J., Hu, Y., Yu, M.: Analyzing netizens' view and reply behaviors on the forum. Physica A: Statistical Mechanics and its Applications 389, 3267–3273 (2010)
19. Clauset, A., Shalizi, C.R., Newman, M.E.J.: Power-law distributions in empirical data. SIAM Review 51, 661–703 (2009)

Performance Evaluation and Scalability Analysis of NPB-MZ on Intel Xeon Phi Coprocessor

Yuqian Li, Yonggang Che, and Zhenghua Wang

National Laboratory of Parallel and Distributed Processing
National University of Defense Technology, Changsha 410073, China
{liyuqian11,ygche,zhhwang}@nudt.edu.cn

Abstract. Intel Many Integrated Cores (Intel MIC) is a novel architecture for high performance computing (HPC). It features large thread parallelism and wide vector processing units, targeting highly parallel applications. The HPC communities are faced with the problem of porting their applications to the MIC platforms. But it is still an open question that how current HPC applications can exploit the capabilities of MIC. This paper evaluates the performance of NPB-MZ programs which are derived from real world Computational Fluid Dynamics (CFD) applications on Intel Xeon Phi coprocessor, the first MIC product. The strong scaling behaviors of the applications with different process-thread combinations are investigated. The performance obtained on the Intel Xeon Phi coprocessors is compared against that obtained on Sandy Bridge CPU based computer nodes. The results show that these programs can achieve good parallel scalability when running with appropriate combinations of processes and threads. But their absolute performance on Intel Xeon Phi coprocessor is significantly lower than that on CPU node, due primarily to the much lower single thread performance. The findings of this paper are of help to the performance optimization of other applications on MIC.

Keywords: Intel MIC, NPB-MZ, performance evaluation, scalability, single thread performance.

1   Introduction

Power is a great challenge for HPC systems in the future. Since the many-core architecture has a high power-to-performance ratio, it is a way to achieve power efficiency for supercomputer [1]. Intel has published the Intel Many Integrated Core (Intel MIC) architecture and recently released the first MIC product, the Intel Xeon Phi coprocessor (Knights Conner). The MIC architecture is designed specifically for high performance computer with the goal to accelerate highly parallel computing tasks. Another outstanding characteristic of MIC is the x86 instruction set, which means there is no need to rewrite codes when running on MIC. In the latest TOP500 supercomputer list, several supercomputers utilized the hybrid CPU + MIC heterogeneous architecture, such as the TACC Stampede (ranked seventh on December 2012), Intel's DISCOVERY, etc [2]. As it provides high computing performance with traditional

W. Xu et al. (Eds.): NCCET 2013, CCIS 396, pp. 143–152, 2013.
© Springer-Verlag Berlin Heidelberg 2013

programming models, the Intel MIC architecture will be a better choice to accelerate HPC applications.

As a typical application field of HPC, CFD (computational fluid dynamics) applications are challenging for today's high-end architectures. It makes great sense to transplant the CFD programs to the MIC platform. NPB (NAS Parallel Benchmark), which was developed by NASA Ames Research Center, is extracted from real world CFD applications. It has become the CFD performance testing standard of high-performance computers. NPB Multi-Zone is the multi-zone version of three applications derived from the NPB benchmark suite. It includes the benchmark programs LU (Lower-Upper symmetric Gauss-Seidel), BT (Block Tri-diagonal) and SP (Scalar Penta-diagonal).   These programs solve the fluid problems on several collections of loosely coupled discretization meshes [3]. This paper evaluates the performance of NPB-MZ on the newly released Intel Xeon Phi coprocessor, with an intention of understanding the performance characteristics of CFD applications on the MIC architecture. The strong scaling behaviors with different process-thread combinations are investigated. After that, we compared the performance obtained on the Intel Xeon Phi coprocessors with that obtained on Sandy Bridge CPU based computer nodes. The results will give some hints for how to optimize CFD applications on MIC.

The reminder of this article is organized as follows. Section 2 briefly describes the architecture and execution mode of MIC. In Section 3, the performance results of the NPB-MZ benchmarks on MIC in native mode under various process-thread combinations for different problem sizes are presented. We draw our conclusions in the last section.

2   Intel MIC Architecture and Execution Modes

2.1   Intel MIC Architecture

Based on Intel MIC architecture, the Intel Xeon Phi comprises of more than 50 cores interconnected by a high-speed bidirectional ring(shown in Figure1).

The cores are in-order dual issue x86 processor cores. Each MIC core has a 512KB L2 cache locally with high-speed access to all other L2 caches, making the collective size over 25M. Also, each core has a 32KB L1 data cache and a 32KB L2 instruction cache. More than 50 cores and four threads on each core result in more than 200 hardware threads available on a single device. With the large number of cores, the 512-bit wide SIMD vectors of each core contribute to the peak double-precision performance of more than 1 TFLOPS [4,6]. As such, it is more important that applications use these multiple hardware threads on Intel Xeon Phi coprocessors than they use hyper-threads on Intel Xeon processors.

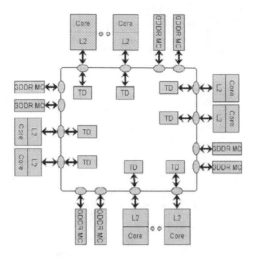

Fig. 1. Intel MIC Architecture

2.2   Execution Modes for Intel Xeon Phi

There are two approaches to involve the Intel Xoen Phi coprocessors in an application, a processor-centric "offload" mode and "native" mode [7]. For offload mode, the highly-parallel phases of the application may be offloaded from the Intel Xeon host processor to the Intel Xeon Phi coprocessor. In this mode, input data and code are sent to the coprocessor from the host, and output data is sent back to the host when offloaded computation completes [9]. Execution may be concurrent on host and coprocessor. For native mode, program runs natively on processors or coprocessors and communicates with each other by various methods.

A key attribute of the MIC architecture is that it provides a general-purpose programming environment similar to that of the Intel Xeon processor. It runs applications written in industry-standard programming languages (FORTRAN, C, C++, etc) and standard parallel programming models (MPI, OpenMP and pthreads). So MPI and OpenMP parallel applications ran on x86CPU can be reused on the Intel Xeon Phi coprocessor in native mode without code modification. What need to be done is just recompilation before it runs. Native mode is the simplest and fastest way to run applications on the Intel Xeon Phi coprocessor.

For developers, the assessment and analysis of application performance in Native mode is important to give full play to the usage of MIC. That's why we study the performance of CFD benchmarks running in native mode. We believe it will be great guidance for accelerating CFD applications with MIC.

3   Experiment Results and Analysis

3.1   Experiment Setup

NPB is a well-known benchmark suite for testing the capabilities of parallel computers and parallelization tools. So we choose the programs from the hybrid MPI+OpenMP version of NPB-MZ to evaluate the performance of programs on MIC. These programs exhibit mostly fine-grain exploitable parallelism and are almost all iterative, requiring multiple data exchanges between processes within each iteration. The hybrid MPI + OpenMP version of NPB-MZ takes advantage of such fine-grain parallelism with a two-level parallelism approach: a coarse grained parallelization among zones and a fine grained parallelization within each zone [5,8]. It uses MPI standard to communicate data related to overlap regions of zones, and OpenMP to parallelize loops within each zone. In detail, the N_Z zones need to be clustered into N_G groups, where N_G is equal to the total number of processes, N_P. Each zone group is then assigned to a process for parallel execution. OpenMP threads are then used to parallel loops within each zone [5].

There are a series of sequentially increasing problem classes in NPB benchmark, S, W, A, B, C, D, E, F [3]. The differences between the eight problem classes are the number of blocks and the size of each block. Among them, S Class and W Class are too small to have a reference value, while D Class can't run on the Xeon Phi coprocessor in Native mode because the memory requirement exceeds the available memory size on a Xeon card. The Class A, B and C are evaluated in our experiments.

For investigating the scalability of NPB-MZ on one Xeon Phi card, we run the benchmark in two types of processor nodes: one Xeon Phi coprocessor and one CPU node. The main performance characteristics of each processor node are summarized in Table 1.

Table 1. Architectural specification of two types of processors

Processor types	Sandy Bridge	Xeon Phi
Cores/nodes	16	57
Treads/cores	2	4
Clock (GHz)	2.59	1.1
Peak FP (Gflops/s)	166.4	1003.2
Peak BW (GB/s)	51.2	352
L1 (KB)	32	32
L2 (KB)	256	512
L3 (MB)	20	None
TDP (W)	115	275

3.2   Experimental Results and Performance Analysis

To investigate the scalability of NPB-MZ on one MIC card, we run the benchmark in two ways: single-process + multi-threads and multi-processes + multi-threads, i.e., pure OpenMP mode and hybrid MPI/OpenMP mode. We also compare the performance on MIC with that on CPU.

3.2.1   Single-Process + Multi-Threads

The MIC card we used in our test has 57 cores, and each with 4 hardware threads. According to that, we set up the threads number with 1, 2, 4, 32, 57, 114 and 228. We use the KMP_AFFINITY environment variable to bind the threads to cores. Thread affinity restricts execution of certain threads (virtual execution units) to a subset of the physical processing units in a multiprocessor computer. In our test, each core runs 1 thread, 2 threads, 4 threads when there is less than 57 threads, 114 threads, 228 threads respectively.

Figure 2, Figure 3, Figure 4 respectively shows the parallel speedup of BT-MZ, LU-MZ, SP-MZ on MIC.

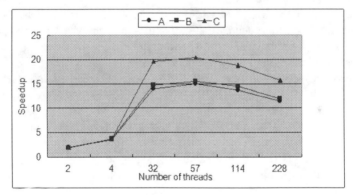

Fig. 2. Speedup of CLASS A, B ,C of BT-MZ on MIC

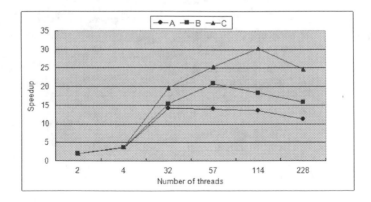

Fig. 3. Speedup of CLASS A, B, C of LU-MZ on MIC

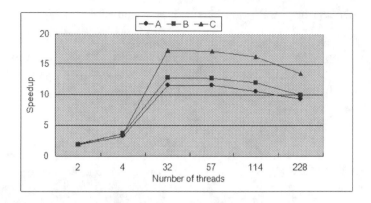

Fig. 4. Speedup of CLASS A, B, C of SP-MZ on MIC

From the above figures, it can be seen that BT-MZ and SP-MZ for Class A, B, C problem size and LU-MZ for Class A, B problem size reach their highest speedup with 57 threads, while LU-MZ for Class C problem size with 114 threads. Beyond that thread number, the speedup decrease slightly. BT-MZ achieves a highest speedup of about 20, while SP-MZ about 17 and LU-MZ about 30. All the three application reach their highest speedup when problem size is CLASS C.

We observed a speedup decrease with the increase of threads number relates to the two-level parallelism approach of NPB-MZ. As all zones are assigned to only one process, there is no parallel execution among zones and no sufficient computing tasks for each thread within each zone. Besides, the threading overhead and memory access conflicts surpass the parallel performance gains of multi-threading when too much threads are used. As a result, the scalability is not so good as we expect. So it's important to balance the number of processes and threads to get the best performance gain.

3.2.2   Multi-processes + Multi-threads

For NPB multi-zone benchmarks, the computation amount of each thread is limited for single process. When the number of threads for single process exceeds 57, the memory access performance is a limited factor for exploiting the MIC performance. Based on the characteristics of NPB programs and MIC architecture, we will investigate the scalability in two steps in this section.

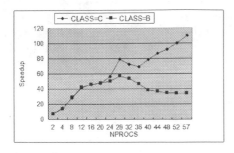

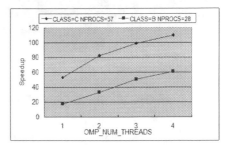

Fig. 5. Speedup of BT-MZ with fixed numbers of threads

Fig. 6. Speedup of BT-MZ with fixed numbers of process

For BT-MZ, we firstly choose process numbers from 1 to 57 with a fixed thread number 4 and plot the speedup of BT-MZ in Figure 5. The curve shows that 57 processes make BT-MZ reaching its highest speedup for Class C and 28 processes for Class B. Next, we set up NPROCS=57 for Class C and NPROCS=28 for Class B and vary threads number from 1 to 4. As shown in Figure 6, the speedup increase linearly as the number of thread increase.

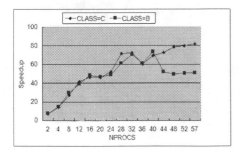

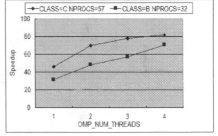

Fig. 7. Speedup of SP-MZ with fixed numbers of threads

Fig. 8. Speedup of SP-MZ with fixed numbers of process

The same test was performed for SP-MZ and Figure 7 and Figure 8 give us a direct impression of the speedup behavior of SP-MZ on MIC. As shown in Figure 3.6 and Figure 3.7, SP-MZ achieves its highest speedup running with 57 processes for Class C and 40 processes for Class B. In the case of best processes number, the speedup increase linearly when traverse the number of threads from 1-4.

The speedup behavior of BT-MZ and SP-MZ match greatly with the architecture features of MIC. The combination of 57 processes with 4 threads per process can exploit the potential of MIC performance for NPB-MZ programs when application size and problem size are large enough. When problem size is smaller, a appropriate number of processes with four threads per process are still the best choice for good performance behavior on MIC.

When NPB-MZ runs with multi-processes and multi-threads, different zone groups are assigned to different processes. Each thread within each process deals with an appropriate amount of tasks to obtain the expected parallel gains. Therefore, good combination of processes and threads makes the performance of the applications scale well on MIC.

3.2.3   Comparison with the CPU Performance

In this section, we compared the performance of NPB-MZ on MIC and that on traditional CPU to obtain a better understanding of how applications behave on MIC. Three column charts Figure 9, Figure 10, Figure 11 show respectively the execution time with single-process + single-thread, the shortest execution time, and the best speedup. We can see from the figures that, the many cores and threads make extraordinary speedup for MIC than traditional CPU. But the actual execution time of application is much longer for MIC than CPU. Considering the Intel MIC architecture, we speculate that the wide performance gap between MIC and CPU is that a single process with a single thread on MIC cannot use the wide vector processing unit(VPU) efficiently, and the memory access performance is worse than that of CPU. To use the wide VPU and optimize the memory access performance are key factors for improving the performance of NPB-MZ programs on MIC.

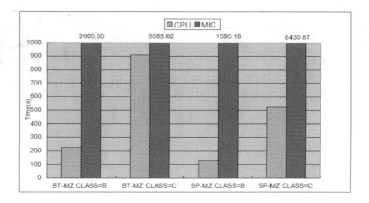

Fig. 9. The execution time for MIC and CPU using a process with a thread

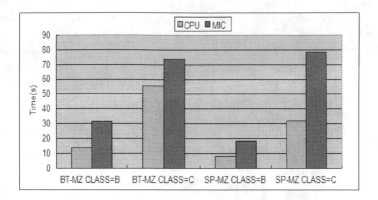

Fig. 10. The best performance of applications on MIC and CPU

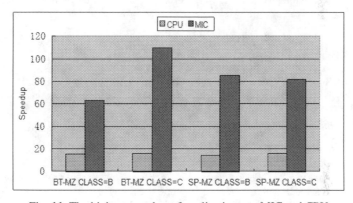

Fig. 11. The highest speedup of applications on MIC and CPU

4   Conclusions and Future Work

In this paper, we evaluated the performance and scalability of NPB-MZ on the Intel MIC architecture. A series of tests are made for the speedup of NPB-MZ under various process-thread combinations and different problem classes. Finally, we compare the results with measurements on CPU nodes. The results show that the program can obtain good scalability when running with a appropriate combination of processes and threads. However, although the many cores and threads make extraordinary speedup for MIC than traditional CPU, the actual execution time of application is much longer for MIC. We attribute the wide performance gap to the poor single-process + single-thread performance on MIC.

For additional performance improvement, we should take into account of vector level parallelism and memory access problem. The Intel Xeon Phi coprocessor is designed with uniquely wide 512-bit SIMD units which contribute a lot to the peak DP performance. How to development vector level parallelism within processes and threads are key factors for improving the performance and scalability of programs on MIC. Furthermore, it's of great significance to investigate how to hide memory access latencies implicit by using concurrent threads.

What's more, when to choose to use an offload model vs. a native execution model relates to the application features. Native model is good for programs that are largely doing operations that map to parallelism either in threads or vectors and are without significant amounts of serial executions. So CFD programs which cannot be made highly parallel consistently throughout most of the application are more appropriate for offload model. Therefore, when porting CFD programs to the MIC platform, offload model is clearly a critical direction for future work.

References

1. Heinecke, A., Klemm, M., Bungartz, H.: From GPGPU to Many-Core: Nvidia Fermi and Intel Many Integrated Core Architecture. Computing in Science & Engineering 14(2), 78–83 (2012)
2. Top500 supercomputer sites (December 2012), http://www.top500.org
3. NASA Advanced Supercomputing Division, http://www.nas.nasa.gov/publications/npb.html
4. Intel: Intel Xeon Phi Coprocessor System Software Development Guide (2012)
5. Van der, W., Jin, H.: Nas parallel benchmarks, multi-zone versions. NASA Ames Research Center, Tech. Rep. NAS-03-010 (2003)
6. Intel@ Xeon Phi^{TM} Coprocessor, http://software.intel.com/mic-developer
7. Jeffers, J., Reinders, J.: Intel Xeon Phi Coprocessor High Performance Programming. Morgan Kaufmann (2013)
8. Jin, H., Van der, W.: Performance characteristics of the multi-zone NAS parallel benchmarks. J. Parallel and Distributed Computing 66(5), 674–685(2006)
9. Newburn, C.J., Deodhar, R., Dmitriev, S.: Offload Compiler Runtime for the Intel® Xeon Phi^{TM} Coprocessor

An Effective Framework of Program Optimization for High Performance Computing

Pingjing Lu, Bao Li, Zhengbin Pang, Ying Zhang, Shaogang Wang, Jinbo Xu, and Yan Liu

School of Computer, National University of Defense Technology
Changsha 410073, China
{pingjinglu,sibaoli,zhbpang,zhying,shgwang,xujinbo,yliu}@nudt.edu.cn

Abstract. The increasing complexity of modern architectures and memory models challenges the design of optimizing compilers. It is mandatory to perform several optimizing transformations of the original program to exploit the machine to its best, especially for scientific, computational intensive codes. Aiming at investigating the best transformation sequence and the best transformation parameters simultaneously, this paper combines polyhedral model and empirical search to create a powerful optimization framework that is capable of fully automated non-parametric transformations and automatic parameter search. The framework employs polyhedral model to facilitate the search of non-parametric code transformation composition, and designs uses Genetic Algorithms to find the optimal parameters. The framework is demonstrated on three typical computational kernels for code transformations to achieve performance that greatly exceeds the native compiler, and is significantly better than state-of-the-art polyhedral model based loop transformations and iterative compilation, generating efficient code on complex loop nests.

Keywords: program optimization, loop transformation, polyhedral model, empirical search.

1 Introduction

Although loop transformations have been applied by compilers for many years, certain problems with the application of transformations have yet to be addressed, including when, where and in what order to apply transformations to get the most benefit, as well as the selection of optimal transformation parameters.

Existing compilers are ill-equipped to address these challenges, because of improper program representations and inappropriate conditioning of the search space structure. They are based on static analysis and a hardwired compilation strategy; therefore they only uncover a fraction of the peak performance on typical benchmarks. Iterative compilation [1] is a maturing framework to address these limitations, but so far, it was not successfully applied because present day iterative compilation approaches select the optimal transformation parameters

W. Xu et al. (Eds.): NCCET 2013, CCIS 396, pp. 153–162, 2013.

at a predefined transformation sequence, and because of the high cost due to multiple, costly "runs" and the combinatorics of the optimization space. The ability to perform numerous compositions of program transformations is key to the extension of iterative optimizations to finding the appropriate program transformations instead of just the appropriate program transformation parameters. The polyhedral model is a well studied, powerful mathematical framework to represent loop nests and their transformations [2][3][5], facilitating compilers to compose complex loop transformations in a mathematically rigorous way to insure code correctness. However existing polyhedral frameworks are often too limited in supporting a wide array of loop transformations required to achieve high performance on today's computer architecture, and they don't allow exploring jointly the best sequence of transformations and the best value of transformation parameters. Usually, the community tries to find the "best" parameter combination when the transformation sequence is fixed [4]. Clearly, there is a need for the infrastructure that can apply long compositions of transformations and find the best transformation parameters in a rich, structured search space.

This paper presents a optimization framework to simultaneously explore the best sequence of transformations and the best value of transformations parameters. It integrates polyhedral model and Genetic Algorithm (GA) based empirical search to create a powerful framework that is capable of fully automated non-parametric code transformations and automatic parameter search. Experimental results validate the effectiveness of our framework.

2   Formal Description

Let P be the source program, τ an arbitrary performance evaluation function (not limited to program execution time, it can be cache miss rate etc.), Ψ a finite set of loop transformations, including l parametric transformation modules $\varphi_i \in \Psi(i = 1, 2, \ldots, l)$. Denote $\circ$ the transformation joint symbol, then applying a finite sequence $\varphi_1, \ldots, \varphi_n$ of transformation modules to P can be represented as $\phi = \varphi_n \circ \varphi_{n-1} \circ \ldots \circ \varphi_1$, and all the sequences form optimization sequence space Φ. Parametric module φ_i contains m_i transformation parameters: $p_{ik} \in Z(k = 1, 2, \ldots, m_i)$, and its upper bound $up_{ik} \in Z$ and lower bound $low_{ik} \in Z$ can be achieved based on domain-specific information. Denote $v = \sum_{i=1}^{l} m_i$, then the optimization parameters $(p_{11}, \cdots, p_{1m_1}, \cdots, p_{l1}, \cdots, p_{lm_l})$ of all parametric transformation modules constitute optimization parameter vector $\overrightarrow{K} \in Z^v$. Applying transformation sequence ϕ to P and adopting optimization parameter vector $\overrightarrow{K}$ results in the program $P' = \phi(P, \overrightarrow{K})$, and the corresponding test result is $\tau(P, \phi, \overrightarrow{K})$. Then the optimal loop transformations problem converts to a combinational optimization problem: having a program P and a set of loop transformation modules Ψ, how to select the optimal transformation sequence ϕ^* and the optimal parameter vector $\overrightarrow{K}$, such that the performance of the final generated program P^* is "optimal" i.e.

$$(\phi^*, \overrightarrow{K}^*) = \arg\min \tau(P, \phi, \overrightarrow{K})$$
$$subject \quad to \quad \begin{cases} \phi \in \Phi \\ \overrightarrow{K} \in Z^v \end{cases} \quad (1)$$

Where $\arg\min$ means that $(\phi^*, \overrightarrow{K}^*)$ are the optimal value of parameters ϕ and $\overrightarrow{K}$ that minimize the object function $\tau(P, \phi, \overrightarrow{K})$, and *subject   to* introduces the requirements that ϕ and $\overrightarrow{K}$ have to satisfy.

3   Polyhedral Model

The polyhedral model is a unified mathematical framework to represent loop nests and their transformations. It represents the code through the iteration domain, affine schedules, and array access functions [3]. We will briefly introduce polyhedral model through matrix multiplication program.

```
for (i = 0; i <= M; i++) {
  for (j = 0; j <= M; j++) {
  S₁: C[i][j] = 0;
    for (k = 0; k <= M; k++) {
  S₂: C[i][j]=C[i][j]+A[i][k]* B[k][j];}}}
```

Fig. 1. Code for matrix multiplication program

3.1   Iteration Domain

Iteration domain is a geometrical abstraction of loop bounds and strides shaping loop structures. The loop control statements surrounding statement S form iteration domain D^S. It can be defined through a set of affine inequalities, which form the parametric polyhedra. Each point in the polyhedra stands for one execution instance. Iteration domain depends on surrounding loop counters and global parameters (e.g. loop bounds). E.g., in Fig.1, surrounding loop counters of statement S_2 is i, j and k, and the scope of loop is bounded by (M, M, M), therefore, the iteration domain of S_2 can be represented as Eq. (2), where (i, j, k) is called an iteration vector, and (M) is called a global parameter.

$$D^{S_2} = \begin{pmatrix} 1 & 0 & 0 & 0 & 0 \\ -1 & 0 & 0 & 1 & 0 \\ 0 & 1 & 0 & 0 & 0 \\ 0 & -1 & 0 & 1 & 0 \\ 0 & 0 & 1 & 0 & 0 \\ 0 & 0 & -1 & 1 & 0 \end{pmatrix} \begin{pmatrix} i \\ j \\ k \\ M \\ 1 \end{pmatrix} \geq \overrightarrow{0} \quad (2)$$

Where $\overrightarrow{0}$ is a vector, and in Formulae (2) $\overrightarrow{0} = (0, 0, 0, 0, 0)^t$.

3.2   Array Access Functions

Array access functions capture the data locations on which a statement operates. In polyhedral model, memory accesses are performed through array references (a variable being a particular case of an array). We restrict ourselves to subscripts of the form of affine expressions which may depend on surrounding loop counters (e.g., i, j and k for statement S_2) and global parameters. Each *Array access functions* is linked to an array that represents a read or a write access.

L^S and R^S are sets of polyhedral representations of array references, describing array references written by S (left-hand side) or read by S (right-hand side), respectively; it is a set of pairs (A, f) where A is an array variable and f is the access function mapping iterations in D^S to locations in A. E.g., in Fig. 1, S_2 reads A[i][k], B[k][j] and C[i][j], and writes the result to C[i][j], so the array access functions of S_2 are:

$$R^{S_2} = \{(A, \begin{bmatrix} 10000 \\ 00100 \end{bmatrix}), (B, \begin{bmatrix} 00100 \\ 01000 \end{bmatrix}), (C, \begin{bmatrix} 10000 \\ 01000 \end{bmatrix})\} \tag{3}$$

$$L^{S_2} = \{(C, \begin{bmatrix} 10000 \\ 01000 \end{bmatrix})\} \tag{4}$$

3.3   Affine Scheduling

θ^S is the *Affine schedule* of S; it is another geometrical abstraction of the ordering of iterations and statements which maps iterations in D^S to multidimensional time stamps, i.e., logical execution dates. Multidimensional time stamps are compared through the lexicographic ordering over vectors, denoted by $\ll$: iteration $\overrightarrow{i}$ of S is executed before iteration $\overrightarrow{i}'$ of S' if and only if $\theta^S(\overrightarrow{i}) \ll \theta^{S'}(\overrightarrow{i}')$. In Fig. 1 the affine schedule of S_1 and S_2 are $\theta^{S_1}(\overrightarrow{i}) = (0, i, 0, j, 0)$, $\theta^{S_2}(\overrightarrow{i}) = (0, i, 0, j, 1, k, 0)$. $\theta^{S_1}(\overrightarrow{i}) \ll \theta^{S_2}(\overrightarrow{i})$, therefore, S_1 executes before S_2.

Assume the loop nest includes d statements, the schedule dimension is s, the iteration vector is $\overrightarrow{x}$, the global parameter is $\overrightarrow{n}$, then each program version can be represented as one point in the optimization space through schedule matrix Θ [5]:

$$\Theta\overrightarrow{x} = \begin{pmatrix} \overrightarrow{i}^1_1 \cdots \overrightarrow{i}^1_d \overrightarrow{p}^1_1 \cdots \overrightarrow{p}^1_d c^1_1 \cdots c^1_d \\ \vdots \\ \overrightarrow{i}^s_1 \cdots \overrightarrow{i}^s_d \overrightarrow{p}^s_1 \cdots \overrightarrow{p}^s_d c^s_1 \cdots c^s_d \end{pmatrix} \begin{pmatrix} \overrightarrow{x}_1 \\ \vdots \\ \overrightarrow{x}_d \\ \overrightarrow{n}_1 \\ \vdots \\ \overrightarrow{n}_d \\ 1 \\ \vdots \\ 1 \end{pmatrix} \tag{5}$$

We can see that in polyhedral model each loop transformation corresponds to a set of matrix operation. An arbitrary complex loop transformation sequence can be applied within one step. Searching the compositions of transformations is equivalent to searching the matrix parameters, therefore, polyhedral model avoids the typical code complexity explosion of long compositions of program transformations, facilitating the composition of complex loop transformations in a mathematically rigorous way.

4   Genetic Algorithm Based Empirical Search

High level program transformations are critical in optimizing the performance of compiled code. Many of these transformations need numerical parameters, which should be carefully selected. Determining the best value of parameter has been a long standing problem in compilers. Iterative compilation approach is a practical means to implement architecture-aware optimizations for high performance applications, outperforming static compilation approaches significantly. Iterative compilation approach generates different program versions, and selects the one that gives the best performance by actually running them on target hardware and using certain search strategies. However, because the optimization spaces (set of all possible program transformations) are large, non-linear with many local minima, finding a good solution may be long and non-trivial, making iterative method quite time consuming.

Genetic algorithm is a class of heuristic biased sampling approach to searching large spaces, which searches only a small portion of the optimization space. This paper utilizes GA to search for the best value for parameterized transformation. GA was invented by John Holland in 1975 [8], which is based on Darwin's principle of evolution and survival of the fittest. GA firstly randomly initializes some number of individual solutions to form an initial population, and then evaluate the fitness value of each chromosome. And then GA performs crossover and mutation to generate a new population from the current chromosomes. The algorithm terminates when some pre-determined termination condition is reached, and outputs the best solution found during the algorithm. The GA based empirical search algorithm is as follows.

Step 1: Initialization. Read the input parameter, and randomly initialize individual solutions to form the initial population Pop_0.

Step 2: Evaluation. For each individual S in the population, take its integral encoding as the parameter and generate the parameter file $paraFile$, run the program, and obtain the execution time $T(S)$.

Step 3: Selection. We use roulette wheel selection scheme and elitists reserved policy for selection. First, a small proportion of individuals, namely elitists, are selected from current population, and are put to the next generation directly. And then select the other individuals based on roulette wheel selection scheme. The proportion of elitists to population size is noted as E_{litist}

Step 4: Reproduction. Perform Arithmetical *crossover* and *mutation* to generate a new population from the current chromosomes. For the new generated individual, take its integral encoding as the parameter and generate the parameter file $paraFile$, run the program, and obtain the execution time.

Step 5: Check Termination. Terminating conditions include: the desired performance is reached, or maximum generation of GA is elapsed. If terminating conditions is conformed, turn to Step 6; otherwise, turn to Step 3.

Step 6: Output. Output the best individual the best solution found during the algorithm.

5   Performance Evaluation

5.1   Environmental Setup

We test matrix multiplication program (mm) with matrix sizes 512 and 1024. Experiments are performed on platform Intel Pentium D 820 listed in Tab.1. Parameter settings for GA are as follows: population size is 50 and the maximum generation is 30, selection pressure is 1.6, E_{litist} is 0.05, crossover probability is 0.2, and mutation probability is 0.05.

Table 1. Experimental platform

CPU	Intel Pentium D 820 2.8 GHz
L1Data cache	2×16(KB)
L1 Instruction cache	2×12 (KB)
L2 cache	2×1024 (KB)
Memory	DDR2 1G
OS	Ubuntu kernel 2.6.15-23-386
Compiler	gcc 4.2.1 -O3 -Dtest_malloc -lm

5.2   Experimental Results

Performance Result after Optimization with Polyhedral Model. This paper makes use of polyhedral transformation tools LeTSeE [6] to apply iterative compilation based on polyhedral model and find the best non-parametric transformation sequence. LeTSeE first builds a search space encompassing legal and distinct program versions, thanks to its algebraic representation, and then traverses the search space, where each point represents a different program version. For each tested point in the search space, it (1) generates the kernel C code with CLooG [7] (2) then integrates this kernel in the original benchmark along with instrumentation to measure running time (3) compiles this code with the native compiler and appropriate options (4) finally run the program on the target architecture and gather performance results, use the information collected to drive the exploration according to user objectives. The transformations implemented in LeTSeE include statement reordering, loop reversal, loop skewing, loop interchange, loop peeling, index-set splitting, loop pipelining/shifting, loop fusion and loop distribution. LeTSeE will generate the best non-parametric transformation sequence. The codes for best transformation with polyhedral mode of mm512 and mm1024 are shown in Fig. 2, from which we can see that by using polyhedral model programs are applied various complex transformations.

```
for (i=0;i<=N;i++) {
    for (j=0;j<=N;j++) {
        S1(i,j) ;     }  }
    for (c1=N+1;c1<=2*N+1;c1++) {
        for (i=0;i<=N;i++) {
            for (j=0;j<=N;j++) {
                S2(i,j,c1-N-1) ; } } }
```

(a) mm512

```
for (c1=-1;c1<=M-1;c1++) {
    for (j=0;j<=M;j++) {
        S1(c1+1,j) ;     }  }
    for (c1=M;c1<=2*M;c1++) {
        for (i=0;i<=M;i++) {
            for (j=0;j<=M;j++) {
                S2(i,j,c1-M) ; } } }
```

(b) mm1024

Fig. 2. The code for best transformation with polyhedral model

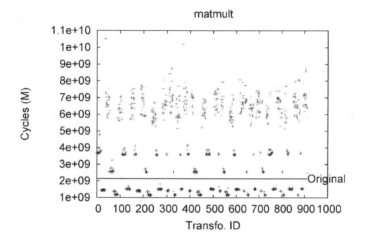

Fig. 3. mm512 performance result with LetSee

Fig.3 and Fig. 4 demonstrate the performance result with LetSee of mm512 and mm1024 respectively, from which we can see that by using polyhedral model the best code version is selected from huge optimization space and the performance of best transformation can greatly improve programs' performance.

Performance Result after Optimization with GA Based Empirical Search. After optimizing programs with polyhedral model, we further employs GA to select the optimal transformation parameters, and finally achieves the best transformation parameters in the best transformation sequence. Fig.5 shows the code for best transformation by combining polyhedral model and empirical search.

Fig.6 compares the performance of original program, optimized program with polyhedral model, and optimized program by combining polyhedral model and empirical search. From Fig.6, we can see that by combining polyhedral model and empirical search, the performance is greatly improved.

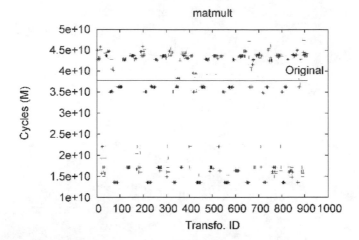

Fig. 4. mm1024 performance result with LetSee

```
for (i=0;i<=N;i++) {
    for (j=0;j<=N;j++) {
        S1(i,j) ;       }   }
for (ii=0;ii<=N;ii+=ct1){
    for (jj=0;jj<=N;jj+=ct2){
        for (c1=N+1;c1<=2*N+1;c1++){
            for (i=ii;i<=min(ii+ct1-1,N);i++){
                for (j=jj;j<=min(jj+ct2-1,N);j++){
                    S2(i,j,c1-N-1) ;}}}}}
```

(a) mm512

```
for (c1=-1;c1<=N-1;c1++) {
    for (j=0;j<=N;j++) {
        S1(c1+1,j) ; } }
for (ii=0;ii<=N;ii+=ct1){
    for (jj=0;jj<=N;jj+=ct2){
        for (c1=N;c1<=2*N;c1++){
            for (i=ii;i<=min(ii+ct1-1,N);i++){
                for (j=jj;j<=min(jj+ct2-1,N);j++){
                    S2(i,j,c1-N) ;}}}}}
```

(b) mm1024

Fig. 5. The code for best transformation by combining polyhedral model and empirical search

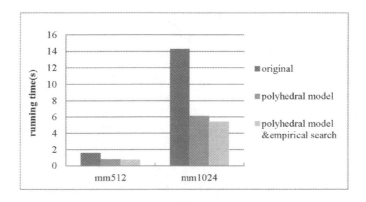

Fig. 6. Performance comparision

6   Related Work and Conclusions

This paper describes a general and robust framework for composing loop transformations for program optimization. We demonstrate the effectiveness of this framework for matrix multiply program that require complex transformations to achieve high performance. As we are developing a framework that supports composition of transformations, the research most closely related to ours is Petit [10], WRaP-IT [7], Pluto [11], CHiLL [9] and LeTSeE. These frameworks all use a polyhedral representation. The main difference of our framework with them is that our work considers a much broader range of loop transformations, and allows exploring the best transformation sequence and best parameter values. By applying this framework to matrix multiply program, we demonstrate that the resulting code quality is quite high than original program and that by only using polyhedral model. These results show that, with a systematic framework, it has now become feasible for compiler-generated code to achieve performance comparable to manually-tuned, even for more complex code constructs than have been previously demonstrated, which makes it a practical and portable means to implement architecture-aware optimizations for high-performance applications.

Acknowledgement. This work was partially supported by the National Natural Science Foundation of China under Grant No. 61103014, No.61003075, No.61202124, and No.61202126, the National High Technology Development 863 Program of China under Grant No. 2012AA01A301.

References

1. Fursin, G.: Iterative Compilation and Performance Prediction for Numerical Applications. Ph.D. Thesis, School of Informatics, The University of Edinburgh, pp. 67–82 (2005)
2. Ananta, T., Chun, C., et al.: Scalable Autotuning Framework for Compiler Optimization. In: Proceedings of the IEEE IPDPS 2009, pp. 1–12 (2009)
3. Feautrier, P.: LCPC, Keynote Speech II: The Polytope Model Past, Present, Future. In: Proceedings of the 22nd International Workshop on Languages and Compilers for Parallel Computing, pp. 4–5 (2009)
4. Sid, T., Denis, B.: On the Decidability of Phase Ordering Problem in Optimizing Compilation. In: Proceedings of the International Conference on Computing Frontiers, pp. 147–156 (2006)
5. Louis, P., Cedric, B., Albert, C., Nicolas, V.: Iterative optimization in the polyhedral model: Part I, one-dimensional time. In: Proceedings of ACM Conf. on Code Generation and Optimization, pp. 144–156 (2007)
6. Louis, P., Cedric, B., Albert, C., Nicolas, V.: Iterative optimization in the polyhedral model: Part II, multidimensional time. In: Proceedings of ACM SIGPLAN Conference on Programming Language Design and Implementation, pp. 90–100 (2008)
7. Sylvain, G., Nicolas, V., Cedric, B., Albert, C., David, P., March, S., Olivier, T.: Semi-automatic composition of loop transformations for deep parallelism and memory hierarchies. Int. J. of Parallel Programming. 34, 261–317 (2006)

 8. Jaume, A., Antonio, G., Josep, L., et al.: Near-Optimal Loop Tiling by means of Cache Miss Equations and Genetic Algorithms. In: Proceedings of Workshop on Compile/Runtime Techniques for Parallel Computing, pp. 568–580 (2002)
 9. Chun, C., Jacqueline, C., Mary, H.: CHiLL: A Framework for Composing High-Level Loop Transformations. Technical report, University of Southern California (2008)
10. Kelly, W., Pugh, W.: A framework for unifying reordering transformations. Tech report, College Park, MD, USA, CS-TR-2995, pp. 1–23 (1993)
11. Bondhugula, U., Hartono, A., Ramanujam, J., Sadayappan, P.: A practical automatic polyhedral program optimization system. In: Proceedings of the 2008 ACM SIGPLAN Conference on Programming Language Design and Implementation, pp. 101–113 (2008)

A Constant Loop Bandwidth Fraction-N Frequency Synthesizer for GNSS Receivers

Dun Yan, Jiancheng Li, Xiaochen Gu, Songting Li, and Chong Huang

School of Electronic Science and Engineering, National University of Defense Technology,
410073 Changsha, China

Abstract. A fully integrated 2.8 GHz to 3.4 GHz frequency synthesizer for satellite navigation RF resciever is implemented in 0.18-μm CMOS process and its area is 0.4 mm^2. A constant and low tuning Gain (K_{VCO}) is achieved by an improved voltage-controlled oscillator (VCO) architecture. The constant loop bandwidth, which is designed to 60 kHz, is implemented by making charge pump current (I_{CP}) match the division ratio N. The synthesizer exhibits phase noise of -85.62 dBc/Hz at 10 KHz offset and -92.78 dBc/Hz at 100 kHz offset, while consuming 18 mW from a 1.8 V supply.

Keywords: Frequency synthesizer, voltage-controlled oscillator (VCO), phase noise, bandwidth.

1 Introduction

As Compass-II provides civil navigational services for Asia-Pacific region since Dec. 2012, multi-constellation Global navigation satellite systems (GNSS) have been achieved formally and the services can be shared through compatible and interoperable collaboration. The growing GNSS market demands lower power and lower cost solutions for integrated receivers. As an essential block of RF receiver, the wideband frequency synthesizer is desired for low power and high performance.

Loop bandwidth affects the capability of GNSS receivers by determining the parameter of the PLL frequency synthesizer, which are phase noise, reference spur and settling time. The system stipulates consistent and stringent phase noise performance over the whole frequency range. However, when output frequency changes to a new frequency or the process, temperature and supply voltage (PVT) bring an offset to the wideband PLL, the bandwidth will lose the optimized state. Until now, the most popular way to get an optimized loop bandwidth is to adopt adaptive [1] and constant loop bandwidth [2]. It is difficult to get the optimized loop bandwidth which limits the use of adaptive loop bandwidth method. Otherwise, A solutions to achieve constant bandwidth is to change charge pump current (I_{CP}) to meet the ratio of VCO tuning gain (K_{VCO}) and division ratio N [3]. The other one is to hold VCO tuning gain (K_{VCO}) overall the output frequency and make I_{CP} to match N [4]. The previous is complicated to achieve due to the difficult to make I_{CP} meet K_{VCO}/N under the influence of PVT. On the contrary it is easy to make I_{CP} match N

W. Xu et al. (Eds.): NCCET 2013, CCIS 396, pp. 163–170, 2013.

and the constant K_{VCO} contribute to the complexity of AFC [5]. Although the constant VCO tuning gain has been achieved in [4], but this method is limited by the process, higher output frequency and lower tuning gain due to particle of varactor.

In this work, a constant loop bandwidth in fraction-N PLL frequency synthesizer is proposed and shown in Fig. 1, which consists of a phase-frequency detector(PFD), a programmable charge pump, a passive loop filter, a constant tuning gain LC-VCO, a programmable divider, an automatic frequency calibration (AFC) block and a 24-bits $\Sigma\Delta$ modulator. Section 2 presents solutions; Section 3 presents the proposed solutions and section 4 show experimental results; Conclusions are in section 5.

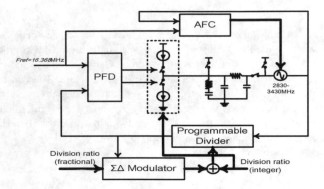

Fig. 1. Architecture of the frequency synthesizer

2   Design Considerations

The PLL loop bandwidth is a very important parameter for loop stability as the PLL system is a closed-loop system, it also affects phase-noise performance variation. So a constant loop bandwidth is demanded in order to minimize the phase-noise variation and stabilize the system over all the wide output frequency range. Generally the open-loop cut-off frequency is selected as bandwidth. For typical forth-order PLL, loop bandwidth is in direct proportion to sink or source current of charge pump (I_{CP}), VCO tuning gain (K_{VCO}) and division ratio N:

$$\omega_c \propto \frac{I_{cp} K_{vco}}{2\pi N}. \tag{1}$$

As discussed previous, the simple way to keep the bandwidth constant is to keep the variety of I_{cp}/N and K_{vco} down.

LC voltage-controlled oscillator is usually employed in frequency synthesizers for RF receivers. The most common way to get wideband output frequency is to achieve closely-spaced multiple frequency tuning curves by employing a switched capacitor bank as shown in Fig. 2(a). Binary weighted capacitor array is switched to shift the output frequency band coarsely while the varactor C_V is controlled by the control voltage to change output frequency continuously.

Fig. 2(b) illustrates typical frequency tuning characteristics of a wideband VCO. VCO tuning gain K_{VCO} is variable for different tuning curves, VCO tuning gain K_{VCO} and frequency spacing $f_{spacing}$ is related to the VCO tuning rang as following [6]:

$$\frac{K_{vco.\,max}}{K_{vco,\,min}} = \frac{f_{spacing,\,max}}{f_{spacing.\,min}} = \left(\frac{f_{o,\,max}}{f_{o,\,min}}\right)^3 . \tag{2}$$

where f_o is the VCO output frequency. Such large variation of $f_{spacing}$ will increase the complexity of structure of AFC.

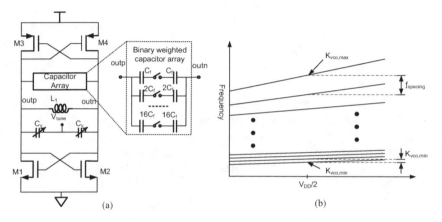

Fig. 2. Conventional topology (a) VCO (b)F-V curve with large variations of K_{VCO}

An improved VCO architecture is presented in [4] to minimize the variations of both the VCO tuning gain and frequency spacing for wideband applications, as shown in fig. 3(a). Instead of using one fixed varactor and a switched capacitor bank, a switched varactor bank and a switched capacitor bank are adopted. At lower frequency bands, more switched capacitor units and more switched varactor are connected into the LC-tank, at the same time, the rest of varactor units are connected to the power supply to get minimum fixed capacitance and the rest of capacitance units are disconnected. The other way round, at higher frequency band, less switched capacitor units and less switched varactor are connected into LC-tank. If a_i ($i=1,2,\cdots,15$) is the ratio of capacitor array units and b_i ($i=1,2,\cdots,15$) is the ratio of varactor array units, so total capacitance $C_{tot,n}$ across the tank at center frequency of the nth sub-band can be expressed as

$$C_{tot,n} = \begin{cases} C_p + C_f + (b_1 + \cdots + b_{n-1})C_{v,\,min} + C_{vn,(0.9)} & (n = 1) \\ C_p + (1 + a_1 + \cdots + a_{n-1})C_f + (b_n + \cdots + b_{15})C_{v,\,min} + (b_1 + \cdots + b_{n-1})C_{vn,(0.9)} & (n = 2,\cdots,14) \\ C_p + (1 + a_1 + \cdots + a_{n-1})C_f + (b_1 + \cdots + b_{n-1})C_{vn,(0.9)} & (n = 15) \end{cases} . \tag{3}$$

In which C_p is the parasitic capacitance and $C_{v,min}$ is minimum capacitance of the varactor, the VCO gain $K_{VCO,n}$ of the nth sub-band can be calculated as

$$K_{VCQn} = \begin{cases} \dfrac{1}{4\pi\sqrt{LC_{tot}^3,_n}} \dfrac{\partial C_v}{\partial V_{tune}}\bigg|_{V_{tune-center}} & (n = 1) \\[4mm] \dfrac{b_i + \cdots + b_{n-1}}{4\pi\sqrt{LC_{tot}^3,_n}} \dfrac{\partial C_v}{\partial V_{tune}}\bigg|_{V_{tune-center}} & (n = 2, \cdots ,15) \end{cases} \tag{4}$$

But as VCO gain $K_{VCO,n}$ is too small or the required center frequency is too high, the varactor units b_iC_V is less than 1 or 2 fF which is too small to be achieved by process. In other words this topology is limited by processes.

3   Circuits Implementations

3.1   Wideband VCO

In order to minimize the VCO tuning gain K_{VCO} and frequency spacing between two adjacent frequency band and to eliminate the limited by processes, a proposed topology is shown in Fig. 3(b). The idea is to use both the switched capacitor bank and switched varactor bank, the varactor C_{V1}, which is the least varactor can be achieved by process, is separated from fixed varactor C_V, and C_{Vi} (i=1,2,$\cdots$,15)can be calculated by formula:

$$C_{Vi} = C_{Va} + b_{i-1}C_V . \tag{5}$$

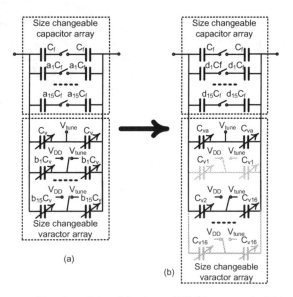

Fig. 3. Improved topology (a) architecture of [4] (b) proposed of this paper

The switched capacitor bank operates as the same with previous architecture and some differences between the switched varactor bank. In this way, only the fixed varactor C_{Va} and switched varactor C_{Vi} are connected to the control voltage, and the rest are connected to the power supply to get minimum sixed capacitance. So total capacitance $C_{tot,n}$ across the tank at the center frequency of the nth sub-band can be expressed as:

$$C_{tot,n} = C_p + (1 + a_1 + \cdots + a_{n-1})C_f + C_{vtot,\min} - C_{vn,\min} + C_{vn,(0.9)} \ (n = 1, \cdots, 16).$$ (6)

Similarly the tuning gain $K_{VCO,n}$ of the nth sub-band can be computed by

$$K_{VCO,n} = \frac{1}{4\pi\sqrt{LC_{tot,n}^3}} \frac{\partial(C_{va} + C_{v,n})}{\partial V_{tune}}\bigg|_{V_{tune-center}} \quad (n = 1, 2 \cdots, 16) \ .$$ (7)

Accordingly, formula and is used to calculate coefficient bi, then C_{V1} is chose to meet the minimize varactor value of the process and the rest of switched varactor is calculated by expression 7. Coefficient bi can be got due to expression. By this way, the VCO tuning gain K_{VCO} and frequency spacing $f_{spacing}$ variations can be greatly reduced immune from the process simultaneously.

3.2   Charge Pump

Due to constant frequency tuning gain, the offset brought by PVT induce no variation of bandwidth. When the output frequency changes to a new frequency by reconfiguring the divider ratio N, the charge pump current will change to match the divider ratio, which indicates the target frequency. So a constant loop bandwidth is achieved by programing the charge pump current (I_{CP}) to make the ratio I_{CP}/N constant.

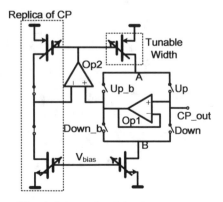

Fig. 4. Schematic of the charge pump

As shown in Fig. 4, some transistor banks can be in parallel with the major current sources and sinks to calibrate the total charging and discharging current via the 4MSBs output of the AFC. Furthermore, the op-amp 1 working as a voltage follower is applied to settle the charge sharing problem [7]. The voltages on parasitic capacitors at nodes A and B are clamped so no charge transfer would occur. To remove current mismatches, the PMOS current sources are biased by op-amp 2 using the self-bias technique to force them to copy the NMOS sink currents precisely [8].

3.3   AFC

AFC is integrated to find an optimal sub-band tuning curve among the curves. Due to the switched capacitor array and switched varactor array, the frequency spacing change ultrafine during the entire output frequency. So the easy way to sense the VCO output center frequency of each tuning curve is to count the output frequency's periodicity per reference period and compare it with the division ratio N, which is indicate the target frequency. The AFC is composed of a frequency detector (PD) and a finite state machine (FSM) as shown in fig. 5.

As the calibration operation starts, the target frequency is represented by multiplying the division ratio N.f and k, which indicates how many reference periods are used to count the VCO frequency. The VCO output frequency is accepted and divided down to $f_{vco}/4$ by a pre-divider. Then the divided signal is counted during k reference periods and a subtractor calculates the frequency error by comparing the count of counter and target frequency k* N.f. Consequently the sign bit indicates whether the frequency of VCO is higher of lower than target frequency. The binary search algorithm simply use the sign bit to adjust the cap code accordingly by the FSM. At the same time, the magnitude of frequency error is compared with the previously stored frequency error to find the min-error code. The least-error code, which represents the optimized code, can be stored by FSM after binary search process. Finally the optimized code is sent to VCO and the PLL loop is closed to achieve phase locking, and AFC is turned off.

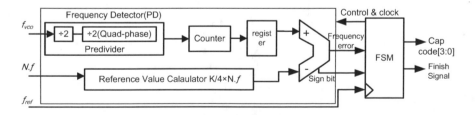

Fig. 5. Diagram of AFC

4   Implementation Results

The fractional-N PLL is fabricated in 0.18-μm CMOS process. The chip micrograph is shown in Fig. 7(b) and the whole frequency synthesizer is 0.4 mm^2. It has been integrated in a GNSS receiver.

The measured VCO tuning rang is 2790 MHz-3480 MHz, which divided by 2 to get 4-phase LO signals for the quadrature mixer to cover the GNSS signal, and closed-loop output frequency is shown in Fig. 6(a). The tuning gain varies from 82 MHz/V to 90 MHz/V, of which the variation is less than 10%.

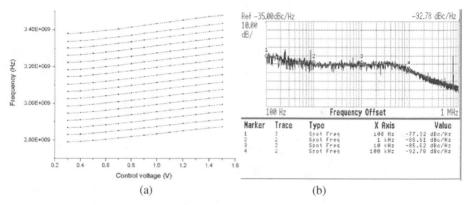

(a)   (b)

Fig. 6. Measured PLL results (a) VCO tuning characteristics (b) Phase noise

The measured phase noise at oscillation frequency of 3130.38 MHz is -85.62 dBc/Hz at 10 kHz offset and -92.8dBc/Hz at 100 KHz offset as shown in Fig. 6(b). The measured bandwidth is shown in Fig. 7(a) which is designed to 60 kHz with a phase margin of 60°. Table I lists the performance comparison of the proposed with other related frequency synthesizers.

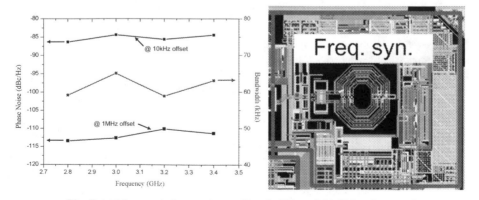

Fig. 7. (a) Measured phase noise and bandwidth and (b) Chip micrograph

Table 1. Comparison of frequency synthesizer

Parameter	This work	Ref. [3]	Ref. [9]	Ref. [10]
Technology	CMOS 180 nm	CMOS 130 nm	CMOS 130 nm	CMOS 130 nm
Center frequency	3.14 GHz	1.48 GHz	3.5 GHz	1.58 GHz
Tuning range	21.7 %	50 %	22.8 %	25 %
Phase noise	-85.62 @ 10 kHz	-93 @ 10 kHz	-82.2@ 10 kHz	-70 @ 100 kHz
(dBc/Hz)	-112 @ 1 MHz	-118 @ 1 MHz	-116 @ 1 MHz	-110 @ 1 MHz
Power (mW)	18	4.5	48	1.2

5   Conclusion

A constant loop bandwidth fractional-N frequency synthesizer for GNSS receivers is reported in this paper, and was fabricated in 0.18-μm CMOS process. A wideband VCO is improved with constant tuning gain which contributes to achieve constant bandwidth. A configurable charge pump with charge sharing and mismatch cancellation is designed to match division ratio to achieve constant bandwidth overall the output frequency and reduces spurs. The frequency synthesizer has been successfully integrated in GNSS RF receivers.

Reference

1. Salvatore, L., Carlo, S., Andrea, B., et al.: Frequency dependence on bias current in 5-GHz CMOS VCOs: Impact on tuning range and flicker noise upconversion. IEEE J. Solid-State Circuits 37(8), 1003–1011 (2002)
2. Kim, J., Horowitz, M.A., Wei, G.Y.: Design of CMOS adaptive bandwidth PLL/DLLs:A general approach. IEEE J. Solid-State Circuits 50, 860 (2003)
3. Xizhen, Y., Shimao, X., Yuhua, J., Qiwu, W., Chengyan, M., Tianchun, Y.: A constant loop bandwidth fractional- frequency synthesizer for GNSS receivers. Journal of Semiconductors 33(4) (2012)
4. Lei, L., Jinghong, C., Yuan, L., Hao, M., Zhangwen, T.: An 18-mW 1.175–2-GHz Frequency Synthesizer with Constant Bandwidth for DVB-T Tuners. IEEE Transactions on Microwave Theory and Techniques 57(4) (April 2009)
5. Jaewook, S., Hyunchol, S.: A fast and high-precision VCO frequency calibration technique for wideband ΔΣ fractional-N frequency synthesizers. IEEE Transactions on Circuits and Systems-I: Regular Papers 57(7) (July 2010)
6. Jongsik, K., Jaewook, S., Seungsoo, K., Hyunchol, S.: A wideband CMOS LC-VCO with linearized coarse tuning characteristics. IEEE Transactions Circuits and Systems-II: Express Briefs 55(5), 399–403 (2008)
7. Rhee, W.: Design of high-performance CMOS charge pumps in phase-locked loops. In: IEEE Int Circuits Syst. Symp., vol. 2, pp. 545–548 (1999)
8. Lee, J., Keel, M., Lim, S., et al.: Charge pump with perfect current matching characteristics in phase-locked loops. Electronics Letters 36, 1907–1908 (2000)
9. Wu, T., Hanumolu, P.K., Mayaram, K.: Method for a constant loop bandwidth in LC. VCO PLL frequency synthesizers. IEEE J. Solid-State Circuits 44, 427 (2009)
10. Cheng, K.W., Natarajan, K., Allstot, D.J.: A current reuse quadrature GPS receiver in 0.13μm CMOS. IEEE J. Solid-State Circuits 45, 510 (2010)

Investigation of Reproducibility and Repeatability Issue on EFT Test at IC Level to Microcontrollers

Jianwei Su[1], Jiancheng Li[2], Jianfei Wu[2], and Chunming Wang[3]

[1] P.O.box 9010 Xiangtan University, 411105 Xiangtan, Hunan, China
[2] National University of Defense Technology, 410073 Changsha, Hunan, China
[3] Freescale Semiconductor Inc., 300457 TEDA, TianJin, China
{away1988,lijc_hh,wujianfei990243}@126.com,
b21150@freescale.com

Abstract. As an important part of EMC, EFT performance at IC level is drawing more and more attentions from IC designers and product engineers. But there is no EFT test standard at IC level exist. CIIM is an influential method proposed for EFT test at IC level and is introduced in this paper. However, this test method is not so perfect and still needs to be improved. Two probes with different internal resistance are tested on a microcontroller to investigate the reproducibility and repeatability issue of the test. It can be very beneficial to the improvement of CIIM test method and the progress of standardization on EFT test at IC level.

Keywords: Microcontroller, EFT, Reproducibility, Repeatability.

1 Introduction

With the widespread usage of modern electronic and electric equipment, the space electromagnetic environment becomes increasingly complex. Electronic and electric devices are suffering from the internal and external electromagnetic interference (EMI). EMC issue is increasingly serious.

At present, EMC research at board level and system level is somewhat mature. A set or test standards are established and EMC approaches such as grounding and shielding are applied. But they are not enough to satisfy the growing concerning of EMC issues. As a key part of modern electronic and electric equipment, ICs are often the source, as well as the victim, of electromagnetic interference. For the continuous decreasing of operation voltage, ICs can withstand less and less noise margin and are more and more susceptible to EMI. Moreover, higher density of IC leads towards higher switch current when IC is working, though the IC's operation voltage is decreased. That is to say ICs get stronger electromagnetic emission ability. So IC's EMC performance has important effects on the EMC of electronic and electric equipment. It is believed that EMC should be focused early at IC level.

Nowadays, EMC performance is becoming another important quality indicator of IC products. Some test standards have been established to quantify the EMC performance at IC level. Methods are specified in IEC 61967 [1] to evaluate the

W. Xu et al. (Eds.): NCCET 2013, CCIS 396, pp. 171–179, 2013.
© Springer-Verlag Berlin Heidelberg 2013

electromagnetic emissions (EME) of ICs and in IEC 62132 [2] to evaluate the electromagnetic susceptibility (EMS) of ICs. The frequency range of those test methods is mostly 150 KHz to 1 GHz while some methods' frequency range can be extended. For example, the measurement range of GTEM cell can extend up to 18 GHz. But there is no test standard exist to evaluate the ICs' transient immunity such as electrostatic discharges (ESD) and electrical fast transient (EFT). A strong demand exists to close this gap and some methods have been proposed in [3-5]. But those methods proposed are not so perfect and little comparability can be found among those test methods.

So far, the evaluation of EMC performance can only rely on EMC testing. However, it is well known that all EMC tests suffer from reproducibility and repeatability problems. A test result uncertainty can be calculated for emission tests while there is no effective method to evaluate the reproducibility or repeatability of the transient immunity tests. In the transient immunity test, the test results may repeat badly if different generators or probes are used, even though the generators or probes all meet the specification of the test standard.

So, an experiment is conducted to investigate the repeatability and reproducibility issue of the CIIM test method [4], a test method proposed to characterize the EFT performance of the ICs. Two probes with different internal resistance are used in this experiment and a further analysis of the two probe's test results is presented in this paper. It can be either beneficial to the improvement of CIIM test method or helpful to the progress of standardization on EFT test method at IC level.

The CIIM test method is briefly introduced in section 2. Section 3 gives a disruption of the experiment and the results. The analysis of the results is presented in section 5 and conclusions are given in section 6.

2   EFT Test Method at IC Level

Electrical fast transient (EFT) test is an important part of the transient immunity test and is a main concern of the EMC problem at system level. EFT is a test that difficult to pass. During system level EFT tests or a real EFT event occurs, disturbance signal can couple into the power supply pins or signal pins of the ICs in the system through different coupling mode (magnetic coupling and electric coupling mode) [6]. They may affect the ICs' normal function which can cause temporary malfunctions or even permanent damages to the ICs. And eventually leads to the fail of the test. Therefore, the system engineers request IC manufacturers to provide the IC level EFT performance of the ICs they used in the system, so that they can estimate the final EFT performance of the system and get their products easier to pass the system level EFT test.

Conducted impulse injection method (CIIM) is an important test method proposed by Günther Auderer to characterize the EFT performance of ICs [4]. This test method can be realized by the Langer IC EFT testing platform [7] which designed by Langer EMV - Technik GmbH from Germany. The block diagram of Langer IC EFT testing platform is shown in figure 1.

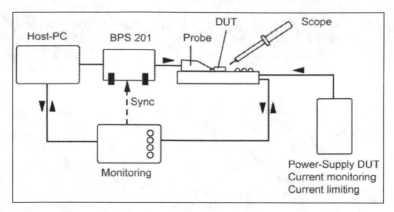

Fig. 1. Block diagram of Langer IC EFT test platform

In this test platform, the device under test (DUT), the IC to be tested, is soldered on a multilayer test board. The test board is embedded in a massive ground plane. The probe tip contacts with the pin of the IC to be tested directly and the probe gets well contacted with the massive ground plane by the magnet in the bottom side of the probe to minimize the current loop-back area. All this guarantees an excellent ground connection which can provide a correct measurement up to the GHz range. The probe is powered by the burst power station BPS201. A host-PC is connected with the BPS201 and can control the parameters of the disturbance signal such as disturbance voltage level, disturbance polarity and burst frequency. During the test, the DUT gets supplied by an external power supply and the test code is operated to detect the software error when the disturbance is injected. The operation status or the software error can be monitored by the different blink combination of the LEDs on the monitor board. Increasing the disturbance voltage level step by step until the voltage limit of the probe or permanent damage occurs on the DUT.

Langer IC EFT provides two series of probes: P200 series and P300 series. P201 and P211 probe from P200 series are current injection probes to simulate the magnetic coupling disturbance to an IC pin. Those two probes have the characteristics of low internal resistance and high coupling capacitance. As to P301 and P311 probe from P300 series, they are voltage injection probes to simulate the electric coupling disturbance to an IC pin. Contrary to P200 series, those two probes have the characteristics of lower coupling capacitance but higher internal resistance. The technical characteristics of those four probes are shown as table 1.

Table 1. Technical characteristics of the four probes

Probe	Pulse shape (rise time/duration)	Coupling capacitance	Internal resistance	Pulse voltage
P201	1.5/5 ns	1.2μF	1Ω	±4.5~36
P211	1.5/5 ns	1.2μF	1Ω	±0.5~5
P301	1.5/20 ns	18pF	100Ω	±140~480
P311	1.5/20 ns	18pF	100Ω	±5~140

In this paper, two P201 probe with different internal resistance are chosen to generate this experiment. The typical waveforms of a single burst of P201 are shown in figure 2.

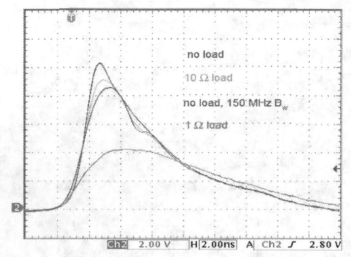

Fig. 2. Waveform of P201 with different load

The waveform of this test method is in accordance with waveform characteristics in system level, which is defined in test standard IEC 61000-4-4 [8]. So the test results of this method can gain high correlation with the results in final system level. For the EFT test with P201, we set a voltage step size of 2V. The burst repetition frequency is 10 KHz and the pulse number is 65535 for each test level, namely the interference burst duration is 6.5525s.

3 Experiment and the Results

We got two P201 probes provided by Langer for this experiment. From the information Langer provided, those 2 probes only have about 16% difference in their internal resistance, which is within the technical specification. We marked the probe with higher internal resistance as P1, while marked the other one as P2.

To analysis the influence of the two probes on the test results, we got them experimented on a microcontroller. The microcontroller we used in the test is designed in 90 nm process with 64 pin LQFP package. The I/Os of this microcontroller use a distributed boosted ESD power rail active MOSFET clamp protection structure, which is widely used in modern I/O protection design. We tested 5 samples (S1 to S5) for each tested pin per polarity.

In terms of the loss of function or degradation of performance of the IC under test, the test results are classified into five grades: A, B, C, D, E. We use different colors to distinguish the five type failures. The representing color and the description of the five grades are shown in table 2.

Table 2. Results representing and description

Result	Color	Description
A		DUT performs as designed during and after exposure of EFT-Burst
B		DUT doesn't perform as designed during exposure, but can return to normal operation after EFT-Burst exposure is removed
C		DUT doesn't perform as designed during exposure. DUT doesn't return to normal until exposure is removed and reset pin is asserted
D		DUT doesn't perform as designed during exposure. DUT doesn't return to normal until exposure is removed and power to DUT is cycled
E		DUT doesn't perform as designed during exposure and can't return to normal due to physical damage or other permanent performance degradation

We picked out the test results listed, such as pin VREFL negative injection shown in figure 3, pin RESET positive injection shown in figure 4 and pin VDD positive injection shown in figure 5.

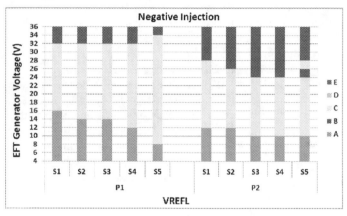

Fig. 3. Results of pin VREFL, negative injection

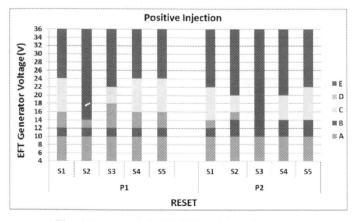

Fig. 4. Results of pin RESET, positive injection

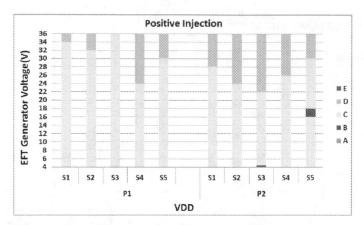

Fig. 5. Results of pin VDD, positive injection

For the analysis of the experiment, we should figure out the final results from the five samples with a certain criterion. Take E as the key consideration, a principle is established for how to figure out the final results as follows:

a.) For the results contains E failure: group the five results by the E failure level within the range of 1 step, and ensure that as much as possible the results can be contained in one group. If five results within one group, the lowest level of this group is the final result. If four results fall in one group and the 5th sample results is defined as outlier, the final result should be the lowest level of the group with four results. If the three results grouped within a range while the rest results grouped in another range, and the maximum voltage level and the minimum voltage level differs with 3 steps, the lowest voltage level of the five results should be reported as the final result. Other cases besides that mentioned above, an in-depth analysis such as check the test configuration or confirm with the designer is needed.

b.) For the results doesn't contain E failure: the worst case should be reported as the final result for each voltage level with the priority of D, C, B, A.

The final results figured out are shown in figure 6.

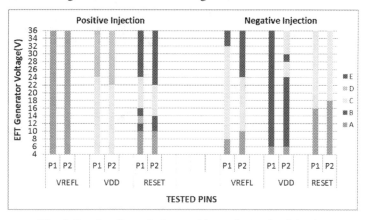

Fig. 6. Results of tested pins, positive and negative injection

4   Discussion and Analysis

From the results we got above, we find that the failure level of P2' is worse than P1's in general. Especially E type failure level on pin RESET positive injection and pin VREFL negative injection, D type failure level on pin VDD positive injection, C type failure on VDD negative injection. That meets our original imagine: lower probe internal resistance lead to worse failure level because of the higher injection current. While there are also some results that don't meet our original imagine. For example, C type failure on pin RESET negative injection.

Also, reproducibility and repeatability issue can be easily found. They are discussed and analyzed as follows:

4.1   Poor Repeatability of B, C, D Type Failure on Each Probe

Repeatability issue can be easily found from figure 3, 4 and 5 on each probe. For E type failure level, the variation range is within 2 steps, which is acceptable. But for D type failure on pin VDD positive injection and C type failure on pin VREFL negative injection, the variation range can be up to 6 steps and 4 steps respectively. And even some B and C type failure occurs occasionally in the five tested samples, such as the results of pin RESET positive injection and pin VDD positive injection. That means B, C, and D type failure get poor repeatability. But what is the root cause?

Many factors can influence the repeatability of the test during EMC testing. In this experiment, what we want to test is the probe, instead of the DUT. So the main influencing factor can be listed as follows: ambient conditions, test equipment, DUT and test method.

The ambient conditions of the lab ate strictly controlled during the test. And every the five samples can be tested in a very short period of time so that the ambient conditions cannot change too much to influence the test. All the test equipments used in the test are also well calibrated at regular intervals. Though slightly difference of the DUT is acceptable for the imperfect of the process, the factor of DUT can be removed because of the acceptable repeatability of E type failure can be found in the test. So the root cause may lay in the test method.

After further analysis, we find that the defined B, C and D type failure are related to the software. They are software failure. CIIM test method operates in asynchronous mode: the execution of test code is asynchronous with the injection of the disturbance signal. During each test, the executed instructions are different when disturbance pulse injects. So the asynchronous operation mode of the test may be the root cause of the poor repeatability of B, C and D type failure.

But for the condition is not permit to conduct an experiment with synchronous mode at present, so we cannot verify it. It would remain to be a part of our later study.

4.2   Bad Reproducibility of E Type Failure Level of the Two Probes

We can get an overview of the results first from figure 6. Disappointedly, bad reproducibility can be found from the results.

For E type failure gets a good repeatability and E type failure is our main concern in the five type failures, we shall figure out the correlation between the two probes' E type failure level. The E type failure level of P2 dropped 1 step by 7.7% on pin RESET positive injection while dropped 4 steps by 12.5% on pin VREFL negative injection compared to P1's. That means no correlations can be found between the two probes' E type failure level. But what should be responsible for it?

As we analyzed above, the test ambient and the test equipment have little influence to the test results in this test. So we should find the answer from DUT and the test method. Different to B, C, and D type failure, E type failure is mainly caused by the electrical over stress (EOS) of I/O protection structure of the tested IC. So the poor correlation may have something to do with the I/O protection circuit of the tested IC. The I/O protection structure of the tested IC is shown in figure 7.

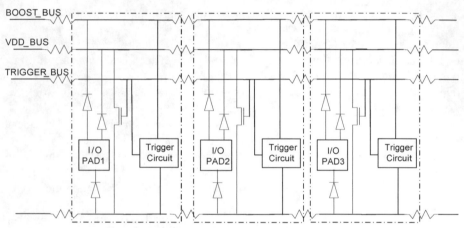

Fig. 7. I/O protection structure of the tested IC

This kind of distributed protection structure is widely used in modern I/O design. Each I/O protection unit contains a trigger circuit and an active MOSFET clamp and they are connected by four whole chip buses forming a pad ring. The design of the pad ring has important influence on the transient immunity performance.

In fact, when EFT event occurs on an I/O PAD, not only the protection unit of this I/O works but the entire protection structure works together. However, only several protection units beside the pin encounter EFT event involved because of the parasitic resistance, capacitance and inductance on the buses. That means different location of the I/O in the pad ring get different current path for the disturbance signal, so their response to the change of the probe's internal resistance may be nonlinear. Sequentially, little correlation can be found between different probes.

So a conclusion can be drawn that bad reproducibility we get when probes with different internal resistance are used in the test. Moreover, poor correlation can be found between the results of the two probes for the reason of the I/O protection structure.

5   Conclusion

An EFT test method at IC level is introduced and two probes with different internal resistance are tested to study the reproducibility and repeatability issue of this test method in this paper. For each probe, only E type failure gets good repeatability while B, C, and D type failure get poor repeatability. A root cause of asynchronous operation mode of the test method is analyzed for the poor repeatability of B, C, D type failure. Besides, bad reproducibility the test gets when different probe is used for the decrease of probe's internal resistance leads to lower failure voltage level. But little correlation can be found between the two probes and a relationship with the I/O protection structure is analyzed.

The research in this paper would be constructive to the standardization of EFT test method at IC level. Also it can be helpful in the I/O protection design.

References

1. IEC 61967: Integrated circuits - Measurement of Electromagnetic Emissions, 150 kHz to 1 GHz. Standard, International Electro-Technical Commission (2004)
2. IEC 62132: Integrated circuits - Measurement of Electromagnetic Immunity, 150 kHz to 1 GHz. Standard, International Electro-Technical Commission (2004)
3. IEC 62215: Integrated circuits - Measurement of Impulse Immunity. Standard Proposal, International Electro-Technical Commission (2005)
4. Auderer, G.: Conducted Impulse Injection Method (CIIM). In: Proceedings of the 5th International Workshop on Electromagnetic Compatibility of Integrated Circuits (2005)
5. Musolino, F., Fiori, F.: Investigation on the susceptibility of microcontrollers to EFT interference. In: IEEE International Symposium on Electromagnetic Compatibility, pp. 410–413. IEEE Press, Chicago (2005)
6. Deutschmann, B., Langer, G., Auderer, G.: Characterizing the Immunity of Integrated Circuits against Electrical Fast Transient Disturbances, http://www.langer-emv.de
7. Guideline IC EFT test, http://www.langer-emv.de
8. IEC 61000-4-4, Electromagnetic Compatibility (EMC)-Part 4-4: Testing and Measurement Techniques - Electrical Fast Transient/Burst Immunity Test. Standard, International Electro-technical Commission (2001)

A Scan Chain Based SEU Test Method
for Microprocessors

Yaqing Chi[1,2,*], Yibai He[1], Bin Liang[1], and Chunmei Hu[1]

[1] College of Computer, National University of Defense Technology,
Deya Str. 109, Changsha, 410073, P.R. China
[2] National Key Laboratory of Science and Technology
on Reliability Physics and Application Technology of Electrical Component,
Dongguanzhuang Str. 110, Guanzhou, 510610, P.R. China
yqchi@nudt.edu.cn

Abstract. A test method based on the scan chain technique is proposed to evaluate the single event upset performance for all the flip-flops in the microprocessors. The single event upset (SEU) performance of a digital signal processor is evaluated using the proposed method and program test method with different working frequencies. Heavy ion irradiation experiment results show that this method is able to capture all the SEUs in the whole chip with no escape and has few infections from the single event transients, which is helpful to study the SEUs precisely in the complicated processors.

Keywords: single event upset, scan chain, microprocessor, heavy ion.

1   Introduction

Single Event effect (SEE) induced by heavy ion irradiation has become a terrible soft error problem for the advanced processors working in the outer space, such as the PowerPC 750 CPU driving the Mars Curiosity Rover. Among all the radiation effects, the single event upset (SEU) is considered to make a major contribution to the global soft error[1]. So the SEU susceptibility evaluation is an essential task for the processors used in space to determine their applied environments before launch.

Usually, the SEU susceptibility evaluation experiments of the complicated processors are carried out by specific test programs, which repeat running calculation processes and reading the results, or reading the data stored in the internal memories to identify the SEU occurred in the calculation units and memories [2-4]. However, only limited flip-flops (FFs) and memories in the processors are accessed and a lot of upsets in the sequential logic cannot be captured directly by the test programs, leading to a reduced SEU cross-section. Design of dedicated test chips for irradiation test is commonly adopted as an additional strategy to evaluate the SEU performance of internal FFs [5-6]. Unfortunately, enormous amount of the same FFs should be

---

* Corresponding author.

W. Xu et al. (Eds.): NCCET 2013, CCIS 396, pp. 180–185, 2013.

implemented in the test chip to improve the statistical accuracy, resulting in extra budget and design time. Furthermore, the distribution and relative distances of the FFs arranged in the test chip are obviously different from the ones placed in the realized processor, which may affect the irradiation test results different between the test chip and realized processor.

In this paper, a test method based on the scan chain technique is proposed to evaluate the SEU performance for the microprocessors. In the scan mode, all the FFs in a processor are configured as several shift register chains, so that all the defects of the transistors in the processor can be detected according to the output data. Under this mode, we captured all the SEU events of the FFs in a microprocessor during the ground heavy ion irradiation test.

2   Scan Chain Based Method

Scan chain is a widely adopted design-for-test (DFT) technique for the processors. This technique facilitates the defect detection by interconnecting nearly all of the flip-flops into one or multiple shift register chains when the scan mode is configured.

Fig. 1 illustrates the schematic diagram of the scan chain design. By setting the signal SCAN_EN high, the circuit operates in the scan mode, and the FFs with multiplexer and some drive buffers are organized into scan chains between ports SCANIN and SCANOUT. A data pattern, such as "static-0" or "static-1", can be loaded into the shift register from port SCANIN. The data sequence will propagate through the chain under the control of CLK until reaching the port SCANOUT. When the heavy ion irradiation upsets a FF, the upset value will also be shifted to the port SCANOUT. So the number of SEUs occurring in the FF chain can be obtained by comparing the data observed at the port SCANOUT with the original ones loaded into port SCANIN.

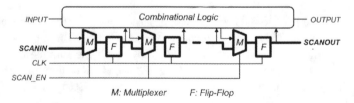

Fig. 1. Schematic diagram of the scan chain design. Bold regions correspond to the data path in the scan mode.

3   Experimental Setup and Procedure

A 32-bit radiation hardened digital signal processor (DSP) was chosen for the SEU performance test, which was manufactured in a 0.18um six-level metal CMOS process. It contains 128KB internal SRAM and 20,200 D-flip-flops (DFFs). The SEU performance of the SRAM can be directly evaluated by some test programs, while the SEU performance of DFFs remains unknown because of their inaccessibility by the test program.

The DSP is tested on a Printed Circuit Board (PCB) at room temperature, which equipped a field-programmable gate array (FPGA) as Fig.2 shows. All the signal pins of the DSP are connected to the FPGA, so the FPGA can control the DSP and monitor its outputs. By setting several specific pin signals to LOW or HIGH, the DSP is configured as the scan mode, and all the DFFs in the DSP are organized into 76 shift register chains, with each containing almost 270 DFFs. The DSP can also be configured as the user mode to execute any programs provided by the FPGA. Fig. 3 illustrates a block diagram of the test system.

Fig. 2. The Photograph of the test board of DSP

For the scan mode test, the SCANIN signal is fixed to static "0" or static "1" during the irradiation with the CLK port stimulated by a 40MHz clock signal. 10MHz and 2.5MHz are also used to investigate the frequency dependence of the SEU rate. The FPGA always monitors all the SCANOUT ports. Once one stage of the scan chain is upset by the heavy ion, the sequent ones in the chain will propagate the upset value until it is read by the FPGA at the SCANOUT port of the chain and recorded as a SEU event.

Setting the same DSP to the user mode, a program test is performed as reference. A specific test program is repeatedly executed to predict the SEU rate of the FFs, which contains the whole instructions set of the DSP to use all the internal components as often as possible but the internal SRAM. The outputs of each iteration are monitored by the FPGA during the irradiation. We assume that a SEU of a DFF will induce wrong results of a running iteration or disturb the instruction flow, then when the outputs are not correct or no output is captured in a specific period, a SEU is recorded and the program reboots.

Heavy-ion irradiation was performed at the HI-13 Tandem Accelerator in China Institute of Atomic Energy. The characteristics of the three ions used in the test are listed in Table I. A fluence of 1E7 ions/cm^2 for every test configuration with the flux about 1000 ions·cm^{-2}·s^{-1}. During the irradiation test, the device currents were constantly monitored in case of potential Single Event Latchup (SEL). Fig. 3 illustrates a block diagram of the heavy ion irradiation test system.

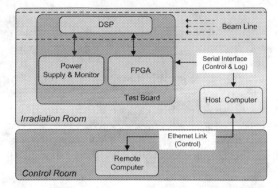

Fig. 3. Heavy ion irradiation test setup of the DSP

Table 1. Heavy Ions used in the irradiation test

Ion	Energy at the Silicon Surface (MeV)	Efficient LET (MeV-cm2/mg)	Incident Angle	Range (um)
Br	225	41.9	0°	31
Ti	175	21.6	0°	36
Cl	145	13.6	0°	41

4   Results and Discussion

The test results in the scan mode with various heavy ion LET values are shown in Fig. 4. In this figure, the cross-section is defined as the average of the static "0" and static "1" test mode for the reason that the data pattern has 50% duty cycle during normal operation. No upsets were observed at the lowest tested LET of 13.6 MeV-cm^2/mg though we tested to a fluence of 1E7 ions/cm^2, so the LET threshold (LET$_{th}$) of upset in FFs is expected to be larger than 13.6 MeV-cm^2/mg. in order to mark the no upset result at the logarithmic coordinate system of Fig. 4, 0.1 errors are assumed to the LET of 13.6 MeV-cm^2/mg, which has no impact on the SEU performance analysis. At higher LET (21.6 and 41.9 MeV-cm^2/mg), the SEU cross-section shows a clear frequency dependence. The measured cross-section is the sum of the upsets of FFs and the single event transients (SETs) occurring in the multiplexers or drive buffers of the scan chains. With higher frequency, the SETs can be more easily latched by the FFs, leading to an increased SEU cross-section. Meanwhile, SETs with larger pulse width can strengthen this effect. In other words, the frequency dependence can be stronger with higher LET value, which can be seen from the Fig. 5.

A comparison of SEU cross-sections of the same DSP measured by the scan mode test at 40MHz and the program test at 160MHz is shown in Fig. 6.The cross-section measured during the program test is much higher than that in scan mode with LET of 13.6 MeV-cm^2/mg. This difference is primarily due to the SETs occurred in the combined circuits used in the program test. However, the experimental data measured at high LETs show that the SEU performance under program test and scan mode test are almost at the same level. This behavior attributes to two contrary effects on the

SEU performance for the program test. In the one hand, the higher frequency and larger combined circuits induced more SET induced soft errors for the program test than for the scan mode test; in the other hand, not all the components in the DSP are working simultaneously during the program test, so the soft errors in the free components cannot change the program results or disturb the instruction flow, which results in lower soft errors. According to the balance of the contrary effects above, the SEU performance under program test and scan mode test are almost at the same level at high LETs. However, the cross-section consistence between the program test and the scan mode test is just coincidence, a lot of complicated factors dominate the test results of the program test, while the scan mode test captured all the SEUs in the whole chip and has few infections from the SETs, which is helpful to study the SEUs precisely in the complicated processors.

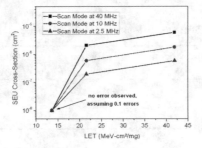

Fig. 4. Cross-section versus LET in the scan mode test

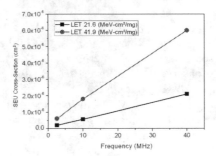

Fig. 5. Cross-section versus frequency in the scan mode test

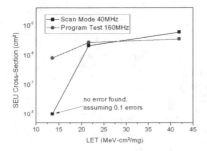

Fig. 6. SEU Cross-sections measured by the scan mode test at 40MHz and program test at 160MHz.

5   Conclusion

Based on the DFT technique of processor-like component, a SEU test method for sequential logic is proposed. Heavy ion data show that this scan chain based method is able to captured all the SEUs in the whole chip and has few infections from the SETs, which is helpful to study the SEUs precisely in the complicated processors. Furthermore, the proposed method is not limited to apply for the processors but could be widely adopted in most processor-like components which realize scan chain techniques.

Acknowledgments. This work supported by the Opening Project of National Key Laboratory of Science and Technology on Reliability Physics and Application Technology of Electrical Component (Grant No. ZHD201202). The authors would like to acknowledge Prof. Guo Gang and members of the HI-13 Tandem Accelerator Group for their long and patient heavy-ion test support.

References

1. Baumann, R.C.: Single event effects in advanced CMOS technology. IEEE NSREC Short Course Text (2005)
2. Joshi, R., Daniels, R., Shoga, M., Gauthier, M.: Radiation Hardness Evaluation of a Class V 32-Bit Floating-Point Digital Signal Processor. In: IEEE Radiation Effects Data Workshop, pp. 70–78 (2005)
3. Lintz, J.P., Hoffmann, L.F., Smith, M.J., Cizmarik, R.R.: Single Event Effects Hardening and Characterization of Honeywell's Pass 3 RHPPC Processor Integrated Circuit. In: IEEE Radiation Effects Data Workshop, pp. 162–166 (2007)
4. Hafer, C., Griffith, S., Guertin, S., Nagy, J., Sievert, F., Gaisler, J., Habinc, S.: LEON 3FT Processor Radiation Effects Data. In: IEEE Radiation Effects Data Workshop, pp. 148–151 (2009)
5. Heijmen, T., Roche, P., Gasiot, G., Forbes, K.R., Giot, D.: A Comprehensive Study on the Soft-Error Rate of Flip-Flops From 90-nm Production Libraries. IEEE Trans. Device and Materials Reliability 7, 84–96 (2007)
6. Warren, K.M., Sternberg, A.L., Black, J.D., et al.: Heavy Ion Testing and Single Event Upset Rate Prediction Considerations for a DICE Flip-Flop. IEEE Trans. Nucl. Sci. 56, 3130–3137 (2009)

Achieving Predictable Performance
in SMT Processors by Instruction Fetch Policy

Caixia Sun, Yongwen Wang, and Jinbo Xu

School of Computer, National University of Defense Technology,
Changsha 410073, Hunan, P.R. China
cxsun@nudt.edu.cn

Abstract. With the applications in embedded systems increasingly complex, future embedded processors will resemble current high performance general purpose processors. Simultaneous multithreading (SMT) is a good choice in embedded processors for its good cost-performance trade-off. However, in SMT processors, the execute time of a thread is unpredictable. The unpredictability is an undesirable feature in embedded systems. In order to apply SMT architecture to embedded processors, the problem of performance unpredictability must be addressed. Among the current researches, a noted one is done by Cazorla et al (we call it Cazorla policy). However, Cazorla policy achieves predictable performance for a time critical thread by shared resources reservation, which weakens the advantage of resources sharing in SMT processors.

In this paper, we propose a novel instruction fetch policy called APP (Achieving Predictable Performance) to control the performance of a time critical thread in SMT processors. Simulation results show that APP can achieve predictable performance for the time critical thread as effectively as Cazorla policy does. Furthermore, APP can make full use of shared resources more effectively to optimize the performance of other co-scheduled threads and overall throughput. Compared with Cazorla policy, overall throughput obtained by APP is increased by 4.9% on average and the performance of other co-scheduled threads is increased by 17.6%.

Keywords: Simultaneous Multithreading, Instruction Fetch Policy, Predictable Performance.

1 Introduction

Applications in embedded systems are increasingly complex, which places an increasingly demand on the performance of embedded processors. To meet these growing demands, future embedded processors will resemble current high performance general purpose processors. How to make general purpose processors suitable for the embedded systems are studying [1–5].

Embedded processors differ from general purpose processors in their concentration on low cost. That is, embedded processors hope to obtain as much performance as possible from each resource. Hence, simultaneous multithreading

W. Xu et al. (Eds.): NCCET 2013, CCIS 396, pp. 186–197, 2013.
© Springer-Verlag Berlin Heidelberg 2013

(SMT) [6–8] architecture is a good option for embedded processors. In SMT processors, multiple threads share hardware resources, and a good cost-performance trade-off can be achieved.

However, co-scheduled threads in SMT processors compete for shared resources. Different threads have different competition abilities. When a thread is co-scheduled with different threads, its performance will be varied.

Figure 1 shows IPC (Instructions Per Cycle) of crafty (a benchmark from SPEC2000) when it runs alone and is co-scheduled with different threads. For multithreaded workloads, ICOUNT [7] fetch policy is used. We can see that the performance of crafty varies with the workload it is executed in.

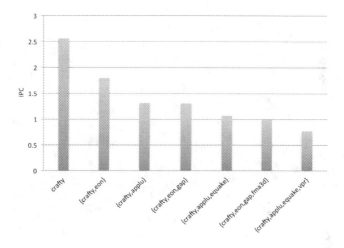

Fig. 1. IPC of crafty for different workloads

As a consequence, in SMT processors, the execute time of a thread is unpredictable. The unpredictability is an undesirable feature in embedded systems. In order to apply SMT architecture to embedded processors, the problem of performance unpredictability must be addressed.

There are few researches that address this problem. Among the current researches, a noted one is done by Cazorla et al. [9–13]. They proposed a hardware mechanism to run a given thread at a desired speed. We call this mechanism Cazorla policy. In Cazorla policy, shared resources are reserved for the time critical thread, and other co-scheduled threads can not occupy the reserved resources, consequently guaranteeing the time critical thread can achieve desired performance. In Cazorla policy, shared resources are allocated explicitly and co-scheduled threads can not compete for resources freely, leading to that the performance of other threads and overall throughput are affected. We will discuss it in detail in section 2.

In this paper, we propose a novel instruction fetch policy to control the performance of a time critical thread in SMT processors. Different from Cazorla policy, our policy allocates shared resources implicitly by fetch control. The goal of our policy is to ensure that the time critical thread can achieve desired performance regardless of the workload it is executed in, at the same time to make full use of shared resources to maximize the performance of other threads and overall throughput.

The rest of the paper is organized as follows. Section 2 introduces Cazorla policy, and discusses it. In Section 3, we detail our new fetch policy and describe how to implement predictable performance for a particular thread by fetch control. Section 4 presents the methodology and Section 5 illustrates the results. Finally, concluding remarks are given in Section 6.

2   Cazorla Policy

Give a workload of N threads and a time critical thread in this workload. The time critical thread is called High Priority Thread (HPT) and other threads are called Low Priority Threads (LPTs) [12]. The goal of Cazorla policy is to ensure that HPT runs at a given target IPC that represents X% of IPC_{alone}. IPC_{alone} is the IPC of HPT when it would run alone on the machine [12].

Cazorla policy is a dynamic resources allocation mechanism, which dynamically adjusts the reserved resources for HPT according to its real performance. Cazorla policy employs two phases:

During the first phase, the sample phase, the processor runs in single-thread mode. HPT runs alone for a certain time. As a result, IPC_{alone} of HPT can be obtained. The target IPC would be achieved correspondingly.

During the second phase, the tune phase, the amount of shared resources dedicated to HPT is varied according to the real IPC of HPT. If the real IPC is lower than the target one, increase the amount of resources deserved for HPT. Otherwise, the amount of resources given to HPT is decreased.

Cazorla policy can implement predictable performance for HPT. However, there are two problems.

- Firstly, HPT achieves the desired performance by shared resources reservation. The reserved resources can only be used by HPT. Co-scheduled threads cannot compete for resources freely. Consequently, the advantage of resources sharing in SMT processors is weakened.
- Secondly, when Cazorla policy adjusts resources allocation every time, the amount of physical registers (integer and floating point) and issue queues (integer, floating point and load/store) given to HPT is changed at the same time. For example, if the real IPC of HPT is lower than the target one, physical registers and issue queues are all increased by a certain amount. In fact, the reason that HPT is incapable of achieving desired performance maybe lack integer registers and integer issue queue, and there is no need to increase the amount of other resources. As a result, resource under-use exists in Cazorla policy.

3   Achieving Predictable Performance by Instruction Fetch Policy

In this section, we introduce our instruction fetch policy. To be simple, in the next of our paper, we call the proposed policy APP (Achieving Predictable Performance). Same to Cazorla policy, the goal of APP is also to ensure that HPT achieves the target IPC, and to implement performance predictability. At the same time, APP tries to make full use of shared resources to maximize the performance of other co-scheduled threads and overall throughput.

3.1   Basic Idea

The basic idea of our policy is to compare the real IPC and the target IPC for HPT, and to adjust the fetch priority of HPT based on the comparison result.

We use ICOUNT2.8 as the default fetch policy. That is, co-scheduled threads are ordered by ICOUNT, the number of threads that can fetch in one cycle is 2, and the maximum number of instructions fetched per thread in one cycle is 8. Furthermore, we define two new policies: PHPT and PLPT.

- **PHPT:** Prioritizing HPT. That is to say, the HPT has the highest fetch priority, and LPTs are ordered by ICOUNT.
- **PLPT:** Prioritizing LPTs. That is to say, the HPT has the lowest fetch priority, and LPTs are ordered by ICOUNT.

Let IPC_{dsr} denote the target IPC of HPT, IPC_{real} denote the real IPC of HPT, and DIPC denote the difference between IPC_{dsr} and IPC_{real}. D_{IPC} is given by equation (1).

$$D_{IPC} = \frac{IPC_{real} - IPC_{dsr}}{IPC_{dsr}} \times 100\% \tag{1}$$

Our policy switches between PHPT2.8, ICOUNT2.8 and PLPT2.8 according to the value of D_{IPC}. If D_{IPC} is smaller that a threshold defined as $Th_{PHPT2.8}$, which means that the HPT has not achieved its desired performance, we use PHPT2.8 to accelerate the execution of HPT. If D_{IPC} is bigger than a threshold defined as $Th_{PLPT2.8}$, PLPT2.8 is used to maximize the performance of LPTs. Otherwise, if D_{IPC} is between $Th_{PHPT2.8}$ and $Th_{PLPT2.8}$, ICOUNT2.8 is used, allowing all co-scheduled threads to compete for shared resources freely and increasing overall throughput.

When PHPT2.8 is used to accelerate the execution of HPT, HPT may not obtain desired performance yet, especially when the target IPC is very high. The reason is that PHPT2.8 fetches instructions from two threads in one cycle. Although HPT has the highest priority, LPTs can still fetch instructions and occupy shared resources, which may cause that HPT has not enough resources to achieve desired performance. So we define a new threshold $Th_{PHPT1.8}$. When D_{IPC} is smaller than $Th_{PHPT1.8}$, PHPT1.8 is used to prevent LPTs from occupying more resources. PHPT1.8 means that only one thread (that is, HPT) can fetch instructions in a cycle.

Figure 2 shows how APP adjusts fetch policy according to the value of D_{IPC}.

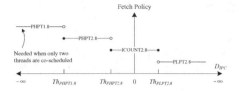

Fig. 2. The relationship between fetch policy and D_{IPC} in APP

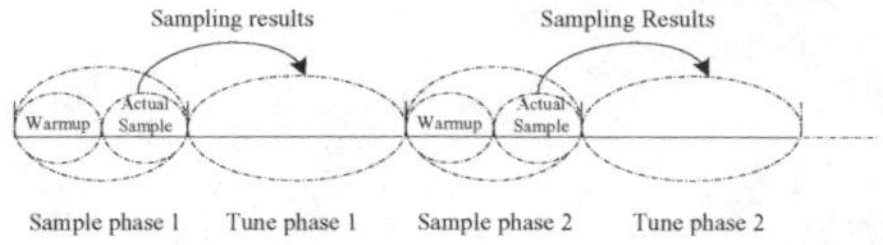

Fig. 3. Sample phase and tune phase in an alternate fashion

3.2   Implementation

To switch between different fetch policies and adjust the fetch priority of the HPT, D_{IPC} must be known, that is, IPC_{dsr} and IPC_{real} are needed. Just as done in [12], we represent IPC_{dsr} as X% of IPC when the HPT runs alone on the machine. Assume that the OS has some goals and decides X% for the HPT. So the hardware needs to know IPC of the HPT when it runs alone, that is, IPC_{alone}. To get IPC_{alone} dynamically, we employ two phases: sample phase and tune phase, just as done in [12].

During the sample phase, HPT runs alone for a certain time. The sample phase is divided two periods: the first period is called warm up period, which is used to remove the pollution by the LPTs from the shared resources and to increase the accuracy of IPC_{alone}. During the second period, IPC_{alone} is measured and IPC_{dsr} is achieved correspondingly.

During the tune phase, all threads are co-scheduled. Each cycle, IPC_{real} and D_{IPC} is re-calculated for HPT. The fetch priority of the HPT is adjusted according to the value of D_{IPC}.

A key point must be considered. Programs experience different phases in their execution in which their IPC varies significantly [14]. Hence, if we want to realize X% of the overall IPC for HPT, we need take into account this variable IPC. Our solution is to execute sample phase and tune phase in an alternate fashion, just as shown in Figure 3.

From the description above, other than switching threshold, three additional parameters are needed to be defined, which are: Lwarm-up, Lactual-sample and Ltune.

- $L_{warm-up}$: the length of the warm up period in the sample phase.
- $L_{actual-sample}$: the length of the actual sample phase.
- L_{tune}: the length of the tune phase.

4   Methodology

In this section, we give the simulator and benchmarks used in our experiments, the metrics employed to evaluate APP, and the values of parameters defined in APP.

4.1   Simulator

Execution is simulated on an out-of-order superscalar processor model derived from SMTSIM [15]. The simulator models all typical sources of latency, including caches, branch mispredictions, TLB misses, etc. It also carefully models execution down the wrong path between branch misprediction and branch misprediction recovery. The baseline configuration of our simulator is shown in Table 1.

Table 1. Baseline Configuration of the Simulator

Parameter	Value
Fetch	Width 8 instructions per cycle
Instruction Queues	64 int, 64 fp
Functional Units	6 int (4 load/store), 3 fp
Renaming Registers	100 int, 100 fp
Active List Entries	256 entries per thread
Branch Predictor	2K gshare
Branch Target Buffer	256 entries, 4-way associative
L1I cache, L1D cache	64KB, 2-way, 64-bytes lines, 1 cycle access
L2 cache	512KB, 2-way, 64-bytes lines, 10 cycles latency
L3 cache	4MB, 2-way, 64-bytes lines, 20 cycles latency
Main Memory Latency	100 cycles

4.2   Benchmarks

Table 2 summarizes the benchmarks used in our simulations. Generally, HPT would be multimedia applications. So we use MediaBench [16] (Denoted as B) as HPT. LPTs are still taken from the SPEC2000 suite [17]. SPEC2000 benchmarks are divided into two groups based on their cache behaviors: those experiencing more than 0.01 L2 cache misses per instruction, on average, over the simulated portion of the code are considered memory-intensive applications, called MEM (denoted as M), and the rest arc called ILP (denoted as I), which have lower miss rates and higher inherent ILP (Instruction Level Parallelism).

Two kinds of workloads are simulated: BI and BM. In BI workloads, LPTs are all taken form ILP benchmarks. In BM workloads, LPTs are all MEM benchmarks. The number of threads included in a workload may be 2, 3 or 4. The simulation ends when HPT is finished.

4.3   Metrics

To quantify the efficiency of APP in achieving predictable performance, we use two metrics: Success Rate (SR) and Maximum Performance Variance (MPV).

If the real IPC of HPT is not less than the target one, APP is successful in achieving predictable performance. Otherwise, it fails. Success Rate is the proportion of success cases to all measured cases.

Table 2. Benchmarks

HPT	LPTs		
adpcm-encode,	ILP	1	gzip, gap, eon, fma3d, mesa
adpcm-decode,		2	{crafty, eon}, {crafty, gzip}, {gzip, fma3d},
epic-encode,			{eon, mesa}, {fma3d, mesa}
epic-decode,		3	{gzip, eon, gap}, {crafty, fma3d, gap}, {eon, fma3d,
mpeg2-			mesa}, {mesa, gap, crafty}, {gap, fma3d, mesa}
encode,	MEM	1	twolf, vpr, swim, applu, lucas
mpeg2-decode		2	twolf, vpr, {twolf, swim}, {applu, lucas},
			{vpr, lucas}, {equake, applu}
		3	{twolf, vpr, lucas}, {applu, swim, equake}, {twolf,
			lucas, swim}, {vpr, equake, applu}, {lucas, swim,
			applu}

Maximum Performance Variance is a metric for the failed cases. Supposed that X_{real} is the percentage of real IPC with respect to IPC_{alone}, and X is the target percentage. Define Performance Variance as equation (2):

$$V_{HPT} = X - X_{real} \qquad (2)$$

For all failed cases, the maximum of VHPT is Maximum Performance Variance. If a policy has a Success Rate of 1, Maximum Performance Variance will be 0.

In addition, we will evaluate the performance of LPTs and overall throughput. IPC is used as the metric.

4.4 Choosing Parameter

Same to Cazorla policy, APP also employs two phases: sample phase and tune phase. When evaluating these two policies, the same length is used, as shown in Table 3.

Table 3. The Values of Phase Length

Parameter	$L_{warm-up}$	$L_{actual-sample}$	L_{tune}
Value	2^{16} cycles	2^{14} cycles	2^{22} cycles

Table 4. The Values of Switching Threshold

Parameter	$Th_{PHPT1.8}$	$Th_{PHPT2.8}$	$Th_{PLPT2.8}$
Value	-3%	-0.1%	0.1%

In APP policy, there are three parameters deciding when to switch fetch policy. Their values are shown in Table 4. These values are determined from plenty of experiments.

5   Results

We first show efficiency of APP in achieving predictable performance. Next, the total throughput and the performance of LPTs obtained by APP are compared to those under ICOUNT. At last, we compare APP policy with Cazorla policy.

5.1 Efficiency in Achieving Predictable Performance

Figure 4 shows SR and MPV results achieved by APP. On the x-axis, the target percentage of HPT is given, ranging from 10% to 90%. For each size of the workload (2, 3, or 4 threads), SR result is given on the left y-axis and MPV result is given on the right y-axis.

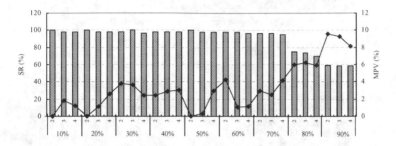

Fig. 4. SR and MPV results of APP

When the target percentage is not more than 70%, for all kinds of workloads, SR is very high, reaching 95% at worst case, and MPV is not more than 5%. However, after the target percentage reaches 80%, SR declines rapidly, and MPV reaches 9.6% for the worst case. The main reason is IPC_{alone} achieved during the actual sample phase can not exactly represent the IPC during the tune phase. If IPC_{alone} sampled is smaller than that of the tune phase, the real performance achieved in the tune phase will be lower than the target one. If IPC_{alone} is bigger, the real IPC will not always exceed the target IPC. For example, assume that IPC_{alone} is 4 and during the tune phase, the IPC of the HPT when it is runs alone is only 3.5. If the percentage is 90%, the desired IPC is 3.6. It is impossible that real IPC reaches 3.6 during the tune phase. But if the percentage is low, the real IPC can exceed the target one, and the final performance meets the target by the complementary effect.

SR is high when the target percentage is lower than 70%, but it does not reach 100%. Fortunately, from the further experiments, we found that using a target percentage higher than actually desired one by 5%, a success rate of 1 can always be achieved. This method is only effective when the target percentage is lower than 70%. When the target percentage is higher than 80%, to ensure that HPT can always achieve desired performance, running HPT alone may be a simple and effective way.

5.2 The Performance of LPTs and Overall Throughput Results

Figure 5 depicts the IPC of LPTs relative to ICOUNT and Figure 6 depicts the total IPC achieved by APP relative to ICOUNT. ICOUNT is a representative fetch policy orienting towards throughput maximization. The performance of LPTs and overall throughput are given as the percentage of those under ICOUNT.

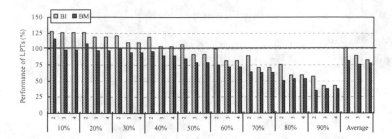

Fig. 5. Performance of LPTs relative to ICOUNT

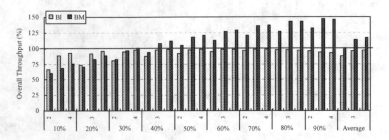

Fig. 6. Overall throughput relative to ICOUNT

For the workload of type BI, the total IPC achieved by APP is always lower than that achieved by ICOUNT. Especially, when the percentage is very slow or very high, the degradation is more severe. The main reason is ICOUNT orients towards throughput optimization of ILP workloads. However, in our policy, to achieve desired performance for the HPT, the fetch priority of HPT is forced to the highest or the lowest sometimes regardless of its real execution state. In fact, if HPT has the highest priority and occupies many resources, resources clogging may occur; if HPT can make forward progress by using the resources not required by LPTs but the HPT has the lowest priority, resources under-use happens. Compared to ICOUNT, the average degradation of overall throughput is not more then 7%.

For the workload of type BM, the total IPC becomes higher as the target percentage increases. When the percentage is very high, APP even outperforms ICOUNT. But for different sizes of workloads, the point at which APP begins to outperform ICOUNT is different. For BM2, BM3 and BM4, the points are 50%, 40% and 30%, respectively. That is to say, the smaller the size of workload is, the higher the percentage is. Now let us give the explanation. When ICOUNT is used, IPC of HPT in BM4 is the lowest, because the competition for shared resources is the most severe. By simulations, we find IPC of the HPT in BM4 under ICOUNT is only 28% of its full speed. However, for BM3 and BM2, the respective values are 33% and 45%. When the target percentage exceeds these values, IPC of the HPT achieved by APP will be higher than that obtained under ICOUNT. The increase of HPT in throughput will lead to the decrease of

LPTs in throughput. But HPT has higher inherent IPC, resulting in the total throughput is increased eventually. Compared to ICOUNT, overall throughput achieved by APP is increased by 10.5% on average.

As a whole, compared to ICOUNT, the performance of LPTs is decreased by not more than 15%, and overall throughput is even increased by 1.8% on average. It can be concluded that to achieve predictable performance for HPT, APP does not sacrifice the performance of LPTs and overall throughput severely.

5.3   Compared with Cazorla Policy

APP is same with Cazorla policy for that they all obtain the target IPC of HPT in sample phase and implement desired performance in tune phase. The difference is the way how to allocate shared resources to ensure that HPT achieves desired performance. Cazorla policy allocates shared resources explicitly by resources reservation for HPT, and APP allocates shared resources implicitly by instruction fetch policy.

In Figure 7, APP is compared with Cazorla policy in success rate and maximum performance variance. Whether in SR or MPV, the results of APP and Cazorla policy are very close. It is concluded that APP can achieve predictable performance for HPT as effectively as Cazorla policy does.

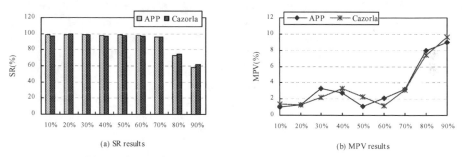

(a) SR results

(b) MPV results

Fig. 7. SR and MPV results of APP and Cazorla policy

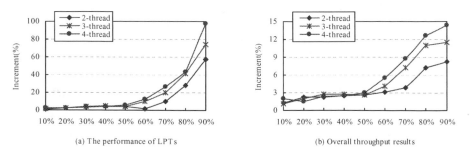

(a) The performance of LPTs

(b) Overall throughput results

Fig. 8. The increment of APP in the performance of LPTs and overall throughput relative to Cazorla policy

Figure 8 shows the increment of APP in the performance of LPTs and overall throughput relative to Cazorla policy. Overall throughput is increased by 4.9% on average and the performance of LPTs is increased by 17.6%. The increment becomes higher as the target percentage increases. When the target percentage is 90%, for two-thread, three-thread and four-thread workloads, the performance of LPTs is increased by 57.7%, 74.5% and 97.7% respectively. Compared to Cazorla policy, APP can more effectively make full use of shared resources to optimize the performance of LPTs and overall throughput.

6   Conclusions

SMT processor is a good option in embedded systems for its good cost-performance trade-off. However, in SMT processors, the execute time of a thread is unpredictable. The unpredictability is an undesirable feature in embedded systems. In order to apply SMT architecture to embedded processors, the problem of performance unpredictability must be addressed.

In this paper, we propose a fetch policy called APP to control the performance of HPT in SMT processors. APP switches between PHPT, ICOUNT and PLPT according to the execution state of HPT, and implements predictable performance for HPT. Simulation results show that when the target percentage is not more than 70%, APP obtains a success rate of over 95%. For the failed cases, maximum performance variance is less than 5%. After the target percentage reaches 80%, SR will decline and MPV is 9.6% for the worst case.

APP is also compared with Cazorla policy, a noted mechanism to address the problem of performance unpredictability in SMT processors. APP can achieve predictable performance for HPT as effectively as Cazorla policy does. Furthermore, APP can more effectively make full use of shared resources to optimize the performance of LPTs and overall throughput. Compared with Cazorla policy, overall throughput is increased by 4.9% on average and the performance of LPTs is increased by 17.6%.

Acknowledgments. This work was supported by Natural Science Foundation of China under grant number 61103011, 61170045 and 61202126.

References

1. Dehnavi, M.M., Hassanein, W.: A Clustered SMT Architecture for Scalable Embedded Processors. In: Proc. PRWT 2006(2006)
2. Berekovic, M., Moch, S., Pirsch, P.: A scalable, clustered SMT processor for digital signal processing. SIGARCH Computer Architecture News 32(3), 62–69
3. Radojkovic, P., Girbal, S., et al.: On the Evaluation of the Impact of Shared Resources in Multithreaded COTS Processors in Time-Critical Environments. In: 7th International Conference on High-Performance Embedded Architectures and Compilers, Paris, France, January 23-25 (2012)

4. Paolieri, M., Quiones, E., et al.: Hardware support for WCET analysis of hard real-time multicore systems. In: ISCA 2009, pp. 57–68 (2009)
5. Ungerer, T., Cazorla, F.J., et al.: Multicore Execution of Hard Real-Time Applications Supporting Analyzability. IEEE Micro 30(5), 66–75 (2010)
6. Tullsen, D., Eggers, S., Levy, H.: Simultaneous multithreading: Maximizing on-chip parallelism. In: Proceedings of the 22nd Annual International Symposium on Computer Architecture, Santa Margherita Ligure, Italy, pp. 392–403 (June 1995)
7. Tullsen, D., Eggers, S., et al.: Exploiting choice: Instruction fetch and issue on an implementable simultaneous multithreading processor. In: Proceedings of the 23rd Annual International Symposium on Computer Architecture, PA, USA, pp. 191–202 (May 1996)
8. Eggers, S.J., Emer, J., et al.: Simultaneous Multithreading: A Platform for next-generation processors. IEEE Micro, 12–19 (September-October 1997)
9. Cazorla, F., Knijnenburg, P., et al.: QoS for high-performance SMT processors in embedded systems. IEEE Micro. Special Issue on Embedded Systems 24(4), 24–31 (2004)
10. Cazorla, F., Knijnenburg, P., et al.: Architectural support for real-time task scheduling in SMT processors. In: Proceedings of International Conference on Compilers, Architectures and Synthesis for Embedded Systems, California, USA, pp. 166–176 (September 2005)
11. Cazorla, F.J., Knijnenburg, P.M.W., Sakellariou, R., Fernández, E., Ramírez, A., Valero, M.: Feasibility of QoS for SMT. In: Danelutto, M., Vanneschi, M., Laforenza, D. (eds.) Euro-Par 2004. LNCS, vol. 3149, pp. 535–540. Springer, Heidelberg (2004)
12. Cazorla, F., Knijnenburg, P., et al.: Predictable performance in SMT processors. In: Proceedings of ACM International Conference on Computing Frontiers, pp. 171–182 (April 2004)
13. Cazorla, F., et al.: Enabling SMT for Real-Time Embedded Systems. In: Proceedings of the 12th European Signal Processing Conference (September 2004)
14. Sherwood, T., Calder, B.: Time varying behavior of programs, Tech. Report UCSDCS99-630, University. of California (August 1999)
15. Tullsen, D.: Simulation and modeling of a simultaneous multithreading processor. In: Proceedings of the 22nd Annual Computer Measurement Group Conference, San Diego, CA, USA, pp. 819–828 (December 1996)
16. MediaBench II Benchmark, http://euler.slu.edu/~fritts/mediabench
17. The standard performance evaluation corporation, WWW cite: http://www.specbench.org

Reconfigurable Many-Core Processor with Cache Coherence

Xing Han, Jiang Jiang, Yuzhuo Fu, and Chang Wang

School of Microelectronics, Shanghai Jiao Tong University
http://icat.sjtu.edu.cn

Abstract. As the number of cores integrated on one processor increases, the cost of on-chip communication becomes more expensive, including the latency and the load on links. This also limits the utilization of the many-core processor. This paper describes a virtual computing group(VCG) model to improve the utilization of the computing resources on NoC-based many-core processor. Each VCG can be reconfigured into different size and topology before the program starts. The token protocol for cache coherence is adopted to improve the performance of memory accessing. Modifications to Token protocol are made to support cache coherence in the local VCG only, which lightens the communication penalty on a large NoC. We implement this reconfigurable system in Gem5 simulator, and the simulation result proves the improvement of the performance.

Keywords: Reconfiguration, Many-core, Cache Coherence, VCG, Parallel Library.

1 Introduction

A current trend for microprocessor is the many-core processor which integrates a great quantity of cores onto one single chip to supply high parallel computing ability. Tilera announced its first many-core processor Tile64[4] in 2007, followed by the Single-chip Cloud Computer(SCC)[1] from Intel in 2009. These serials of processors contains tens to hundreds of cores, using network-on-chip(NoC) as their interconnection. The report of ITRS2011[7] shows that the number of cores per chip increases at the speed of 1.4x each year, and predicts that more than one hundred cores will be integrated on one processor by the year 2016 in SoC design. Although some researches, such as TRIPS[13], put a lot of efforts in processing element(PE) design to make the best use of each computing components, the researches on many-core processors nowadays usually focus on two aspects: interconnection and memory hierarchy.

In the single-core and even some multi-core processors, bus is the most commonly used interconnection among processing cores. However, as the number of cores increases, the exclusive accessing to bus becomes the bottleneck for data exchanging. Some other interconnections are designed to reduce communication latency, such as crossbar and NoC. Compared to crossbar, NoC has higher

W. Xu et al. (Eds.): NCCET 2013, CCIS 396, pp. 198–207, 2013.

accessing latency, but it need fewer physical links and is much easier for extending. A lot of researches are made to improve the performance of NoC in the past two decades, which cover topology designing and link optimization, such as application-specific NoC design from Xu[16], 3D NoC from Xie[17], and link addition and removal from Jiao[8]. Some other researches focused on avoiding deadlock for some specified NoC topology, which are mainly based on the theory of William Dally[3], such as routing algorithms on Torus[15]. For NoC, the Mesh topology is the most used in research.

Memory hierarch is another aspect to be considered in many-core processors. In multi-core processors, cache is widely used to reduce the penalty for memory accessing. Using of cache introduces the coherence problem, which could be easily solved in the system using bus as inter-core connection. Protocols, snoopy for example, could work effectively and correctly under this situation. However, in the environment of NUMA architecture, coherence protocols like Directory Protocol or Token Protocol are more complex. More interactions should be done to keep the cache data synchronized. And also, while the number of core increases, the performance of coherence protocol decreases dramatically, which is called Coherence Wall[9]. Tilera modified the Directory protocol, allowing to migrate the cache data to the nearby directory controller[4], and Ros introduced a Di-Co protocol[12] to reduce the latency in directory querying. SCC uses a genius cache tactic to avoid this problem, dividing memory space into private and shared one[1].

With such a great quantity of cores on chip, how to improve the utilization of many-core processor is a sharp problem due to the reasons mentioned above. In fact, many parallel programs require different computing resources in each period, such like Fork-Join and Map-Reduce Model. Partitioning, which is widely used in MPP system, is now introduced into many-core gradually. Computing resources in TRIPS[13] are divided into four parts statically, and SCC can run like a MPP on chip with hardware support of MPI[1]. Tile64 introduced the Multicore Hardwall[4] to supply protection domains on the network, which disallow the outbound traffics and an interrupt will be generated to the system software once outbound transmission happens. Any way, partitioning from the traditional MPP system provides a new way to make good use of many-core processor.

In this paper, we introduce the reconfigurable Virtual Computing Group(VCG) to improve the utilization of many-core processor. A adapted cache protocol based on Token Protocol could supply cache coherence in the local VCG only. This mechanism could reduce both the penalty of memory accessing and the load on links, as showed in our simulation with Gem5.

2   Motivation and Background

2.1   Phase in Parallel Programs

As mentioned above, many parallel programs have different phases while running. A further example is the Strassen Matrix Multiplication algorithm[5], as is shown in Figure 1 taken from Vydyanathan's work[14]. Each cycle marked with + or * stands for a ADD or MULTI operation to the sub-matrix and could be design as one single thread. The arrows stands for the control dependency between two threads. Any threads with control dependency satisfied could run in parallel.

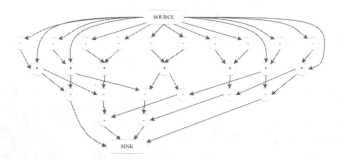

Fig. 1. Strassen Matrix Multiplication(From Vydyanathan)

Generally speaking, we could group all the threads into several phases according to the control dependency among them. However, the threads without control dependency may have shared data accessing, and we call this communication dependency. We could use the communication dependency as directives to map the threads onto many-core processor for a better performance. In another word, the communication dependency could, somehow, impact the positions of each thread on the chip.

Finally, the parallel program could be reorganized into phases, and each phase contains different number of threads. When we map one phase onto the many-core processor, it forms a VCG. VCG is the basic unit of computing resources in our reconfigurable many-core architecture.

2.2   Reconfiguration in Many-Core Processors

In the typical many-core architecture shown in Figure 2, different processes could run on the many-core processor at the same time. The bolded gray boxes are the VCGs in section 2.1. The cache coherence messages and the communications among the cores may be broadcasted to all the nodes on Mesh. This will introduce unnecessary communication and latency, which will enlarge the penalty of memory accessing. For this, partitioning becomes necessary for a large many-core processor. However, statically partitioning, as is used in TRIPS, is less flexible to fit different applications, especially our VCGs. To satisfy different kinds of VCGs, the reconfigurable many-core processor should supply separated computing resources to each VCG, either in a logical or in a physical way. For NoC, using subnet could solve this problem. Blocking the communications on some specified links will make the VCG separated from any other. However, for some irregular topology, it is difficult to implement a dead-lock free routing algorithm

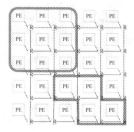

Fig. 2. VCGs on Many-Core Processor

supplying the shortest path, so supply subnet in a logical way is much more reasonable.

If we want to break the Coherence Wall on the many-core processor, we have to reduce the penalty in synchronizing the data in each cache controller. The mechanism of sharing memory without cache in Intel SCC shows us a reasonable way to solve this. We could supply cache coherence in the VCG only, for one process will never exceed the range of its VCG. Due to this, we have to implement a reconfigurable cache coherence for a dynamic region on the many-core processor. In a small region, such as one separated VCG or a small Mesh, Token protocol has higher performance than Directory protocol[11], and its character of using broadcasting makes reconfiguration much more convenient.

3   Reconfigurable Design for Many-Core

3.1   Overview

The structure of reconfigurable many-core processor covers both software library and hardware support, as is shown in Figure 3. The library is an interface for the upper programmers to reconfigure the hardware, and also maps each VCG onto one subnet.

The software library is wrapped from the parallel library pthread with our thread scheduler. It supplies a programming model which takes the threads and dependency information as input and generates phases of the program. Then the library requests the computing resources needed and maps the first phase onto these cores, according to the data dependency, of course. At the end of each phase, the scheduler adjusts the resources and maps a new phase. In this way, all the phases executes in order. In order to speedup the phase switching, any thread in the following phase could be executed if and only if all the control dependencies are satisfied.

Another important job for the scheduler is configuring the hardware including NoC and cache coherence protocol. While mapping a phase, a VCG is generated. The computing resources specified for the VCG will be organized into one subnet,

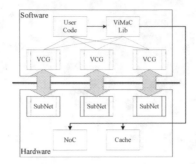

Fig. 3. Structure of Reconfigurable Many-Core Processor

on which the cache coherence protocol will be set to work locally. This means the information of subnet should be passed to the hardware. And the cache protocol running on the local region also takes much less penalties. These mechanisms will be introduced in the following sections.

3.2 Reconfigurable Subnet Design

The idea of separating a subnet is not novel. We just cut off the traffics at the edge of the subnet. However, considering the design of deadlock-free routing algorithm, as mentioned in section 2.2, we use a physical subnet to cover the logical one. The logical subnet is a subnet managing the same computing resources with its VCG. According to the requirement of the application, the logical subnet may have different topologies , even not a regular mesh.

Let us consider about the VCG at bottom right in Figure 2. It seems reasonable to divide the subnet directly from the whole mesh, but the XY routing can't work on such an irregular topology. Using Turning Model or virtual channels does work, but we make a tradeoff under this situation. We use a regular mesh to cover the logical subnet, which is called physical subnet and is used to supply routing path for the logical subnet. We do leak some communications to the other VCGs, but we can make XY routing work with irregular subnet.

Another aspect to consider is the broadcast, which is used a lot in Token protocol. When any device, such as a cache controller, sends a broadcast request, the message should pass the Network Interface(NI) before going into the router. A set of configuration registers in NI, which could be reconfigured, stores the nodes belonging to the same subnet in the form of bitmap. When a broadcast message comes in, the address in this message will be masked with this register. The destinations not in the same subnet will be discarded. And then, the message will be routed as it used to be. In each router on its journey, the router computes whether it need to be duplicated according to the destinations. If yes, the flit will be duplicated into several copies and be sent to correct directions.

By now, we restrict the network messages into the local subnet. However, if we simply use the Token protocol on it, some caches may never finish their cache request because of lacking of tokens.

3.3   Reconfigurable Cache Coherence Protocol Design

Cache coherence protocol is an important component in our works. For the reason we mentioned in section 2.2, we will build our cache protocol based on Token protocol. Based on Token protocol, we make the necessary modifications so that the protocol could work locally on a reconfigurable Mesh topology. We maintain the cache coherence in the VCG, because the VCG belongs to one process only. The synchronization between two processes should work in a explicit way, under the programmer's control.

The typical Token protocol[11] maintains the coherence according to the number of tokens possessed. For a many-core processor with N tokens for each cache line, there is one among these N tokens called OWNER token, and the others are SHARER tokens. Only the node possessing all the tokens has permission to write data to cache line. The nodes having no token could not write or read the cache line. And so, if one node wants to update the data in its cache, it must broadcast a request GETX to get all the token for this cache line. Then any other node could send a broadcast GETS to get a SHARED token from the node possessing more than one token.

The cache in our many-core system contains private L1 cache, shared L2 cache and shared directory controller, which is also the basic structure in Gem5 simulator. With the help of subnet, we could avoid the modifications to the broadcast mechanism in L1 cache controller. In order to supply separated cache coherence in different VCG or subnet, the shared L2 cache and directory controller should distinguish the entries according to the subnet id. We extended the cache lines in L2 and directory, adding a subnet domain in it to distinguish one subnet from the other, which means we maintain one set of tokens for each subnet. In this way, each subnet maintains its own coherence protocol.

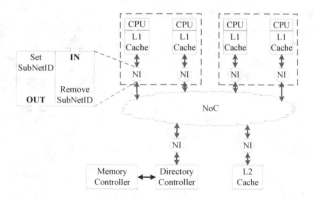

Fig. 4. Reconfigurable Cache Coherence Protocol

As shown in Figure 4, when one L1 cache controller broadcast a GETX, the address of this message will be masked in NI, so the broadcast will be restricted into the local VCG. A tag will also be attached in this NI, which stores the subnet id. If the right copy of the requested data exists in another L1 cache, that L1 cache will send its data with all the tokens to the requestor. The subnet id will be removed before entering the requestor. So far, one cache request succeeds. Under this situation, caches works the way it used to be.

However, if any of the L2 cache and directory controller, which are shared by all the L1 cache, having the requested data, things become different. Taking L2 cache controller for example, when the message GETX from subnet A arrives,

- if L2 cache has no cache line marked as subnet A for requested address, it forward the request to directory controller. The subnet id tag in the request message will be reserved so that the directory controller could return the data and token to the requestor correctly. Then directory controller will lose the tokens of subnet A only.
- if L2 cache has the cache line for requested address and it is marked with subnet A, L2 cache will send all the tokens and switch the cache line state into INVALID. Other cache lines not marked as subnet A will not be influenced, even the cache line address matches the request message.

In any of these two cases, the requestor could get the tokens it need, and so the cache request succeeds.

We shows one possible cache request above, and all the cache controllers works in a similar way for any other requests. The key point is that the subnet id tag in the request should be reserved in L2 cache controller and directory controller, so that the shared components could know which subnet the current request is in and which cache line it should operate on.

When the VCG is reconfigured, the new cache protocol may crash because nodes newly added bring in some tokens and the nodes removed also carry out some. So when one VCG need to be reconfigured, a message will be broadcasted to the whole subnet and all the cache lines are locked. Then all the tokens will be returned back to the shared nodes such as L2 cache controller and directory controller, depending on which has the OWNER token for each cache line. For the cache data in the same VCG keep synchronized all the time, cache data is not necessary to be sent back in most cases, except the cache data marked with dirty on the L1 cache. So the L1 cache could write back the dirty data only.

4   Simulation

4.1   Simulation Platform

We verify our reconfigurable many-core system on the Gem5 simulator[2]. Gem5 has a cycle-accurate components for memory hierarchy simulation called Ruby, which is also one popular plugin for memory system in SIMICS with GEMS. Gem5 also supply the SLICC language to describe the cache coherence protocol and a well designed Token protocol. Ruby supplies the Mesh topology we need, with two kinds of router architecture which are fixed-pipeline and flexible-pipeline.

In our works, we modified the structure of NI in Gem5 to support subnet with fixed-pipelined Mesh topology. The broadcast packet will be duplicated into multiple copies in NI and then be sent to each node in original Gem5. We modified this mechanism and implement this in a multicast way. The flits are duplicated when needed only. Because the duplication of flits happens in the router, the pipeline in the router should be stalled while duplicating. And also, the deadlock should be avoid during the broadcast, which is deeply discussed in Lin's works[10].

For the cache coherence protocol, we modified the structure of cache entry as described above, and some necessary messages such as token collecting message during the reconfiguration.

4.2 Simulation Results

In our simulation, we take MiBench[6] form University of Michigan. MiBench has five serials of benchmarks, including automotive, consumers, security, telecom and network. The programs we select from the MiBench are listed below, covering the situations with the character of either computing or memory accessing. The inputs of these benchmarks are supplied with the source code.

- **fft**: Discrete fast fourier transforms on an long array;
- **dijakstra** Find the shortest path for each node on a graphic with 100 nodes;
- **qsort**: Quicksort on the strings, stored in a 1536KB file;
- **sha**: A hashing algorithm on a 3172KB file;
- **jpeg**: The image compressing algorithm on a 192KB picture.

In order to get the real performance of each kind of benchmarks, we run each programon the many-core system to get the latency of memory accessing and the network load, with the simulation parameters listed in Table 1. We choose ALPHA because it has a simple architecture and has a better simulating speed. The latencies of accessing memory controller and directory controller are default values in Gem5.

Table 1. Simulation Parameters

Parameters	Values
Topology	4 × 4 Mesh
CPU Type	ALPHA
System clock	2GHz
L1 Cache	16KB for data cache and instruction cache each
L2 Cache	2MB with 8-way set associate
Cache Line	64 Bytes
Memory controller	Latency of 5 Cycles
Directory controller	Latency of 12 Cycles

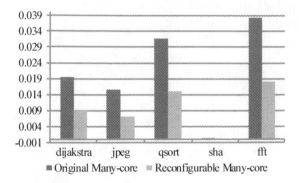

Fig. 5. Average Link Utilization(flits per cycle)

In our experiments, we aim to evaluate the average link utilization and the cache request latency for the five benchmarks.

The average link utilization results are listed in Figure 5. The statistics show that link loads on the many-core drop 50% because VCGs on many-core could reduce a lot of broadcast messages of Token coherence protocol. The SHA benchmark has the lowest link load, which are 0.000375677 flits per cycle for original and 0.000155677 flits per cycle for reconfigurable many-core, because the computing of hashing takes much more CPU cycles for each memory access, and the cache miss happens about only once for each block of size. Benchmarks such as fft and qsort have much heavier link loads because little computing is needed for each memory access.

Table 2. Latency for each stage on the many-core(in Cycles)

Benchmarks	Network	NI Queueing	Average
dijakstra	21.1538	10.754	31.9077
dijakstra(VCG)	19.7205	3.13783	22.8584
jpeg	21.2268	10.8176	32.0444
jpeg(VCG)	19.7669	3.08165	22.8486
qsort	21.0818	10.5155	31.5973
qsort(VCG)	19.5559	2.9968	22.5527
sha	20.8703	10.808	31.6783
sha(VCG)	19.3075	2.87522	22.1827
fft	21.4747	10.7725	32.2472
fft(VCG)	20.108	3.10057	23.2086

The results of cache request latency do not drops so much as the average link utilization. From Table 2, we could find out that the latency for queueing at NI drops a lot, while the network latency drops less. Using the VCGs on many-core processor restricts range of broadcasting and this reduced a lot of flit copying. This introduces much less stalls in the pipeline of the NoC, which means that the flits queueing at NI will be sent in time. The average network latency drops because VCGs restrict the broadcast into a local subnet on Mesh and a request over the whole chip never happens.

5   Conclusion

In this paper, we proposed a reconfigurable many-core system with a reconfigurable cache coherence in it. VCGs in the many-core system could partition a large many-core into small ones dynamically, according to the requirements of the applications. Each process is mapped to one single VCG, so we do not need to maintain the cache coherence among the VCGs. However, the area of a VCG is variable, so we design a cache coherence protocol over a dynamic subnet, based on the Token protocol. The simulation result on the Gem5 simulator shows that the reconfigurable many-core system could reduce the latency of cache request and the load on the links.

References

1. Baron, M.: The single-chip cloud computer - intel networks 48 pentiums on a chip. Microprocessor Report (2010)
2. Binkert, N.: The gem5 simulator. SIGARCH Computer Architecture News 39(2) (2011)
3. Dally, W., Seitz, C.: Deadlock free message routing in multiprocessor interconnection networks (1985)
4. David, W.: On-chip interconnection architecture of the tile processor. Micro 27(5) (2007)
5. Golub, G.H., Loan, C.F.V.: Matrix computations, 3rd edn. Johns Hopkins University Press (1996)
6. Guthaus, M.R.: MiBench: A free, commercially representative embedded benchmark suite. In: IEEE 4th Annual Workshop on Workload Characterization (2001)
7. ITRS2011, International technology roadmap for semiconductors: System drivers (2011)
8. Jiao, J., Fu, Y.: Multi-application specified link removal strategy for network on chip. In: Fourth International Joint Conference (2011)
9. Kumar, R., Mattson, T., Pokam, G., van der Wijngaart, R.: The case for message passing on many-core chips
10. Lin, X., McKinley, P.K., Ni, L.M.: Deadlock-free multicast wormhole routing in 2d mesh multicomputers (1992)
11. Martin, M.: Token Coherence. University of Wisconsin-Madison (2003)
12. Ros, A.: A direct coherence protocol for many-core chip multiprocessors. IEEE Transactions on Parallel and Distributed Systems 21(12) (2010)
13. Sankaralingam, K.: The distributed microarchitecture of the trips prototype processor. In: 39th International Symposium on Microarchitecture (2006)
14. Vydyanathan, N., Krishnamoorthy, S., Sabin, G.: An integrated approach for processor allocation and scheduling of mixed-parallel applications. In: ICPP (2006)
15. Wu, C.: Design and simulation of a torus structure and route algorithm for network on chip. In: 7th International Conference (2007)
16. Xu, J., Wolf, W.: A design methodology for application-specific network-on-chip. ACM Transaction on Embedded Computing System 5(2) (2005)
17. Ye, Y., Xie, Y.: 3d optical networks-on-chip (noc) for multiprocessor systems-on-chip (mpsoc). In: 3D System Integration 2009, 3 DIC (2009)

Backhaul-Route Pre-Configuration Mechanism for Delay Optimization in NoCs

Xiantuo Tang, Feng Wang, Zuocheng Xing, and Qinglin Wang

School of Computer, National University of Defense Technology,
410073, Changsha, Hunan, China
tangxiantuo@nudt.edu.cn

Abstract. The paper proposes a backhaul-route pre-configuration mechanism (BRPCM) for the round-trip communication pattern, which is suited for the backhaul packets traversal. With previous communication patterns, BRPCM pre-configures a converse crossbar connection creating backhaul-route within a single router during the previous flits traversal. Combining with appropriate route reuse and termination mechanism, the subsequent packets satisfied with the comparative conditions are expected to reuse the backhaul-route and directly forward to crossbar without SA stage, and hence to reduce the average latency for packets traversal. Our evaluation with traces from Splash-2 Benchmark shows the average performance improvement for BRPCM can be achieved by up to 53.5%, 40.1% and 16.4% respectively compared to the BASE 、 BASE_LR 、 BASE_LR_SPC routers. Evaluated with synthetic workload traffic, BRPCM shows performance improvement by up to 51.5%, 36.3% and 10.2% at most while compared to the BASE, BASE_LR and BASE_LR_SPC router under the Uniform-random, Bit-reverse, Shuffle and Transpose traffic mode at the low-load traffic.

Keywords: backhaul-route, round-trip communication, BRPCM, routing transform mechanism.

1   Introduction

The rapid development of semiconductor technology has driven the chip design into multi-core era, the constantly increasing number of cores on a single chip results in the exacerbation of inter-core communication delay, which has become a dominated performance bottleneck for multi-core system-on-chip. Aimed to such bottleneck, on-chip networks (NoCs) is proposed and became an appealing solution for multi-core system-on-chip [1][2][6][9]. Currently, multi-core system-on-chip must adopt corresponding coherence protocol to maintain the consistency of shared data, on chip communication is mostly responsible for the miss of reading and writing of shared data, as well as maintaining the coherence protocol. When a node in multi-core system-on-chip fails to read or write a shared data, the node must sends a read-request or write-request packet to an appropriate node according to the coherence protocol adopted. After the requested node receives the request packet, it performs the

W. Xu et al. (Eds.): NCCET 2013, CCIS 396, pp. 208–217, 2013.
© Springer-Verlag Berlin Heidelberg 2013

requested operation and sends a corresponding read-reply or write-reply packet to the original node in a certain probability, showing a round-trip communication pattern between the request nodes and response nodes. Under such a kind of communication pattern, a response packet is usually preceded by a request packet [3]. In this paper, we assume that the request packets due to miss of reading or writing of shared data are named source packets, while the response packets are called backhaul packets.

According to the coherence protocol adopted, source packets and backhaul packets exist in pairs with a certain probability. Given certain Coherence protocol, the proportion of backhaul packets is mainly determined by actual applications. Fig.1 shows the proportion of backhaul communication for eight actual applications in the splash-2 [5] benchmark. Among these applications, the average proportion for backhaul packets and backhaul flits is up to 22.7% and 59% respectively. Inspired by it, the paper proposes a backhaul-route pre-configuration mechanism, i.e. BRPCM, which is specially optimized for backhaul communication based on the original optimization principles and trying to improve the backhaul communication performance as well as the overall communication performance.

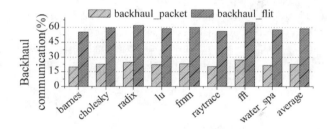

Fig. 1. Backhaul communication

2   Related Works

Traditionally, source packets and backhaul packets belonging to the round trip communication pattern are regarded as a separate network traffic, which means that such two packets can't utilize related routing and arbitration information of each other as they traverse on the network. Their average delay mainly depends on the average number of hops for packets traversal and per-hop router delay.

The average number of hops mainly depends on router's radix and the topology of network as the scale of network is constant. Many researchers and organizations have carried out a lot of works and proposed some effective techniques for on-chip networks to reduce the average number of hops, such as high-radix router [7] and novel network topology [8] for specific applications. Once the network scale and its topology have been chosen, the average latency for packets traversal is mainly determined by per-hop router delay. Several prior techniques have been proposed to reduce per-hop router delay. A speculative virtual-channel router architecture [9] is introduced which optimistically arbitrates for the crossbar switch in parallel with allocating an output virtual channel to reduces 1 pipeline stage. Pseudo-Circuit [10] has proposed to bypass switch arbitration by reusing the previous arbitration information to accelerate communication under repeated communication patterns. Hiroki Matsutani et al proposes a Prediction router architecture [11] that predicts the output channel to be used by the next packet transfer and speculatively completes the switch arbitration to reduce communication latency. Robert Mullins et al presents a low-latency on-chip network router [12] which removes control overheads (routing and arbitration logic) from the critical path in order to minimize cycle-time and latency. Token flow control [13] allows packets to use tokens to find routes along which intermediate nodes can be bypassed, and hence make the packets bypass all nodes between their source and destination in the best case. Express Virtual Channel (EVC) [14] enable packets to virtually bypass intermediate routers by forming an express channel within a single dimension using latches in the intermediate routers, thus minimizing per-hop router delay when packets keep traversing in the same dimension.

3   Backhaul-Route Pre-Configuration Mechanism

As yet other low-latency router architecture, the key design goal of the proposed BRPCM is to reduce communication delay by reusing backhaul-route preconfigured in previous packets traversal. In this section, we firstly describe several general router architectures widely used in on-chip interconnection networks, and then present our BRPCM which enable the subsequent packets satisfied with the comparative conditions to reuse partial intermediate route, and hence to improve communication performance.

3.1   General Router Architecture

Fig.2 [6] illustrates a classical virtual-channel router, which includes five input ports and five output ports respectively, supporting 4 VCs per input port. Each router is composed of input VC buffers, routing unit, VC allocator, switch arbiter and 5*5 cross switch and so on. When a packet arrives at an input VC buffer of the router,

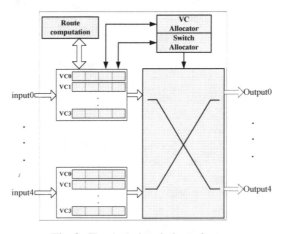

Fig. 2. Classical virtual-channel router

they must firstly perform the route computation to determine the output port to which the packet can be forwarded. After the route computation, the packet requests an available VC from the VC allocator. Once a route has been determined and a VC allocated, each flit of the packet is forwarded over the VC by allocating a time slot on the switch using the switch allocator and forwarding the flit to the appropriate output unit during this time slot[6]. Finally, the output unit forwards the flit to the downstream router, as shown in fig5(a).

A lookahead routing technique is introduced in [9], which removes the serialization delay due to routing computation by determining the route of a packet one hop in advance, and hence removing the control dependency between the routing computation and VC allocation in order to perform them in parallel, as shown in fig.5(b). Another well-known technique to reduce the number of pipeline stages in a router is the speculative transfer, which optimistically arbitrates for the crossbar switch in parallel with allocating an output virtual channel to reduce 1 pipeline stage. Combined with the lookahead techniques, the router pipeline stage can be reduced to only two cycles, as shown in fig.5(c).

3.2   Backhaul-Route Pre-Configuration

The main consideration of our proposed BRPCM is to trigger a converse connection from an input port to an output port of crossbar within a single router as previous flits traversal, which is expected to be reused by the subsequent backhaul packets and other packets satisfied with the comparative conditions in the near future.

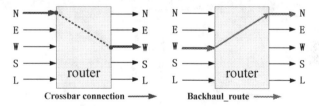

Fig. 3. Backhaul-route pre-configuration

A backhaul-route is defined as a converse crossbar connection from an input port to an output port within a single router made by the switch arbiter using related arbitration information of previous flits. Each flit traversal in a router can create a backhaul-route after its switch arbitration, as shown in fig.3. To realize the backhaul-route pre-configuration, we consider to setting up a backhaul-route registry at each input port, which is used to hold the essential information of backhaul-route and provide some necessary information for a simple comparison between the backhaul-route and the routing information of incoming packets, as fig.4 shows.

Each backhaul-route registry contains three ingredients. backhaul_outport indicates the output port of backhaul-route, which is corresponding to the input port of the crossbar connection created by previous flits. When a flit establish a crossbar connection from an input port to an output port by switch arbiter, put the number of input port write into the backhaul_outport register at the corresponding input port. Since the first part of the switch arbiter arbitrates the input VCs, each backhaul-route should hold an input VC number for route pre-configuration. For simplicity, we consider to select a fixed VC, such as VC0, and put its number write into the backhaul_vc register of backhaul-route registry, so the subsequent flits are expected to come to the VC0 in order to reuse the backhaul-route. Meanwhile, the available VC0 has the higher priority to be allotted to incoming packets in the VA stage. backhaul-valid is used to indicate whether the backhaul-route preconfigured is valid currently.

Once a backhaul-route is pre-configured, the backhaul-route remains connected unless there is another recent backhaul-route conflicting with the backhaul-route. If the backhaul-route is connected, it is ready to send flits directly to the crossbar switch without SA stage.

3.3   Backhaul-Route Reuse

In order to judge whether the flit can traverse the backhaul-route, the router needs to compare the routing information of incoming flit with the backhaul-route information. To implement it, we plan to setup a simple comparator combined with backhaul-route registry at each input port, as shown in fig.4.

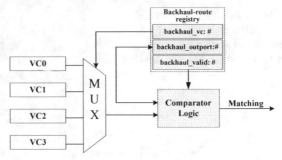

Fig. 4. Backhaul-route Comparator logic

The comparator performs a simple comparison between the routing information of incoming flits and the backhaul-route. If it asserts a matching signal, the flit can traverse the backhaul-route, and hence to bypass SA stage, as shown in fig.5(d). Otherwise, the flit must experience the original pipeline stages as fig.5(c) shows. It is well-known that the routing information is always carried by header flits, once the header flit has matching routing information with the backhaul-route, the following flits coming to the same VC can bypass SA until the backhaul-route is terminated.

Since the comparison of backhaul-route reuse is in parallel with the VC allocation, no additional delay is required in VA for current flit traversal. Therefore, BRPCM has no additional overhead in delay analysis. Meanwhile, the area overhead of the logic is very small compared to the other router control logical, we assume the hardware overhead of BRPCM is negligible.

3.4   Backhaul-Route Termination

In order to avoid negative influences to the communication performance, it is necessary to build a corresponding termination mechanism to terminate partial backhaul-route in real time. There are three conditions for backhaul-route termination:

(1) If either the input port or the output port of backhaul-route is assigned to another backhaul-route, the previous backhaul-route must be terminated because one input or output port cannot have more than one backhaul-route.

(2) If another flit at the different input port claims the same output port with the current backhaul-route, a new backhaul-route is created and the previous backhaul-route must be terminated.

(3) If the downstream router connected to the output port is congested, the previous backhaul-route must be terminated. Since the switch arbiter performs arbitration based on the credit availability in the downstream routers, the backhaul-route existence must guarantee credit availability of the corresponding output port.

As the updating and termination of backhaul-route is in parallel with crossbar switch setup after switch allocation of previous flits, no additional delay is required in SA for the current flit traversal. Meanwhile, backhaul-route termination does not need any performance overhead on the network, which only disconnects crossbar switch while clearing the valid bit at the corresponding backhaul-route registry. Once the backhaul-route is terminated, no flit is accepted for the terminated backhaul-route without SA because there is no backhaul-route.

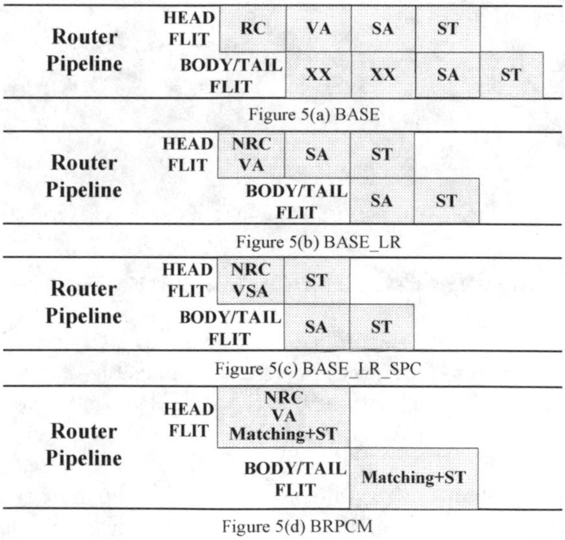

Router Pipeline	HEAD FLIT	RC	VA	SA	ST	
	BODY/TAIL FLIT	XX	XX	SA	ST	

Figure 5(a) BASE

Router Pipeline	HEAD FLIT	NRC VA	SA	ST	
	BODY/TAIL FLIT		SA	ST	

Figure 5(b) BASE_LR

Router Pipeline	HEAD FLIT	NRC VSA	ST	
	BODY/TAIL FLIT		SA	ST

Figure 5(c) BASE_LR_SPC

Router Pipeline	HEAD FLIT	NRC VA Matching+ST	
	BODY/TAIL FLIT		Matching+ST

Figure 5(d) BRPCM

Fig. 5. Router pipeline Stages

3.5   Routing Transform Mechanism

In order to reuse the backhaul-route for backhaul packets, we propose a routing transform mechanism (RTM) to guarantee that a pairs of source packets and backhaul packets take the same route if one packet's destination is the other's source, which adopts different routing strategy according to the different type of packets. For simplicity, if the incoming packet belongs to a source packet, adopts XY routing strategy; while the incoming packet affiliates to a backhaul packet, the packet must transform its routing strategy to ensure the backhaul packet to enter the same router as source packet traversal, as shown in fig.6.

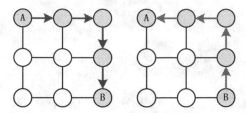

Fig. 6. RTM

Fig.7 shows the influence of RTM on the communication performance normalizes to XY routing strategy based on baseline router. As shown in figure, the average variability of communication performance is less than 0.3% and can be negligible in quantitative description, which implied that RTM has little impacts on the application communication performance.

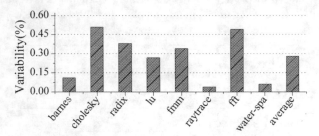

Fig. 7. The performance variability for RTM

4   Experiment and Performance Evaluation

In order to evaluate the communication performance of BRPCM, we implement the proposed router architecture based on HS [15], as well as the classical virtual-channel router (BASE), Look-ahead router (BASE_LR) and speculative router (BASE_LR_SPC) architecture for comparison. Both routers are connected as an 8*8 2D mesh network in our simulation. To have a fair comparison, each routers have five input/output ports, and adopt the deadlock-free XY routing strategy except for RTM. In our simulation, we provide eight communication traces extracted from actual applications by using the full system simulator GEMS. We also adopt the Uniform-random, Bit-reverse, Shuffle and Transpose traffic mode for synthetic workloads.

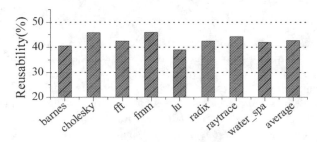

Fig. 8. Backhaul-route reusability

Fig.8 shows the backhaul-route reusability in eight benchmark applications. Backhaul-route reusability is defined as the percentage of flits reusing backhaul-route. Among these applications, the application fmm shows the biggest reusability by up to 45.93%, and the average backhaul-route reusability is about 42.7%. Generally, the higher backhaul-route reusability is, the greater communication performance improvement is expected.

Fig.9 shows the average latency for packets traversal normalized to the BASE router. As we can see from the figure, BRPCM router has the lowest latency compared to the other three routers in all cases. Among these applications, the application fmm shows the highest improvement by up to 54.7%, 41.6% and 18.1% due to the highest reusability compared to BASE, BASE_LR and BASE_LR_SPC routers, while the average communication performance improvement can be achieved up to 53.5%, 40.1% and 16.4%, respectively. The communication performance improvement of BRPCM is mainly determined by the backhaul-route reusability of actual applications, which is very sensitive to the backhaul communication characteristics of applications as well as the injection rate of networks. BRPCM hardly reduces communication latency in high-load traffic due to contentions between flits.

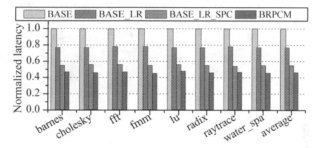

Fig. 9. Normalized latency comparison

Fig.10 shows the communication performance comparison for four kinds of router architectures in the synthetic workload traffic. As shown in the figure, BRPCM router performs better than other three routers at any traffic load before saturation in all synthetic workload. At the low-load traffic, BRPCM router can achieved performance improvement by up to 10.2%, 7.1%, 7.3% and 6% respectively under the Uniform-random, Bit-reverse, Shuffle and Transpose traffic mode while compared to BASE_LR_SPC router. When compared to the BASE and BASE_LR routers, BRPCM router can achieved performance improvement by up to 51.5%, 48.3%, 49.2%, 47.9% and 36.3%, 32.5%, 33.5%, 31.4% respectively. It is expected that uniform-random has less round-trip communication because the next packet can be destined to any random destination. However, these two consecutive communications may have a common path with the backhaul-route in dimension order routing algorithms. Since BRPCM exploits backhaul-route reusability within a single router, it can improve performance within the common path.

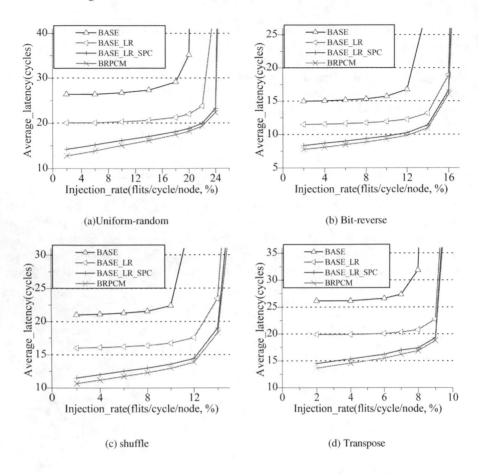

Fig. 10. Performance comparison with synthetic workload traffic

5   Conclusion

The paper proposes a novel flow control mechanism, i.e. BRPCM which pre-configures a corresponding backhaul-route as previous packets traversal to enable the subsequent packets satisfied with the comparative conditions to bypass the SA stages, and hence to improve communication performance. Our evaluation with traces from Splash-2 Benchmark shows the average performance improvement for BRPCM can be achieved up to 53.5%, 40.1% and 16.4% respectively compared to the BASE、 BASE_LR 、 BASE_LR_SPC routers. Evaluated with synthetic workload traffic, BRPCM shows performance improvement by up to 51.5%, 36.3% and 10.2% at most while compared to the BASE, BASE_LR and BASE_LR_SPC router under the Uniform-random, Bit-reverse, Shuffle and Transpose traffic mode at the low-load traffic. Note that, as the premise of backhaul-route pre-configuration and reuse is the route of packets traversal without shifting with the network communication status,

BRPCM only applies to the deterministic routing strategy. Meanwhile, BRPCM can hardly achieve communication performance improvement in high-load traffic due to contentions between flits.

Acknowledgment. This paper is supported by the National High-Tech 863 Project of China (2009AAOIZ102) and the National Natural Science Foundation of China (60873016, 61170083).

References

1. Benini, L., de Micheli, G.: Networks on chips: A new SoC paradigm. IEEE Computer 35(1), 70–78 (2002)
2. Goossens, K., et al.: Æthereal network on chip: Concepts, architectures, and implementations. In: IEEE Des. and Test of Comp. (2005)
3. Fang, Z., Hallnor, E.G., et al.: Boomerang: Reducing Power Consumption of Response Packets in NoCs with Minimal Performance Impact. IEEE Computer Architecture Letters 9(2) (2010)
4. Martin, M.M.K., et al.: Multifacet's general execution-driven multiprocessor simulator (gems) toolset. SIGARCH Comput. Archit. News 33, 92–99 (2005)
5. Woo, S.C., Ohara, M., Torrie, E., Singh, J.P., Gupta, A.: The Splash2 Programs: Characterization and Methodological Considerations. In: Proceedings of the 22nd Annual International Symposium on Computer Architecture, ISCA 1995 (1995)
6. Dally, W.J., Towles, B.: Principles and Practices of Interconnection Network. Morgan Kaufmann, San Francisco (2004)
7. Kim, J., Dally, W.J., Towles, B., Gupta, A.K.: Microarchitecture of a High Radix Router. In: 32nd Annual International Symposium on Computer Architecture, ISCA (2005)
8. Grot, B., Hestness, J., Keckler, S.W., Mutlu, O.: Express Cube Topologies for on-Chip Interconnects. In: IEEE 15th International Symposium on High Performance Computer Architecture, HPCA (2009)
9. Peh, L.-S., Dally, W.J.: A Delay Model and Speculative Architecture for Pipelined Routers. In: Proceedings of the 7th International Symposium on High-Performance Computer Architecture, HPCA (2001)
10. Ahn, M., Kim, E.J.: Pseudo-Circuit: Accelerating Communication for On-Chip Interconnection Networks. In: Proceedings of the 43rd Annual IEEE/ACM International Symposium on Microarchitecture, MICRO (2010)
11. Matsutani, H., et al.: Prediction Router: A Low-Latency On-Chip Router Architecture with Multiple Predictors. IEEE Transactions on Computers 60(6) (June 2011)
12. Mullins, R., West, A., Moore, S.: Low-Delay Virtual-Channel Routers for on-Chip Networks. In: Proceedings of the 31st Annual International Symposium on Computer Architecture, ISCA 2004 (2004)
13. Kumar, Peh, L.S., Jha, N.K.: Token Flow Control. In: 41st IEEE/ACM International Symposium on Microarchitecture, MICRO 2008 (2008)
14. Kumar, Peh, L.-S., Kundu, P., Jha, N.K.: Express Virtual Channels: Towards the Ideal Interconnection Fabric. In: Proceedings of the 34th Annual International Symposium on Computer Architecture, ISCA 2007 (2007)
15. Chen, Y., Xie, L., Li, J., Shi, Z., Zhang, M., Chen, X., Lu, Z.: A trace-driven hardware-level simulator for the design and verification of network-on-chips. In: Proceedings of International Conference on Computers, Communications, Control and Automation, CCCA 2011 (2011)

A Novel CGRA Architecture and Mapping Algorithm for Application Acceleration

Li Zhou, Hengzhu Liu, and Dongpei Liu

Institute of Microporcessor and Microelectronics, School of Computer,
National University of Defense Technology
410073 Changsha, Hunan, China
{zhouli06,hengzhuliu,liudongpei}@nudt.edu.cn

Abstract. Coarse grained reconfigurable array (CGRA) is an architecture which offers hardware like high performance and software like flexibility. The two characteristics make CGRA an effective candidate for computational intensive applications. In this paper, we propose a novel cluster base CGRA architecture which achieves high efficiency of CGRA. The reconfigurable processing elements in CGRA clusters share complex function units and registers. Area is reduced due to the resource sharing and the performance is improved. Besides, an ant colony based mapping algorithm is proposed. Experiments show that the cluster base CGRA outperforms some existing architectures in the efficiency; the proposed mapping algorithm also outperforms other mapping heuristics.

Keywords: CGRA, cluster based architecture, resource sharing.

1 Introduction

As the rapid development of modern microelectronics, the number of transistors in a microprocessor is increasing rapidly in recent years. Although the performance of microprocessor has been improved, there are still some challenges for microprocessor executing computational intensive applications. The microprocessor's architecture ensures the adequate flexibility for different tasks, but it has relative lower performance than the application specific integrated circuit (ASIC). Due to specialization of hardware unit, ASIC usually is more suitable for dedicated task. However, the flexibility support of ASIC is poor. In some application domain such as software defined radio (SDR), high performance is necessary because of complex digital signal processing. Moreover, hardware platform requires a certain kind of flexibility to sustain multiple wireless protocols. Neither microprocessor nor ASIC can meet these requirements efficiently in the same time.

The coarse grained reconfigurable array (CGRA) is an architecture which the function unit in it can be configured each cycle. Thus, CGRA can change its operation to be performed easily. CGRA is a kind of reconfigurable computing, just like field programmable gate array (FPGA). The context controlled function unit makes it

W. Xu et al. (Eds.): NCCET 2013, CCIS 396, pp. 218–227, 2013.

flexible enough for different applications. In another aspect, the configuration granularity of CGRA is word level where FPGA is bit level. The coarse grained characteristic improves the efficiency (both in computation capability and power) of CGRA which lead to much higher performance than FPGA for executing operations. The hardware like performance and software like flexibility in CGRA make it a effective platform for SDR and other applications which require these two features. However, there are still a gap between ASIC and CGRA. Design an efficient architecture and adapt CGRA to a dedicated application is the key factor to improve its performance.

In this paper, we present a novel cluster based CGRA architecture and a heuristic mapping algorithm. The cluster based architecture has a better utilization of hardware resource and more efficient. We also use heuristic based algorithm to explore parallelism. The rest of this paper is organized as follows. Section 2 gives related work of CGRA research. Section 3 shows the detailed cluster based CGRA architecture. Section 4 describes the ant colony algorithm for CGRA mapping. Section 5 presents the experimental evaluations, and Section 6 concludes the paper.

2   Related Work

The CGRA architecture becomes popular in about 10 years [1]. Several architectures and techniques for CGRA have been studied. ADRES [2] is 2D mesh array tightly coupled with VLIW processor. It uses share register for data communication. However, the application running on the VLIW processor and the code accelerated on CGRA can not be execute concurrently. DRRA [3] is an array of reconfigurable data path units which connected by bus. Each data path unit has its own register file and to minimize the movement of data. The bus in DRRA is locally connected and cannot be used out of the range of 3 hops; this makes data communication inefficient and hard to manage. SmartCell [4] is a CGRA for stream based application. It tiles many simple microprocessors in single chip with multi-layered communication. The nodes in SmartCell are microprocessors with instruction pipeline whose efficiency is lower compared with function unit, similar to a many core architecture. EGRA [5] is a template so that its function unit can be customized according to a dedicated application. The specification of function unit will eventually loose flexibility in some extent.

These CGRA architectures all have some drawbacks either in the data communication or the efficiency of hardware. But they do have some inspiration for us to design a new architecture. First, the shared register file for data communication is more suitable than bus in the CGRA. It has less constraint when transferring data. Second, the locally connected architecture has the benefit of minimized the movement of data, which is an important factor for achieving high performance. Third, the specification of function unit and processor like node are still a trade off between performance and flexibility in CGRA, which need carefully consideration. The aroused cluster based architecture we designed turned out to be a highly efficient CGRA with performance improved. The novelty will be described in the following section.

3   Cluster Base CGRA

3.1   Overview

The cluster based CGRA is composed of a number of reconfigurable clusters as showed in Figure 1. A reconfigurable cluster consists of 4 generic PEs and 1 shared PE. It is connected with neighboring clusters in 8 dimensions. Generic PE (GPE) implements ordinary arithmetic and logic operations, it is a common PE which can be used by all applications. GPE only have data communication within the cluster. The shared PE (SPE) contains register file and LD/ST unit to retain intermediate result and exchange data with external RAM. The most important feature of SPE is that the function unit in SPE is usually complex and area consuming. Some special function unit for application domain can also be place in SPE. The interconnection network of intra cluster is managed by SPE.

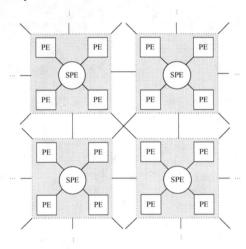

Fig. 1. CGRA constructed by reconfigurable clusters

A SPE shared by several GPEs is appropriate for acceleration applications for two reasons. First, a number of function units in CGRA are inactivated during execution. Thus, some function units in the array are not necessary for all PEs. The hardware overhead will be huge if complex hardware was added in all PEs. The hardware share technique will lead to more efficient PE utilization. Second, the SPE ensures local connectivity which is very important to enhance performance.

3.2   GPE Architecture

In our design, 4 generic PEs and 1 SPE construct a reconfigurable cluster. The GPE in cluster is similar to most PE in existed CGRA. Figure 2 shows the detail architecture of generic PE. A GPE is only connected to SPE inside the cluster. It gets data for computing from SPE (port IN1 and IN2). Only ALU is enclosed in the generic PE's function unit. All operations performed on ALU cost single cycle and the data path width is 16 bit. Config word stored in SPE determines which operation to be executed and where the 2 source operands from. Communication of GPE within the cluster is done by shared register file in the SPE. Thus, there are no registers inside the GPE and the connection network between GPE is not needed.

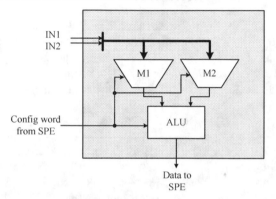

Fig. 2. GPE architecture

3.3 SPE Architecture

Unlike GPE, complex operation units such as multiplier and other customized special function unit can be implemented in the SPE. Detailed architecture of SPE is depicted in Figure 3. MUL in SPE is fully pipelined so that we can start an operation at each cycle. In order to exchange data with external RAM, LD/ST unit is also necessary for SPE. This is distributed memory structure makes CGRA scalable and reduces workload in the interconnect network.

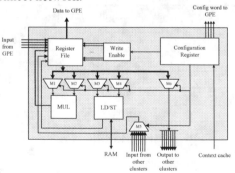

Fig. 3. SPE architecture

SPE has a 64×16 register file for the intermediate storage. The input port for the register file includes 7 parts: 4 data from generic PEs, input from other cluster, results from MUL(2X16 bits) and LD/ST. Accordingly, the register file is divided into 7 subsets. Each subset can only be written by its corresponding data source in order to avoid complex data permutation. Thus, there are 8 write ports for register file. Write enable signals are generated according to all the destination operands indicated in config word. The configuration register loads config word from context cache each cycle which defines the behavior of whole reconfigurable cluster.

3.4   Configuration of CGRA

Table 1 lists the structure of config word for GPE. 19 bits are used to config a GPE. ALU supports 16 types of arithmetic and logic operations including shift. The control signal for multiplexer M1 and M2 choose source operands from 64 registers so that it is 6 bit width. The destination register of ALU's result is 3 bits; therefore each GPE owns 8 registers in SPE which is sufficient for local intermediate storage.

Table 1. GPE configuration structure

Field	Number of bits	Meaning
OPR	2×6	Operand 1 and operands 2 selection
OPC	4	Operation to be executed
DST	3	Destination register index

Table 2 presents the structure of config word for SPE. 3 bits FUEN field indicates whether to perform the multiply, load or store operation. There is 8-to-1 multiplexer M5 to choose the input data from 8 neighboring clusters. Other multiplexers in SPE all have 6 bit width control signal. Note that the output of MUL maybe more than others so that there is 1 more bit in DST field for registers indexing.

Table 2. SPE configuration structure

Field	Number of bits	Meaning
OPR	4×6	Operands selection, 2 for MUL 2 for LD/ST
FUEN	3	Function units enable for MUL, LD and ST
IN	3	Input data selection
OUT	6	Output data selection
DST	4+3	Destination register index 4 bits for MUL, 3 bits for LD/ST

4   Mapping Algorithm for Cluster Based CGRA

4.1   Problem Definition

A kernel of applications is represented by the data acyclic graph (DAG): $G =< V, E >$, where vertices $v \in V$ represent operations in the kernel. Each vertex has an attribute 'type' which indicates the category it belongs to (ALU or multiply operation etc). The edge $e =< v_1, v_2 > \in E$ represents the fact that operation v_1 is data-dependent on v_1. Given a target CGRA, we use a directed graph $C =< P, L >$ to represent the computation resource it contains. P is the set of PEs and the type of operations which can be executed on PE p is denote by the set $p.type$. The edge $l = < p_1, p_2 > \in L$ represents that p_2 can use the result of p_1 directly either through connection network or register files. $t(v, p)$ denotes the execution cycles of operation v on PE p. We assume that the multi cycle PE is pipelined so that we can start an operation each cycle. When mapping a DAG onto CGRA, the placement and execution time of operations is concerned. So, two functions $M_v : V \rightarrow P$, $M_t : V \rightarrow N^+$ is defined to represent the location and start time of operations. In addition, intermediate PEs for routing an edge $e = < v_1, v_2 > \in E$ are needed if $< M_v(v_1), M_v(v_2) > \notin L$.

Given the definition of temporal mapping problems, ILP emerges as the preferred method in obtaining the optimal answer. However, the mapping time is intolerable. The technique used in loop pipelining on CGRA limits operations in a certain initial interval and can not be applied to mapping DAG directly. So, a heuristic temporal mapping algorithm is urgently needed for the problem.

4.2   Methodology

Ant colony optimization (ACO) is proved to be superior to genetic algorithms and simulated annealing in scheduling problem. In the algorithm, ants are placed at start point to construct their solutions step by step. At each step, there is a set of candidate decisions which is 'visible' to the ant, and one will be chosen according to the 'visibility' of these decisions. The measurement of 'visibility' for a decision is related to how good the decision can get. The more benefit a decision can get, the higher probability will be defined for selecting the decision. This is the local heuristic. Ants release pheromones after decision was made, which are used in the next iteration. Pheromone is the global heuristic which prevents algorithm from falling into local optimized result. The min-max ant colony system (MMAS) is a modification of ant colony optimization. It only allows the ant which finds the best solution to release pheromone in order to speed up the convergence procedure. It also limits the pheromone within $[\tau^{min}, \tau^{max}]$ to ensure enough exploration of algorithm.

In the CGRA mapping problems, the candidate decisions are denoted by a set $S = \{s = (v, p) | v \in V, p \in P, v.type \in p.type\}$. Each $s_i = (v_i, p_i) \in S$ means mapping operation v_i onto PE p_i. The initial candidate set S is defined as:

$$S = \{s = (v, p) | \forall v' \in V, < v', v > \notin E\} \tag{1}$$

Once a decision s_i is selected, the candidate set will change accordingly. Equation (1) shows that if all parents of an operation are mapped yet, then the operation and its possible location should be added into candidate set. The set D denotes the decisions that have been selected. D is initialized with Φ and updated by $D = D \cup \{s_i\}$ each time after s_i is selected.

$$S = (S / \{s_i\}) \cup \{u = (v, p) \mid \forall v' \in V, < v', v > \in E \Rightarrow \exists p' \in P, (v', p') \in D\} \tag{2}$$

At the d th step, the probability of choosing s_i can be calculated by:

$$p_{d,s_i} = \frac{\tau_{d,s_i}^{\alpha} \cdot \eta_{d,s_i}^{\beta}}{\sum_{s_j \in S} \tau_{d,s_j}^{\alpha} \cdot \eta_{d,s_j}^{\beta}} \tag{3}$$

where τ_{d,s_i} is the information left by ants in previous iterations, η_{d,s_i} is the expectation of taking s_i as decision at this step. α and β indicate the importance of the global heuristic and local heuristic. After all ants end exploring, the pheromones left on the road are updated by:

$$\tau_{d,s_i}(t+1) = \rho\tau_{d,s_i}(t) + \Delta\tau_{d,s_i} \tag{4}$$

$$\tau_{d,s_i} = \tau^{min} \text{ if } \tau_{d,s_i} < \tau^{min}, \tau_{d,s_i} = \tau^{max} \text{if} \tau_{d,s_i} > \tau^{max} \tag{5}$$

where ρ indicates the evaporation factor of pheromone and $\Delta\tau_{d,s_i} \neq 0$ only if the choice of s_i is included in the best solution.

The local heuristic η_{d,s_i} for a decision $s_i = (v_i, p_i)$ is related to the earliest time that v_i can be executed on p_i. The earlier it can be executed, the higher η_{d,s_i} it will get. It is calculated by the formula

$$\eta_{d,s_i} = \frac{1}{startTime(s_i)} \tag{6}$$

$$startTime(s_i) = \max_{<v',v_i> \in E} \{M_t(v') + t(v', p') + route(M_v(v'), M_t(v'), p_i)\} \tag{7}$$

The $startTime(s_i)$ is estimated according its parent operations' execution time $t(v', p')$ and the routing latency for delivering data from producer PE to p_i. The function $route(M_v(v'), M_t(v'), p_i)$ finds routing PEs by maze route technique and returns the path's latency according to PE reservation table. It starts the breath first search from the slot $(M_v(v'), M_t(v') + t(v', p') - 1)$ until a free slot of p_i is reached. There may be conflicts for PEs when maze routing more than one data dependency of v_i. Thus, we ensure that the longer path is prior in using routing PEs when conflict occurs to balance the length of paths as much as possible. The entire procedure is depict in Algorithm 1

Algorithm1: MMAS for CGRA mapping

Initialize pheromones;
while exploration is not terminated
  for each ant
    Initialize PE occupy table;
    Initialize candidate set S using Eq.(1);
    while S is not empty
      for each node s in S
        Calculate the earliest start time of s using Eq.(7);
      end for
      Select a node to move onto according to Eq.(3);
      Update PE occupy table;
      Update candidate set S by Eq.(2);
    end while
  end for
  Update pheromones and only the ant who found the best solution release pheromone according to Eq.(4) and Eq.(5);
end while

All pheromones are initialized with a certain value. Then the algorithm takes several iterations for exploration. In each step of the algorithm, ants in colony make decisions step by step through local heuristic η_{d,s_i} and pheromones left by the ants of last iteration. When a decision is selected, it is deemed as assigning an operation to a certain PE. The routing PEs for data transfer is found while calculating the local heuristic. Thus, each ant will construct a feasible mapping. After updating pheromones several times, the algorithm will gradually converge to an optimized solution. This methodology can be applied to optimize other metric of application mapping such as power consumption by adjusting the way of estimation of local heuristic.

5 Evaluation

We describe the CGRA in Verilog HDL and utilize Synopsys design compiler for logical synthesis of the whole CGRA, Chartered 90nm CMOS technology was used for standard cells. The total area of the array (without SRAM) composed of 4 reconfigurable clusters (16 PEs with 4 SPEs) is 1.82 mm^2. If synthesized separately, a single PE costs 0.056 mm^2 and SPE costs 0.235 mm^2. The maximal frequency of CGRA is 667 MHz, note that the MUL is divided into 4 stages for pipelining so that higher clock rate is achieved.

5.1 Experimental Setup

We choose the SDR as our target application domain to implements the CGRA. Several frequently appeared kernels in various wireless digital signal processing programmes were extracted for analysis. Number of operations in these kernels varies from 78 to 1258. We also use the ant colony base algorithm to map data acyclic graph of a kernel to the CGRA designed in section.

5.2   Results

Table 3 gives the comparison of cluster base CGRA with other existing architectures. Hardware overhead and the execution performance of SDR kernels are concerned. We can conclude from the results that cluster based CGRA architecture offers a good computational performance with higher utilization of hardware resource. In the means of efficiency, our architecture outperforms the other 2 CGRA because of the function units sharing is sufficient for most applications. The shared register file in clusters structure can reduce communication workload due to the locality of application which will improve the performance of execution.

Table 3. Compare the cluster base CGRA to others

Architecture	Description	Clock frequency (MHz)	Cycle count	Area (mm^2) SRAM included	Efficiency 1/(latency × area)
Proposed	4 clusters, 16 GPE, 4 SPE	667	10021	2.05	32.5
SmartCell	64 PE connected in mesh grid each PE contains one multiplier	295	2066	5	28.5
EGRA	A heterogeneous customizable CGRA template, 9 ALU , 4 multipliers, 2 memory access unit	495	14180	1.14	30.6

Table 4. Compare the proposed mapping algorithm to other heuristics

Algorithm	Mapping time (sec)	Cycle count	Variance
Proposed	9663	5621	9.41
SA	10491	6037	9.63
GA	10537	5904	9.52

Table 4 shows the comparison of proposed mapping algorithm with other heuristic method. The genetic algorithm (GA) and the simulated annealing (SA) are chosen for comparison. The kernel we used is 1024-point fast Fourier transformation (FFT). To evaluate them, we give the average cycle count each algorithm get and the variance when the 3 algorithms runs 50 times.

Table 4 shows that proposed mapping algorithm has the least mapping time and more robust compared with SA and GA. The better average cycle count indicates that the proposed algorithm achieves a globally optimal result in more cases than SA and GA. It is also more stable since it obtains a lower variance.

6   Conclusion

In the paper, cluster based CGRA architecture is presented with an ant colony based mapping algorithm. This novel architecture is constructed by reconfigurable clusters. It is highly efficient because of the sharing of complex function units which reduces area while performance can be improved by utilization of locality to avoid long path communication. This architecture is suitable for accelerating computational intensive applications such as SDR and multi media. The cluster based CGRA outperforms some existing CGRA architecture and shows better efficiency; the proposed mapping algorithm also outperforms other mapping heuristics.

Acknowledgments. This work is supported by Research Fund for the Doctoral Program of Higher Education of China (No. 20114307130003).

References

1. Compton, K., Hauck, S.: Reconfigurable computing: A survey of systems and software. ACM Computing Surveys 34(2), 171–210 (2002)
2. Mei, B., Vernalde, S., Verkest, D., Man, H.D., Lauwereins, R.: ADRES: An Architecture with Tightly Coupled VLIW Processor and Coarse-Grained Reconfigurable Matrix. In: Cheung, P.Y.K., Constantinides, G.A. (eds.) FPL 2003. LNCS, vol. 2778, pp. 61–67. Springer, Heidelberg (2003)
3. Shami, M.A., Hemani, A.: Partially reconfigurable interconnection network for dynamically reprogrammable resource array. In: IEEE 8th International Conference on ASIC, pp. 122–125. IEEE Press, New York (2009)
4. Liang, C., Huang, X.: Mapping Parallel FFT Algorithm onto Smart-Cell Coarse-Grained Reconfigurable Architecture. IEICE Transactions on Electronics E93-C(3), 407–415 (2010)
5. Ansaloni, G., Bonzini, P., Pozzi, L.: EGRA: A Coarse Grained Reconfigurable Architectural Template. IEEE Transactions on Very Large Scale Intergration (VLSI) Systems 19(6), 1062–1074 (2011)

Tunable Negative Differential Resistance of Single-Electron Transistor Controlled by Capacitance

Xiaobao Chen*, Zuocheng Xing, and Bingcai Sui

Institute of Microelectronics, School of Computer,
National University of Defense Technology, Changsha, Hunan, 410073, P.R. China
chenxb@nudt.edu.cn

Abstract. The characteristic of specifically tunable negative differential resistance (NDR) of single-electron transistor (SET) controlled by capacitance which is noted accidentally in our experiment is studied in this paper. Tunable NDR of SET controlled by single source, drain and gate capacitances are simulated, respectively, then it is also done by controlling more than one capacitance. From the simulation results, it is seen that NDR of SET can be modulated by changing the value of capacitance of SET. Moreover, the cause of the phenomenon of tunable NDR of SET controlled by capacitance is given a qualitative analysis based on macro model.

Keywords: tunable negative differential resistance, controlled by capacitance, tunneling rate, single-electron transistor.

1 Introduction

Single-electron transistor (SET) is a promising candidate owing to ultra-low power and ultra-high density [1], and there is a very important phenomenon which is negative differential resistance (NDR) in SET. Since C. P. Heij et al. found the NDR characteristic in double-island SET for the first time in the year of 1999 [2], there already exist many reports concerning exhibiting NDR in SET [3,4,5]. In addition, Kousuke Miyaji et al. and Sejoon Lee et al. reported NDR in SET with discrete quantum energy levels at room temperature, respectively [6,7]. At the same time, theoretical investigation about origin of NDR attracted some attention, too [8,9]. However, there is scarcely any affecting factor investigation and special utilization of NDR of SET and SET circuit, which is different from a lot of characteristic researches and applications about NDR of metal-oxide-semiconductor field-effect transistor (MOSFET) circuit [10,11].

In this paper, The specifically tunable NDR of SET controlled by capacitance which is noted accidentally in our experiment is studied. Based on the existed NDR characteristic in SET, tunable NDR of SET is investigated by adjusting the value of capacitance of SET. Above all, the NDR of SET will show tremendous

---

* Corresponding author.

W. Xu et al. (Eds.): NCCET 2013, CCIS 396, pp. 228–234, 2013.
© Springer-Verlag Berlin Heidelberg 2013

change when the value of the source, drain and gate capacitances is adjusted seperately, and the NDR of SET shows prodigious variety when the value of the source, drain and gate capacitance are adjusted at the same time, in a word, it can be seen that NDR will be modulated by controlling capacitance in SET. Then, the phenomenon of tunable NDR of SET controlled capacitance is analyzed and discussed based on macro model. Finally, the conclusions of the whole paper is given, and it is deduced that the tunable NDR of SET controlled by capacitance can be very useful for fabrication and special application of SET.

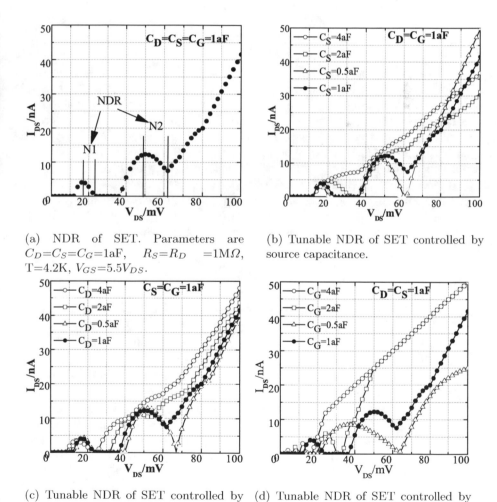

(a) NDR of SET. Parameters are $C_D=C_S=C_G$=1aF, $R_S=R_D$ =1MΩ, T=4.2K, V_{GS}=5.5V_{DS}.

(b) Tunable NDR of SET controlled by source capacitance.

(c) Tunable NDR of SET controlled by drain capacitance.

(d) Tunable NDR of SET controlled by gate capacitance.

Fig. 1. Tunable NDR of SET controlled by single capacitance

2   Tunable NDR of SET Controlled by Capacitance

We note that NDR of SET can be modulated specifically by changing the value of capacitance of SET accidentally in our experiment. Based on the notice, we study the phenomenon by changing the value of single source, drain or gate capacitance, respectively, and by changing two or all of these three capacitances together. We study three ports SET, namely, back gate capacitance and resistance are ignored to accord with general form of SET.

Fig. 1a shows NDR characteristic of pure SET in which the parameters are $C_D=C_S=C_G=1aF$, $R_S=R_D=1M\Omega$, $T=4.2K$, $V_{GS}=5.5V_{DS}$ according to our preview research [9], where C_D, C_S, C_G denote drain, source, gate capacitance, R_D, R_S denote drain, source resistance, T denotes the temperature (in Kelvin), V_{GS} denotes the voltage between gate and source, V_{DS} denotes voltage between drain and soure, respectively. In this chart, there are two obvious segments of NDR in the $I_{DS}-V_{DS}$ line. Fig. 1b, fig. 1c and fig1. d show NDR can be modulated by changing the value of single source, drain or gate capacitance of SET, respectively. For the sake of convenience of comparison, all external conditions except capacitance are invariable, namely, $R_S=R_D=1M\Omega$, $T=4.2K$, $V_{GS}=5.5V_{DS}$ in the latter experiment, and the line with blcak solid circle denotes drain source current I_{DS} of SET which varies along with drain source voltage V_{DS} when $C_D=C_S=C_G=1aF$ in all charts.

Fig. 1b shows the change of NDR when source capacitance is adjusted solely. If $C_S=0.5aF$, the first NDR segment keep steadiness and the second NDR segment become more obvious than that at $C_S=1aF$. If $C_S=2aF$, the first NDR segment keep invariability and the second NDR segment disappears. If $C_S=4aF$, the first and second NDR segments vanish synchronously. In all, it is seen that NDR can be modulated by changing the value of the source capacitance in SET.

The change of NDR is shown from Fig. 1c when drain capacitance is adjusted solely. If $C_D=0.5aF$, the first NDR segment keep steadiness and the second NDR segment become more obvious than that at $C_D=1aF$. If $C_D=2aF$, the first NDR segment keep invariability and the second NDR segment almost disappears. If $C_D=4a$, the first NDR segment keeps the shape all the same, while the second NDR segment vanishes completely. Obviously, it is seen that NDR can be modulated by changing the value of the source capacitance in SET, too.

In the same way, fig. 1d shows the change of NDR when gate capacitance is modulated solely, If $C_G=0.5aF$, these two NDR segments keep the same shape while the region that they stand zoom in according to the same rate with the value of 2. If $C_G=2aF$ and If $C_G=4aF$, these two NDR segments also keep the same shape while the region that they stand zoom in according to the same rate with the value of 0.5, 0.25, respectively. It is shown from the chart that NDR can be modulated by changing the value of the source capacitance in SET.

Fig. 2 shows NDR can be modulated when more than one of source, drain and gate capacitances are adjusted synchronously. We simulate it with several typical condition, in the figure, the open up-triangle line denotes the NDR of SET when $C_S=C_D=0.5aF$,$C_G=1aF$, the open square line denotes the NDR of SET when $C_S=2aF$,$C_D=0.5aF$,$C_G=1aF$, the open circle line denotes the NDR

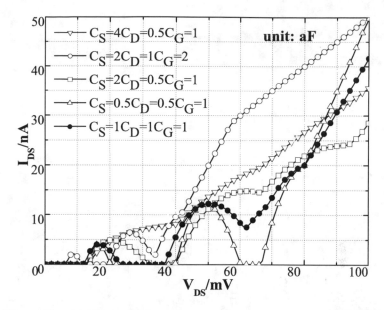

Fig. 2. Tunable NDR of SET controlled by more than one capacitance

of SET when C_S=2aF,C_D=1aF,C_G=2aF, the open down-triangle line denotes
the NDR of SET when C_S=4aF, C_D=0.5aF,C_G=1aF. The fore lines show that
the NDR of SET changes when more than one of capacitances alter. In all, it is
seen from Fig.1 and Fig.2 that NDR can be modulated by changing one of or
more than one of the source, drain and gate capacitances in SET.

3   Analysis and Discussion

Which factors do NDR of SET decide? Johann See et al. made theoretical investigation about origin of NDR and drew a conclusion that the tunneling rate
of electron leads to NDR in SET completely [8], he began with Schrodinger
equation and got to tunneling rate equation as follows:

$$\begin{cases} \Gamma_{elec \to Dot} = \sum_{\varepsilon_{Dot}} \frac{2\pi}{\hbar} |M|^2 \rho(\varepsilon_{Dot}) l_{\varepsilon_{Dot}} f(\varepsilon_{Dot}) \\ \Gamma_{Dot \to elec} = \sum_{\varepsilon_{Dot}} \frac{2\pi}{\hbar} |M|^2 \rho(\varepsilon_{Dot}) g_{\varepsilon_{Dot}} [1 - f(\varepsilon_{Dot})] \end{cases} \tag{1}$$

However, the eq. (1) can not explain how the capacitance affects the NDR of
SET concretely. Therefore, we try to calculate the tunneling rate of electron in
SET and explain the phenomenon based on macro model of SET. The equivalent
circuit and macro model of SET are shown in the Fig. 3, according to orthodox
theory, namely, quantum kinetic energy and co-tunneling are ignored, a single-
electron tunneling in SET can happen only if a transition produces a negative
change in electrostatic energy, The tunneling rate $\Gamma(\Delta E)$ given by Eq. (2) [12]

$$\Gamma(\Delta E) = \frac{\Delta E}{e^2 R_T (exp(\Delta E / k_\beta T) - 1)} \tag{2}$$

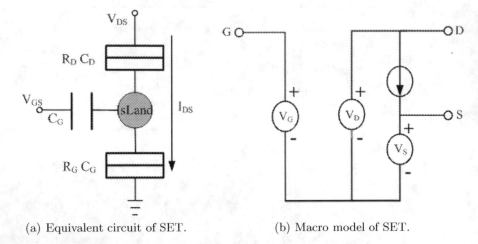

(a) Equivalent circuit of SET.   (b) Macro model of SET.

Fig. 3. Equivalent circuit and macro model of SET

where ΔE is free energy of electron tunnel, e, R_T, k_B and T are the electron charge, junction resistance of SET, Boltzmann constant and the temperature (in Kelvin), respectively. In these parameters, e, R_T, k_B and T are constants generally and only ΔE is a variable, therefore, the tunneling rate $\Gamma(\Delta E)$ is decided just by free energy of electron tunnel ΔE.

In the macro model of SET as Fig. 3b, free energy of four tunnel events can be obtained (Eq. s (3)-(6)) based on orthodox theory of single electronics

$$\Delta E_{di} = \frac{e}{C_\Sigma}[-(C_S + C_G)V_{DS} + C_G V_{GS} - ne - \frac{e}{2}] \tag{3}$$

$$\Delta E_{id} = \frac{e}{C_\Sigma}[(C_S + C_G)V_{DS} - C_G V_{GS} + ne - \frac{e}{2}] \tag{4}$$

$$\Delta E_{is} = \frac{e}{C_\Sigma}[-C_D V_{DS} - C_G V_{GS} + ne - \frac{e}{2}] \tag{5}$$

$$\Delta E_{si} = \frac{e}{C_\Sigma}[C_D V_{DS} + C_G V_{GS} - ne - \frac{e}{2}] \tag{6}$$

where e is the electron charge, C_Σ is the total capacitance of SET and $C_\Sigma = C_D + C_S + C_G(C_B = 0)$, the initial electrons in island is $Q_0 = ne$, and s, d and i denote source, drain and island, respectively. From eq.s (3)-(6), it can be seen that capacitances which include source, drain and gate capacitance is one of the decision factors of free energy of electron tunnel ΔE.

Thus, it will be draw a conclusion that NDR can be modulated by changing the value of capacitance in SET associated the proposition of Johann See with our deduction. Furthermore, the fabrication of SET will be guided by the characteristic of tunable NDR of SET controlled capacitance if it is necessary, and the characteristic will be useful at special application such as multiple-valued logic.

4   Conclusion

This paper notes, simulates and analyzes tunable NDR of SET controlled by capacitance, which is a new phenomenon of NDR of SET and noted accidentally in our experiment. Tunable NDR of SET controlled by source, drain and gate capacitance is simulated, respectively, then it is also done by controlling more than one capacitance, the simulation results show that NDR of SET can be modulated by changing the value of capacitance of SET. Based on these, we explain and analyze the cause of the phenomenon elementarily based on macro model . The simulation and analysis results indicate that NDR of SET can be modulated by changing the value of capacitance of SET, which will be very useful for the fabrication and special application such as multiple-valued logic of SET.

Acknowledgments. This work was supported in part by the National Natural Science Foundation of China (Grant No. 61170083), in part by the National Science Foundation for Young Scientists of China (Grant No. 61106084), and in part by the Ph.D. Programs Foundation of Ministry of Education of China (Grant No. 20114307110001).

References

1. Likharev, K.K.: Single-Electron Devices and Their Applications. Proceedings of the IEEE 87(4), 606–632 (1999)
2. Heij, C.P., Dixon, D.C., Hadley, P., Mooij, J.E.: Negative differential re-sistance due to single-electron switching. Appl. Phys. Lett. 74, 1042–1044 (1999)
3. Lee, B.H., Jeong, Y.F.: A novel SET/MOSFET hybrid static memory cell design. IEEE Trans. Nanotechnol. 3, 377–382 (2003)
4. George, H.C., Pierre, M., Jeh, X., Orlov, A.O., Sanquer, M., Snider, G.L.: Application of negative differential conductance in Al/AlO$_X$ single-electron transistors for background charge characterization. Appl. Phys. Lett. 96(4), 042114 (2010)
5. Kaasbjerg, K., Flensberg, K.: Image charge effects in single-molecule junctions: Breaking of symmetries and negative-differential resistance in a benzene single-electron transistor. Phys. Rev. B 84(11), 115457 (2011)
6. Miyaji, K., Saitoh, M.: Compact Analytical Model for Room-Temperature-Operating Silicon Single-Electron Transistors With Discrete Quantum Energy Levels. IEEE Trans. Nanotechnol. 5(1), 167–173 (2006)
7. Lee, S., Miyaji, K., Kobayashi, M., Hiramoto, T.: Extremely high flexibilities of Coulomb blockade and negative differential conductance oscillations in room-temperature-operating silicon single hole transistor. Appl. Phys. Lett. 92(7), 073502 (2008)
8. See, J., Dollfus, P., Galdin, S.: Theoretical Investigation of Negative Differential Conductance Regime of Silicon Nanocrystal Single-Electron Devices. IEEE Trans. on Electron Devices 53(5), 1268–1273 (2006)
9. Sui, B., Fang, L., Chi, Y., Zhang, C.: Analysis of negative differential conductance of single-island single-electron transistors owing to Coulomb oscillations. IET Circuits Devices Syst. 4(5), 425–432 (2010)

10. Chen, S.L., Griffin, P.B., Plummer, J.D.: Negative Differential Resistance Circuit Design and Memory Applications. IEEE Trans. on Electron Devices 56(4), 634–640 (2009)
11. Ramesh, A., Park, S.Y., Berger, P.R.: 90 nm 32×32 bit Tunneling SRAM Memory Array With 0.5 ns Write Access Time, 1 ns Read Access Time and 0.5 V Operation. IEEE Trans. on Electron Devices 58(10), 2432–2445 (2011)
12. Wasshuber, C.: Computational Single-electronics. Springer, New York (2001)
13. Mahapatra, S., Ionescu, A.M.: Realization of Multiple Valued Logic and Memory by Hybrid SETMOS Architecture. IEEE Trans. Nanotechnol. 4(6), 705–714 (2005)
14. Gan, K.J., Tsai, C.S., Chen, Y.W., Yeh, W.K.: Voltage-controlled multiple-valued logic design using negative differential resistance devices. Solid State Electron. 54(6), 1637–1640 (2010)

Modeling and Electrical Simulations of Thin-Film Gated SOI Lateral PIN Photodetectors for High Sensitivity and Speed Performances

Guoli Li, Yun Zeng*, Wei Hu, Yu Xia, and Wei Peng

School of Physics and Microelectronics Science, Hunan University,
Changsha 410082, People's Republic of China
{yunzeng}@hnu.edu.cn

Abstract. Thin-film gated SOI lateral PIN (LPIN) photodetectors was proposed, with ITO deposited on topside as transparent gate electrode. This paper investigates performances of the photodetectors versus the P-doping level in the intrinsic region (I-region), with gate voltage applied. We present analytical model and two-dimensional Atlas simulations of the current characteristics, sensitivity and speed performance. At a $400nm$ wavelength, the output photocurrent approximately reaches the available photocurrent, the internal quantum efficiencies yield over 90%, even nearly 100% with various dopings. In terms of speed performances, the total -3dB frequencies of the photodetectors are up to a few tens of MHz with the intrinsic length of $8um$. And dark currents as low as $10^{-14}A$ can give a high ratio of more than 10^7 between illuminated to dark currents under low-voltage operation. With such advantageous electrical characteristics, thin-film gated SOI LPIN photodetectros appear highly suitable for optical storage systems and blue DVD applications.

Keywords: lateral PIN photodetector, SOI, intrinsic region, fully depleted, P-doping.

1 Introduction

Fast and efficient photodetectors, with high sensitivity, responsivity, speed performance and low dark current are increasingly required for short distance optical communications[1] and optical storage systems [2]. Thanks to the particular silicon-on-insulator (SOI) structure and its advantages such as high-speed operation and low-power consumption, thin-film SOI integrated detectors are excellent candidates to cope with these specifications. In 2005, Afzalian and Flander proposed lateral PIN (LPIN) photodiodes fabricated on SOI structure in Ref.[3]. These diodes are indeed capable of high interest for short distance optical communications [4], and achieve high responsivity and sensitivity with low dark

---

* This work has been supported by the National Natural Science Foundation of China (No. 61040061), and Hunan Provincial Innovation Foundation for Postgraduate Students of China (No. 11JJ2034).

W. Xu et al. (Eds.): NCCET 2013, CCIS 396, pp. 235–243, 2013.

236   G. Li et al.

current, low capacitance at short wavelengths [5][6]. However, photodetection in PIN photodiodes is usually modeled considering pn junction with extended depletion region thanks to the low doped region sandwiched between the highly P- and N- doped regions. Under low-voltage operation and device parameters of actual SOI CMOS processes, the intrinsic region (I-region), corresponding in fact to a body P-doping, is not fully depleted and other phenomena have to be taken into account like volume recombination and surface recombination. High reverse voltage must be applied to make the I-region fully depleted, which is not propitious to low-voltage operation, low-power consumption or microelectronic integration for the small input resistance.

In order to address this issue, novel thin-film gated SOI LPIN photodetector has firstly been proposed by Zeng et al., 2011 [7]. Based on standard SOI technology and CMOS process, the photodetector structure resembles lateral PIN photodiode, but only with ITO deposited on the topside as transparent gate electrode. In such device, voltage applied to the gate is assumed to make the I-region fully depleted, achieve low carriers recombinations and efficient collection of photogenerated carriers. The device performances are optimized under low-voltage operation. Practically, photodetectors are fabricated in different SOI materials such as UNIBOND, SIMOX, ZMR, the I-region corresponds to various P-doping levels [8]. Here, the present paper investigates the influence of P-doping in I-region on the ultimate performances of thin-film gated SOI LPIN photodetectors, with gate voltage applied topside.

2   Model Description and Electrical Simulations

In our model, we consider the device parameters of 0.18um SOI CMOS process, as the schematic cross-section of a thin-film gated SOI LPIN photodetector shown in Fig.1. d_{Si}, d_{ox2} and d_{ox1} are, respectively, the thin silicon film, the top oxide and the buried oxide thicknesses, equal to $800nm, 30nm$ and $400nm$. L_{PN},

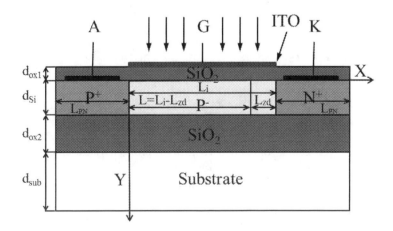

Fig. 1. Schematic cross-sectional view of a thin-film gated SOI LPIN photodetector

the length of the contact N+ and P+ regions, is equal to $1um$. There N+ and P+ dopings are both about $10^{20}cm^{-3}$. L_i, the length of the I-region, is equal to $8um$. Here, we consider photodetectors made on different SOI materials, the I-regions correspond to various P-doping levels: $6 \times 10^{14}, 8 \times 10^{14}, 1 \times 10^{15}, 2 \times 10^{15}, 5 \times 10^{15}$ and $1 \times 10^{16} cm^{-3}$. The dopings can greatly influence photocurrent and dark current characteristics, sensitivity, and speed performances of the devices.

2.1   Phorocurrent

With a steady flow of photons incident on surface of the photodetector, the source photocurrent, I_S, can be given by [3]

$$I_S = q\Phi = q\frac{P_{opt}\lambda}{\hbar c} \tag{1}$$

where Φ is the photon flux ($= P_{opt}\lambda/\hbar c$), P_{opt} is the optical power, λ is the incident wavelength.

Within the depletion region, we assume the quantum efficiency is unity. The electron-hole generation rate along the y direction is:

$$G(y) = \Phi_0\alpha\exp(-\alpha y) \tag{2}$$

where α is the optical absorption coefficient, Φ_0 is the incident photon flux per unit area, given by $(1 - R)P_{opt}\lambda/A\hbar c$, R is the reflection coefficient, A is the device area.

The available photocurrent for a monochromatic source can be obtained by

$$I_A = -qW \int_0^{L_i} \int_0^{d_{Si}} G(y)\mathrm{d}y\mathrm{d}x \tag{3}$$

Under steady-state conditions, the total photocurrent through the device is given by

$$I_{tot} = I_{dr} + I_{diff} \tag{4}$$

where I_{dr} is the drift current due to carriers generated within the depletion region and I_{diff} is the diffusion current due to carriers generated outside the depletion region then diffusing and contributing to the total current. Here, the total photocurrent I_{tot} equals to the cathode current ($I_{tot} = I_k$), related to the carriers transport and dependent on the condition of the I-region.

Without gate voltage (V_G), the I-region is partially depleted, carriers diffuse with significant volume recombination outside the depletion region, and surface recombination at the front and back oxide interfaces cannot be negligible. The total photocurrent of Equ.(4) can be rewritten as

$$I_{tot}(L_i) = I_{dr}(L_{zd}) + I_{diff}(L) \simeq I_{diff}(L) - qW \int_0^{L_{zd}} \int_0^{d_{Si}} G(y)\mathrm{d}y\mathrm{d}x \tag{5}$$

where the current item $I_{diff}(L)$ can be calculated in Ref.[4], and L_{zd} is the length of the depletion region under reverse cathode voltage V_K,

$$L_{zd} = \sqrt{\frac{2\varepsilon_{Si}}{q} \cdot \frac{(V_0 + V_K) \cdot (N_A + N_D)}{N_A \cdot N_D}} \simeq \sqrt{\frac{2\varepsilon_{Si}}{q} \cdot \frac{(V_0 + V_K)}{N_A}} \qquad (6)$$

where V_0 is the built-in contact potential, N_A, N_D are the doping levels of the I-region and the N+ region, respectively.

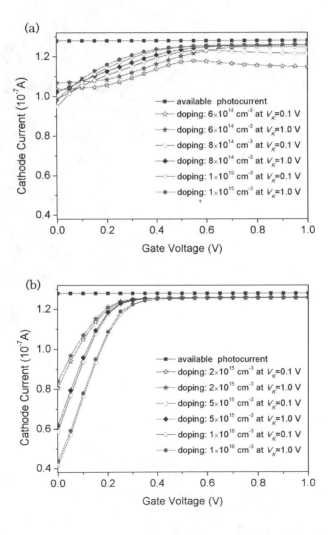

Fig. 2. Photocurrent versus gate voltage at $\lambda = 400nm$, $P_{in} = 5W/cm^2$ and $V_K = 0.1, 1.0V$ for the photodetectors corresponding to various P-doping levels: (a) $6 \times 10^{14}, 8 \times 10^{14}, 1 \times 10^{15} cm^{-3}$; (b) $2 \times 10^{15}, 5 \times 10^{15}, 1 \times 10^{16} cm^{-3}$.

The depletion region widens with gate voltage applied. Until the I-region is fully depleted, carriers drift across the whole I-region accelerated by the lateral reverse-biased electric field. In this condition, the carriers recombinations can be totally negligible, $I_{diff} \approx 0$. Therefore the total photocurrent is dominated by the drift current I_{dr} and approximately equal to $I_A(L_i)$.

$$I_{tot}(L_i) \simeq I_{dr} = I_A(L_i) = -qW \int_0^{L_i} \int_0^{d_{Si}} G(y)\mathrm{d}y\mathrm{d}x \qquad (7)$$

Two-dimensional (2-D) Atlas numerical measurements and electrical simulations are performed to validate this model [10]. As shown in Fig.2, we present the photocurrent characteristics with gate voltage for the photodetectors related to different doping levels in the I-region. Since the carriers recombination term can be very small for low doping levels, the majority of the photogenerated carriers can be collected with $V_G = 0V$, and a high value of the electrode photocurrent can be obtained as shown in Fig.2a. In comparison, there exists significant carriers recombinations especially recombination in volume with doping levels increasing, which leads to sharp decrease in the photocurrent under partially-depleted conditions in Fig.2b.

Increasing with gate voltage, the output photocurrents of photodetectors can achieve the maximum, approximately the value of the available photocurrent, when the I-region is fully depleted and the carriers drift across the whole I-region with the perfect collection. Also, it can be observed on the Atlas simulation curves, the effect of cathode voltage on the photocurrent decreases with doping level. Even for doping levels of $2 \times 10^{15}, 5 \times 10^{15}$, and $1 \times 10^{16} cm^{-3}$, the photocurrent curves present obvious gate-controlled characteristics, with totally negligible influence of the cathode.

2.2   Quantum Efficiency

One factor of merit for sensitivity is the quantum efficiency (QE). It is the product of the internal quantum efficiency (QI) by the ratio of absorbed power P_{abs} to total impinging power P_{in}

$$QE = QI \cdot \frac{P_{abs}}{P_{in}} \qquad (8)$$

the ratio($\eta = P_{abs}/P_{in}$) strongly depends on d_{Si} and the wavelenfth λ, represents the maximum QE under reach.

For $\lambda = 400nm$ and d_{Si} greater than $1/\alpha$, all the light transmitted in thin silicon film is almost absorbed before reaching the buried oxide layer, there is no resonant cavity effect (RCE) in the SOI photodetectors [11]. Therefore, the losses due to the reflection at the device surface dominate, we can get

$$\eta = (1 - R) \cdot (1 - e^{-\alpha d_{Si}}) \qquad (9)$$

Here, QI is defined as the ratio of the cathode photocurrent to the available photocurrent. We perform measurements of QI between thin-film gated SOI

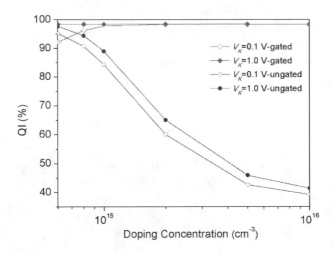

Fig. 3. Comparison of QI measured on gated and ungated SOI LPIN photodetectors at $V_K = 0.1, 1.0V$ for P-doping levels of $6 \times 10^{14}, 8 \times 10^{14}, 1 \times 10^{15}, 2 \times 10^{15}, 5 \times 10^{15}$, and $1 \times 10^{16} cm^{-3}$.

LPIN photodetectors and the ungated, the evolution is illustrated in Fig.3. To thin-film gated SOI LPIN photodetectors, the I-region can be fully depleted with gate voltage applied to reduce carriers recombinations and make all the charges collected. At $V_K = 0.1V$ and $1.0V$, QI can both yield in excess of 90%, even approximately 100%. Contrastingly, the carriers recombinations of the ungated photodetectors can significantly increase with doping level, which makes QI decrease sharply, achieving just around 40% for doping of $1 \times 10^{16} cm^{-3}$ as shown.

2.3   Speed Performance

The speed performances depend on a trade-off between carriers transit time frequency, f_{tr}, and RC cut-off frequency, f_{RC}.

Under partially-depleted condition, carriers transit is dominated by a slow diffusion mechanism in the I-region, the related -3dB frequency is f_{diff}. As long as the entire I-region is fully depleted with proper gate voltage applied, the transit time limit is due to fast drift, with the related -3dB frequency, f_{drift}. The -3dB frequency related to the total transit time (drift and diffusion) can be obtained as [12]

$$f_{tr} = (\frac{1}{f_{drift}} + \frac{1}{f_{diff}})^{-1} \tag{10}$$

Combined with the input impedance of the readout circuit, the photodetectors also exhibit a capacitor which leads to a RC -3dB frequency, f_{RC}. The capacitive component involved in f_{RC} is mainly due to the depletion capacitance of the PIN photodetectors, with much lower value for thin film SOI than in bulk [13].

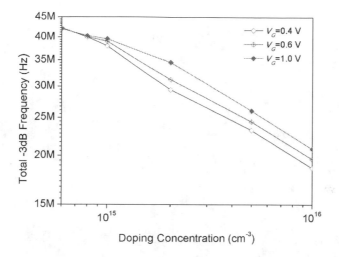

Fig. 4. Evolution of the total -3dB frequency with P-doping levels for $\lambda = 400nm$, $P_{in} = 1mW/cm^2$ and $V_K = 0.1V$, at $V_G = 0.4, 0.6, 1.0V$.

Speed response to a small signal optical source of $1mW/cm^2$ can be obtained by 2-D Atlas simulations, as the results can be viewed in Fig.4. With gate voltage applied to form the fully-depleted condition, carriers drift through the I-region accelerated by the reverse-biased electric field cause by cathode voltage. With intrinsic length $L_i = 8um$, the total -3dB frequencies of thin-film gated SOI LPIN photodetectors all can reach a few tens of MHz at $V_K = 1.0V$ operation, also decrease with doping levels as seen in Fig.4.

2.4   Dark Current

The device dark current is originated from the thermionic emission of carriers, dependent on the carriers concentration in I-region, and related to their transport process, recombination and generation. We finally analyze the photodetectors dark current as a function of gate voltage for various P-doping levels at $V_K = 1.0V$. As can be seen in Fig.5, dark currents in thin-film gated SOI LPIN photodetectors are just in the order of $10^{-14}A$ and increase with gate voltage. When gate voltage exceeds $0.3V$, the version charges occur in the I-region, corresponding to relatively low P-doping levels ($6 \times 10^{14}, 8 \times 10^{14}, 1 \times 10^{15} cm^{-3}$), which leads to higher value of dark currents. Seen from Fig.2 and Fig.5, the results can yield a high ratio of more than 10^7 between illuminated to dark currents under low-voltage operation.

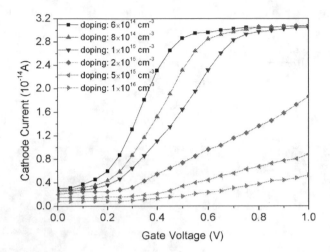

Fig. 5. Dark current versus gate voltage arranging from $0.0V$ to $1.0V$ at $V_K = 1.0V$ for various P-doping levels of $6 \times 10^{14}, 8 \times 10^{14}, 1 \times 10^{15}, 2 \times 10^{15}, 5 \times 10^{15}$, and $1 \times 10^{16} cm^{-3}$.

3   Conclusions

Thin-film gated SOI LPIN photodetectors realized in $0.18um$ SOI CMOS technology with ITO deposited on topside as transparent gate electrode. Gate voltage can be applied to control the depleted condition in the I-region, which corresponds to various P-doping levels. Under fully-depleted condition, carriers drift across the whole I-region with negligible recombinations, the device can achieve advantageous electrical characteristics and benefits.

Photocurrent and dark current characteristics, sensitivity, and speed performance of thin-film gated SOI LPIN photodetectors have been investigated versus doping levels in the I-region. The device shows a net improvement of its sensitivity and speed performance, being one of the best results ever reported in the literature. At the incident wavelength $\lambda = 400nm$, the output photocurrent maximum approximately reaches the value of the available photocurrent, and the internal quantum efficiencies yield over 90%, even nearly 100% for various doping levels. Meanwhile, the total -3dB frequencies for the intrinsic length $L_i = 8um$, all can reach a few tens of MHz with gate voltage applied. And the dark currents of the photodetectors are very low, just in the order of $10^{-14}A$, which can lead to a high ratio of more than 10^7 between illuminated to dark currents under low-voltage operation.

With optimized device performances, the photodetectors have potential applications in optical storage systems, and appear highly suitable for blue DVD applications.

References

1. Mueller, T., Xia, F.N., Avouris, P.: Graphene photodetecors for high-speed optical communications. Nature Photon. 4, 297–301 (2010)
2. Nemecek, A., Zach, G., Swodboda, R., Oberhauser, K., Zimmermann, H.: Integrated BiCMOS p-i-n photodetectors with high bandwidth and high responsivity. IEEE J. Select. Top. Quantum Electron. 12(6), 1469–1475 (2006)
3. Afzalian, A., Flander, D.: Physical modeling and design of thin-film SOI lateral PIN photodetectors. IEEE Trans. Electron Dev. 52(6), 1116–1122 (2005)
4. Afzalian, A., Flander, D.: Characterization of quantum efficiency, effective lifetime and mobility in thin film ungated SOI lateral PIN photodetectors. Solie-State Electron. 51(2), 337–342 (2007)
5. Bulteel, O., Flander, D.: Optimization of blue/UV sensors using p-i-n photodiodes in thin-film SOI technology. In: 215th Electrochemical Society (ECS) Meeting, San Francisco (2009)
6. Navo, C., Giacomini, R., Afzalian, A., Flander, D.: Operation of lateral SOI photodiodes with back-gated bias and intrinsic length variation. In: 223th Electrochemical Society (ECS) Meeting. Toronto (2013)
7. Xie, H.Q., Zeng, Y., Zeng, J.P., Wang, T.H.: Analysis and simulation of lateral PIN photodiode gated by transparent electrode fabricated on fully-depleted SOI film. J. Cent. South Univ. Technol. 18, 744–748 (2011)
8. Rudenko, T., Rudenko, A., Kilchytska, V., Critaloveatu, S., Ernst, T., Colinge, J.P., Dessard, V., Flander, D.: Determination of film and surface recombination in thin-film SOI devices using gated-diode technique. Solie-State Electron. 48, 389–399 (2004)
9. Sze, S.M., Ng, K.K.: Physics of semiconductor devices. Wiley Interscience Press, New Jersey (2007)
10. ATLAS User's Manual Device Simulation Software. Silvaco Inc., Santa Clara (2010)
11. Kinshino, K., Unlu, M.S., Chyi, J.I., Reed, J., Arsenault, L., Morkoc, H.: Resonant cavity-enhanced (RCE) photodetectors. IEEE J. Quantum Electron. 27(8), 2025–2034 (1991)
12. Afzalian, A., Flander, D.: Speed performances of thin-film lateral SOI PIN photodiodes up to tens of GHz. In: 2006 IEEE International SOI Conference Proceedings, New York, pp. 99–100 (2006)
13. Zimmermann, H.: Integrated Silicon Opto-electronics. Springer Press, Berlin (2010)

A Full Adder Based on Hybrid Single-Electron Transistors and MOSFETs at Room Temperature

Xiaobao Chen*, Zuocheng Xing, and Bingcai Sui

Institute of Microelectronics, School of Computer,
National University of Defense Technology, Changsha, Hunan, 410073, P.R. China
chenxb@nudt.edu.cn

Abstract. A full adder based on hybrid single-electron transistors (SET) and MOSFETs (SETMOS) at room temperature is proposed in this paper. Because the SET can play the same role as compensatory MOSFETs, we design a fuller adder with hybrid SETMOS. Further more, we simulate the logic element by HSPIC and the simulation result shows that the logic element implements the function of a full adder. To compare our work with conventional CMOS logics, which significantly reduces area and power consumption.

Keywords: full adder, hybrid single-electron transistors and MOSFETs, single-electron transistor, room temperature.

1 Introduction

Semiconductor industry has closely followed the trend predicted by Moores law which states that the number of transistors per chip doubles roughly every 2 years. This trend has been achieved by continuously shrinking the minimum physical dimensions of the device. With this trend in the miniaturization of transistor sizes towards the nanometer scale, it is obvious that we would hit a point in the near future when it would be impossible for further shrinkage. It is generally accepted that, sooner or later, it will become impossible to reduce MOSFET-based circuits further in (feature) size due to fundamental physical restrictions. Therefore, many researchers have begun to investigate other technologies that will replace MOSFET devices. Single-electron transistor (SET) is a promising candidate owing to ultra-low power and ultra-high density [1].

However, because the SET fabricated by the current technology cannot avoid the problems at room temperature, a hybrid solution based on SET and MOSFET is the key to the practical application of the SET for the IC industry [2]. As the most attractive candidate for post-CMOS era, hybrid SETMOS can potentially deliver high device density and power efficiency at a good speed [3]. The solution of hybrid SETMOS technology [4] has attracted much attention [5,6] as such integration can offer new functionalities [7,8], which are very

---

* Corresponding author.

W. Xu et al. (Eds.): NCCET 2013, CCIS 396, pp. 244–250, 2013.

difficult to achieve either by pure CMOS or pure SET approaches. In recent years, new architectures based on hybrid circuits consisting of SET and MOS-FET transistors are developed to efficiently exploit the unique functionality of room-temperature-operating SETs. Representative examples include the hybrid SETMOS multivalue logic circuits [9], analog pattern matching circuits [10], multiband filtering circuits [11], reconfigurable threshold logic circuits[12], etc. In the CMOS field, pseudo-NMOS logic [13,14] is an attempt to reduce the number of transistors required to implement a given logic function, often at the expense of reducing robustness and extra power dissipation, which prevents it from very large scale application. Based on the technology of hybrid SETMOS, can it vary the state?

In this paper, we design a full adder based on hybrid SETMOS and simulate the circuit by HSPICE. From the simulation results, the design accords with the expect that is the logic element implements the function of a full adder. Finally, the conclusions of the whole paper is given, and it is deduced that the logics based on hybrid SETMOS can be very useful for reducing logic-gate density and power consumption significantly.

2   Full Adder with Hybrid SETMOS

Figure 1 shows a SET, where electrons are manipulated one by one through two junctions under the control of bias and gate voltages applied to the coulomb island, the left and right terminals are denoted as source and drain, respectively. SET by an island connected to two tunnel junction composed of the gate electrode through the coupling capacitor and the island phase, with a dual-gate SET structure shown in figure 1, where C_G is the gate capacitance, R_D, R_S are the junction resistance, and C_D, C_S are junction capacitance, respectively.

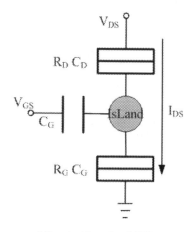

Fig. 1. Sketch of SET

A full adder adds binary numbers and accounts for values carried in as well as out. A 2-input full adder often written as A, B, and C_{in}; A and B are the operands, and C_i is a bit carried in from the next less significant stage. The full-adder is usually a component in a cascade of adders, which add 8, 16, 32, etc. bit wide binary numbers. The circuit produces a two-bit output, output carry and sum typically represented by the signals C_o and S.

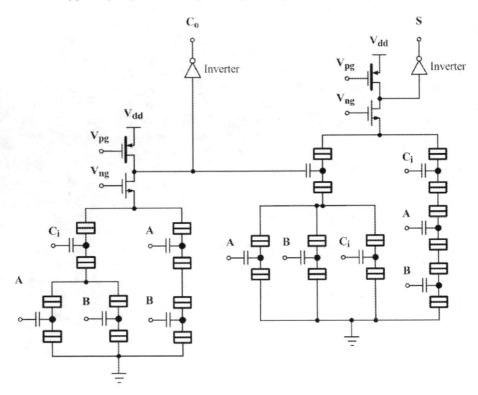

Fig. 2. Structure of a bit full adder

A full adder can be implemented in many different ways such as with a custom transistor-level circuit or composed of other gates. 2-input full adder implementation is with

$$C_o = AB + BC_i + AC_i \tag{1}$$

and

$$
\begin{aligned}
S &= A \oplus B \oplus C_i \\
&= A\bar{B}\bar{C}_i + \bar{A}B\bar{C}_i + \bar{A}\bar{B}C_i + ABC_i \\
&= ABC_i + \bar{C}_o(A + B + C_i).
\end{aligned}
\tag{2}
$$

Based on these, 2-input full adder based on hybrid SETMOS is shown as Fig. 2.

3   Experiments and Discussion

SET-based circuits are normally simulated using the Monte Carlo-based method such as SIMON [15] and SECS [16], however, these methods are extremely time consuming for large circuit simulations, and they do not offer a cosimulation environment with MOSFET devices. Several SPICE simulation methods for the SET have been reported [17]-[19], and the compact macromodel [17] based on SPICE method, whose correctness and precision have been verified by both MONTE CARLO simulator SIMON [15] and experiments [20,21], can be used to co-simulate the hybrid SETMOS circuit effectively. Thus, throughout this letter, the compact macromodel is used for SETs and the BSIM4.0 model is used for MOSFETs, and all simulations are conducted using SPICE simulator of Synopsys Inc based on the 16-nm CMOS technology. Moreover, since there is only current model and no voltage model for SET in the compact macromodel, we make slight modifications and insert voltage model for the simulation of the serial logic of SET.

Table 1. Parameters of The Devices of The Full Adder

Device	Parameter	Value
	C_s, C_d	0.09aF
SET	R_s, R_d	90KΩ
	C_g	0.1aF
	W_p	16nm
	L_p	48nm
	t_{oxe}	0.95nm
	t_{oxp}	0.7nm
PMOS	C_{gdo}, C_{gso}	50pF/m
	C_{gbo}	2.56pF/m
	C_{gdl}, C_{gsl}	265.3pF/m
	V_{th}	-0.43V
	W_n	16nm
	L_n	24nm
	t_{oxe}	0.95nm
	t_{oxp}	0.7nm
NMOS	C_{gdo}, C_{gso}	50pF/m
	C_{gbo}	2.56pF/m
	C_{gdl}, C_{gsl}	265.3pF/m
	V_{th}	0.48V
	V_{dd}	0.8V
Bias Voltages	V_{pg}	0.4V
	V_{ng}	0.4V
	$V_{in1}...V_{inn}$	0('0'), 0.8V('1')
Temperature	T	300K

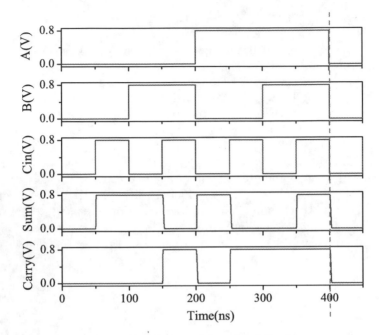

Fig. 3. Simulation of the a bit full adder

In this paper, we use a 16-nm MOSFET transistor to simulate the behavior of the MOSFET transistors. The W/L ratio of the MOSFET is set to $1/3$ or $2/3$, which is completely different from conventional digital practice. The parameters of the PMOS are $W = 16$nm, $L = 48$nm, $V_{pg} = 0.4$V and $V_{dd} = 0.8$V. The parameters of the NMOS are $W = 16$nm, $L = 24$nm and $V_{ng} = 0.4$V. The SET is a completely symmetrical one, its parameters are $C_d = C_s = 0.09$aF, $C_g = 0.1$aF and $R_d = R_s = 90$KΩ. The simulation temperature is 300K. All experimental parameters is shown in Table 1. Further more, all parameters keep constant in the whole paper except separate one that will be asserted in concrete simulation.

Fig. 3 shows the detailed timing diagram of the 2-input full adder. The top three panels indicate time variation of the input signals A, B and C_i, the 4th and 5th panel indicates time variation of the output signals S and C_o. The simulation results show that the element achieves the function of 2-input full adder. From Fig. 3, it is obvious that the simulation result is consistent with the analysis in section 2. Therefore, the function of the logic gate based on hybrid SETMOS is completely the same to the one based on pure CMOS.

To compare our work with compensatory MOSFETs logic based on pure MOSFET, we investigate the key performance parameters in terms of power dissipation, the worst delay, voltage swing and area. We use the same technical MOSFETs, namely, a 16-nm MOSFET transistor to simulate the behavior of the MOSFET transistors of 2-input full adder. The technics parameters of the MOSFETs and the size of the SETs are as shown in table 1. We simulate

$\overline{Sum}$, Sum, $\overline{Carry}$, $Carry$ of 2-input full adder based on hybrid SETMOS, and Sum, $Carry$ of 2-input full adder based on conventional CMOS, respectively. All logics are simulated at the same condition as that in section 2. To implement correct function and make the performance close to the optimal according to the optimization principle of the power-delay product (PDP) which is a quality measures for a logic gate [14], we adjust the size of MOSFETs of compensatory MOSFETs logic. The concrete size of CMOS are $W = 32$nm and $L = 16$nm.

Table 2. Comparison of Performance of CMOS Logic And Hybrid SETMOS Logic. Simulation Temperature Is 300K.

Type	Signal	Delay(ns)			V_o Swing(mV)		$V_o/V_i(\%)$	Area		Power
		t_{pHL}	t_{pLH}	t_p	V_{oH}	V_{oL}		No. of MOSFETs	No. of SETs	
Hybrid SETMOS logic	Sum	0.205	0.975	0.59	786	23	95.38	8	12	58.83
	Sum	0.981	0.213	0.60	799.5	0.6	99.86			
	$Carry$	0.202	0.814	0.51	789	23	95.75			
	$Carry$	0.824	0.215	0.52	799.5	0.6	99.86			
CMOS logic	Sum	0.014	0.016	0.015	799.5	0.6	99.86	28	0	195.10
	$Carry$	0.008	0.006	0.007	799.5	0.6	99.86			

4   Conclusion

This paper proposes a full adder based on hybrid SETMOS at room temperature. Because the SET can play the same role as compensatory MOSFETs, we design a fuller adder with hybrid SETMOS. Further more, we simulate the logic element by HSPIC and the simulation result shows that the logic element implements the function of a full adder. To compare our work with conventional CMOS logic based on pure MOSFET, we investigate the key performance parameters in terms of power dissipation, the worst delay, voltage swing and area, and it is deduced that the logics based on hybrid SETMOS can be very useful for reducing logic-gate density and power consumption significantly. Additions, the full-adder is usually a component in a cascade of adders, which add 8, 16, 32, etc. bit wide binary numbers.

Acknowledgments. This work was supported in part by the National Natural Science Foundation of China (Grant No. 61170083), in part by the National Science Foundation for Young Scientists of China (Grant No. 61106084), and in part by the Ph.D. Programs Foundation of Ministry of Education of China (Grant No. 20114307110001).

References

1. Likharev, K.K.: Single-Electron Devices and Their Applications. Proceedings of the IEEE 87(4), 606–632 (1999)
2. Wang, W., Liu, M., Hsu, A.: Hybrid nanoelectronics: Future of computer technology. J. Comput. Sci. Technol. 21(6), 871–886 (2006)

3. Ionescu, A.M., Declercq, M.J., Mahapatra, S., Banerjee, K., Gautier, J.: Few Electron Devices: Towards Hybrid CMOS-SET Integrated Circuits. In: Proceedings of 39th Design Automation Conference, pp. 323–328 (June 2002)
4. Mahapatra, S., Ionescu, A.M.: Hybrid CMOS Single Electron Transistor Device and Circuit Design. Artech House Publication (2006)
5. Venkataratnam, A., Goel, A.K.: Design and simulation of logic circuits with hybrid architectures of single-electron transistors and conventional MOS devices at room temperature. Microelectronics Journal 39, 1461–1468 (2008)
6. Parekh, R., Beaumont, A., Beauvais, J., Drouin, D.: Simulation and Design Methodology for Hybrid SET-CMOS Integrated Logic at 22-nm Room-Temperature Operation. IEEE Trans. Electron Devices 59(4), 918–923 (2012)
7. Uchida, K., Koga, J., Ohba, R., Toriumi, A.: Programmable singleelectron transistor logic for future low-power intelligent LSI: Proposal and room-temperature operation. IEEE Trans. Electron Devices 50(7), 1623–1630 (2003)
8. Sui, B.C., Chi, L.F.Y.Q., Zhang, C.: Nano-Reconfigurable Cells With Hybrid Circuits of Single-Electron Transistors and MOSFETs. IEEE Trans. on Electron Devices 57(9), 2251–2257 (2010)
9. Inokawa, H., Fujiwara, A., Takahashi, Y.: A multiple-valued logic and memory with combined single-electron and metal-oxide-semiconductor transistors. IEEE Trans. Electron Devices 50(2), 462–470 (2003)
10. Saitoh, M., Harata, H., Hiramoto, T.: Room-temperature demonstration of integrated silicon single-electron transistor circuits for current switching and analog pattern matching. In: IEDM Tech. Dig., San Francisco, CA, pp. 187–190 (2004)
11. Song, K.W., Lee, Y.K., Sim, J.S., Jeoung, H., Lee, J.D., Park, B.G., Jin, Y.S., Kim, Y.W.: SET/CMOS Hybrid Process and Multiband Filtering Circuits. IEEE Trans. Electron Devices 52(8), 1845–1850 (2005)
12. Wei, R.S., Chen, J.F., Chen, S.C., He, M.H.: Reconfigurable Threshold Logic Element with SET and MOS Transistors. Chin. Phys. Lett. 29(2), 028502 (2012)
13. Chandrakasan, A.P., Sheng, S., Brodersen, R.W.: Low-Power CMOS Digital Design. IEEE Journal of Solid State Circuits 27(4), 473–484 (1992)
14. Rabaey, J.M., Chandrakasan, A., Nikolic, B.: Digital Integrated Circuits: A Design Perspective, 2nd edn. Pearson Education (2003)
15. Wasshuber, C., Kosina, H., Selberherr, S.: SIMON-a simulator for single-electron tunnel devices and circuits. IEEE Trans. Comput. Aided Design 16, 937–944 (1997)
16. Zardalidis, G., Karafyllidis, I.G.: SECS: A New Single-Electron-Circuit Simulator. IEEE Trans. Circuits Syst. I, Reg. Papers 55(9), 2774–2784 (2008)
17. Inokawa, H., Takahashi, Y.: A compact analytical model for asymmetric single-electron tunneling transistors. IEEE Trans. Electron Devices 50(2), 455–461 (2003)
18. Mahapatra, S., Vaish, V., Wasshuber, C., Banerjee, K., Ionescu, A.M.: Analytical modeling of single electron transistor for hybrid CMOSSET analog IC design. IEEE Trans. Electron Devices 51(11), 1772–1782 (2004)
19. Zhang, F., Tang, R., Kim, Y.-B.: SET-based nano-circuit simulation and design method using HSPICE. Microelectron. J. 36(8), 741–748 (2005)
20. Inokawa, H., Takahashi, Y.: Experimental and simulation studies of single-electron-transistor-based multiple-valued logic. In: Proc. 33rd Int. Symp. Multiple-Valued Logic, pp. 259–266 (May 2003)
21. Zhang, W., Wu, N.J., Hashizume, T., Kasai, S.: Novel Hybrid Voltage Controlled Ring Oscillators Using Single Electron and MOS Transistors. IEEE Trans. Nanotechnol. 6(2), 146–157 (2007)

Author Index

Printed in the United States
By Bookmasters